DATE DUE

WITHDRAWN
UTSA LIBRARIES

Organizational Olympians

Other titles in the trilogy

ORGANIZATIONAL EPICS AND SAGAS: Tales of Organizations
MYTHICAL INSPIRATIONS FOR ORGANIZATIONAL REALITIES

Also by Monika Kostera

CRITICAL MANAGEMENT RESEARCH IN EASTERN EUROPE:
Managing the Transition *(edited with Mihaela Kelemen)*

Organizational Olympians

Heroes and Heroines of Organizational Myths

Edited by
Monika Kostera

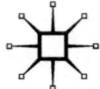

Selection and editorial matter © Monika Kostera 2008
Individual chapters © contributors 2008

All rights reserved. No reproduction, copy or transmission of this publication may be made without written permission.

No paragraph of this publication may be reproduced, copied or transmitted save with written permission or in accordance with the provisions of the Copyright, Designs and Patents Act 1988, or under the terms of any licence permitting limited copying issued by the Copyright Licensing Agency, 90 Tottenham Court Road, London W1T 4LP.

Any person who does any unauthorized act in relation to this publication may be liable to criminal prosecution and civil claims for damages.

The authors have asserted their rights to be identified as the authors of this work in accordance with the Copyright, Designs and Patents Act 1988.

First published 2008 by
PALGRAVE MACMILLAN
Houndmills, Basingstoke, Hampshire RG21 6XS and
175 Fifth Avenue, New York, N.Y. 10010
Companies and representatives throughout the world

PALGRAVE MACMILLAN is the global academic imprint of the Palgrave Macmillan division of St. Martin's Press, LLC and of Palgrave Macmillan Ltd. Macmillan® is a registered trademark in the United States, United Kingdom and other countries. Palgrave is a registered trademark in the European Union and other countries.

ISBN-13: 978–0–230–51571–0
ISBN-10: 0–230–51571–1

This book is printed on paper suitable for recycling and made from fully managed and sustained forest sources. Logging, pulping and manufacturing processes are expected to conform to the environmental regulations of the country of origin.

A catalogue record for this book is available from the British Library.

Library of Congress Cataloging-in-Publication Data
Organizational olympians : heroes and heroines of organizational myths / edited by Monika Kostera.
   p. cm.
Includes bibliographical references and index.
ISBN 0–230–51571–1 (alk. paper)
 1. Organizational effectiveness. 2. Myth. I. Kostera, Monika, 1963–
HD58.9O743 2008
658.4′09—dc22
                                          2008000190

10 9 8 7 6 5 4 3 2 1
17 16 15 14 13 12 11 10 09 08

Printed and bound in Great Britain by
CPI Antony Rowe, Chippenham and Eastbourne

Contents

List of Tables	x
List of Figures	xi
Acknowledgements	xii
Notes on the Contributors	xiii

Introduction to the Trilogy: Mythologies of Organizational Everyday Life — 1
Monika Kostera

Myths and human beings	2
Organizational mythmaking	4

Introduction to *Organizational Olympians: Heroes and Villains of Organizational Myths* — 9
Monika Kostera

Structure of the book	12

1 **Louhi, the Mistress of Northland: The Power of the Loner** — 17
Iiris Aaltio

Introduction	17
The *Kalevala* as spoken tradition: the origins of Louhi	18
Louhi and the story of the Sampo	19
The loneliness of Louhi	26
Final words	28

2 **Engaged Leadership: Living the Myth and Embodying the Legend of the Olympian Athlete** — 30
Elena P. Antonacopoulou

Introduction	30
The virtues of engaged leadership	31
Olympian ideals and Olympic athletes as vision for leadership	34

The Olympics of organizing: living the myth
and embodying the legend of the Olympian athlete   36
Conclusions   38

3 From Managers to Artists and Priests: On Transformation and Development of Organizational Leaders 40
Dorota Bourne

Introduction   40
Research design   41
Two locations, two different pasts   42
Leaders in General Motors   43
Conclusions   48

4 The Uncanny Organization Man: Superhero Myths and Contemporary Management Discourse 50
Alf 'Orgspawn' Rehn and Marcus 'Analysator' Lindahl

Introduction   50
On universes   51
Tales of capes and champagne   53
Management, get ready to Rrrrumble!   55
'Chainsaw', 'Neutron' and the rest of the boys   56
References   58

5 From Rags to Riches: A Fairy Tale or Living Ethos? Stories of Polish Entrepreneurship during and after the Transformation of 1989 59
Małgorzata Ciesielska

Prologue   59
The 1989 business begins   62
Jeans, cassettes and paints   63
Epilogue   66
'It was like on a stupid film on business': reflections on
   Polish e-tales after the transformation of 1989   66
Some final remarks   68

6	**'I Could Have Been Like Lou Barlow, But I'm More Like Ken Barlow': Long-Stayers as Heroes or Failures** *Yvonne Guerrier*	**71**
	The changing history of careers and attitudes to staying and leaving	73
	What do they know?	77
	The end	79
7	**Little Johnny and the Wizard of OS: The PC User as a Fool Hero** *Dariusz Jemielniak*	**80**
	ID10T	82
	Interpretation and conclusions	88
8	**An Emerging Legend of a Kosovar Heroine: Narrating Female Entrepreneurs** *Lena Olaison*	**92**
	In search of female entrepreneurs in Kosovo/a	92
	Emerging myths and legends	93
	Narrating female entrepreneurs in Kosovo/a	94
	Discussion: tracing the legend(s) of a Kosovar heroine	97
9	**Gender-Content Myths and their Role in Nation Forming** *Elżbieta Pakszys*	**102**
10	**Adulation, Abandonment and Amputation: Images of Women in Vedic Mythology** *Sumohon Matilal*	**108**
	Living women: women in myth	108
	Adulation: the story of Durga	109
	Abandonment: the story of Sita	110
	Amputation: the story of Draupadi	111
	Perceptions of women	114

11 Romanian Socialist Directors: Heroes or Tricksters?   119
Mihaela Kelemen and Dirk Bunzel

    The centrality of language forms to understanding organizations   119
    The context of Romanian economic leadership   120
    The role of fairytales   121
    Directorship self-portraits   123
    Conclusions   128
    Appendix I: Greuceanu – the Heavy and the Great Man   129

12 The Hard-working Hero/ine among Phantoms, Donors and Dark Forces: On Mythical Features in Polish Organizational Imagination   132
Katarzyna Wolanik Boström

    Introduction   132
    Helpers and donors   133
    Trials, challenges, harassments   135
    Favourite phantoms   138
    Images of paradise   140
    Mission impossible accomplished   141

13 Mighty McManus: Mystery, Myth and Modernity   142
Tony Watson

    It's good to see you again   142
    Enter McManus   143
    Myths and the shield against terror   144
    A spooky diversion: the Nazi spymaster and the philosophical anthropologist   145
    Myths and sacred forces   146
    McManus: hero and villain   147
    The beautiful Maria-Vittoria   149
    McManus and masculinity: capturing, shooting and taking   151
    Modernity and the demise of gods, heroes and devils?   152
    Modernity and a continuing role for the mythical   152

14 Myth and Charisma as Symbolic Capital: The Case of Architecture 155
Alexander Styhre and Mats Sundgren

Introduction	155
The nature of architecture	156
Myth and charisma as symbolic capital	158
Architecture and symbolic capital	159
Discussion and conclusion	162

15 Paradise Lost: Impartiality of an Arbitrator 165
Joanna Jemielniak

Introduction	165
Absolute justice	166
Leaving paradise	169
Conclusion	174

16 The Film Producer: A Scapegoat or/and a Midwife in the Film Making Process? 175
Marja Soila-Wadman

Introduction	175
The scapegoat myth and its enactment through ritual	176
Ideas of art work and its organizing	179
The producer in the role of a scapegoat	180
A need for a new myth: the producer as a midwife	181
Conclusion	182

17 The Witchcraft of Professionalism: The Attractiveness of Ideal Types of Professions 184
Karin Jonnergård

Professions as the lackeys of modernism	185
Undressing the professionals: knowledge as a bits and pieces	186
Late modernity and the use of professionalism	189
Letting the witches back in	190

Bibliography 195

Index 213

List of Tables

I.1	Structure of this volume	13
8.1	Tracing an emerging legend of a Kosovar heroine	98
17.1	Ideal types built upon the 'profession(-alism)' figure of thought	191

List of Figures

7.1 The Fool in the *Rider-Waite Tarot Deck*   89
7.2 Till Eulenspiegel   90

Acknowledgements

I am very fortunate to be surrounded by friends and colleagues who have in many ways contributed to the appearance of this book. Our many conversations provided me with ideas and counter-ideas, as well as awoke my curiosity to the point where I felt I wanted to collect texts on the topic of myths and archetypes and decided to send out a call for contributions. While, for lack of space, many of them will remain unnamed, I wish to direct special thanks to the few to whom I owe special gratitude.

First and foremost, I wish to thank all the authors who responded to my call for contributions and wrote the chapters that make up this book. It was a real joy to work with you all.

I would also like to thank the friends and colleagues whose texts and conversations with me have provided me with inspiration and ideas in my thinking and writing about myths and archetypes. They are many, but let me use this opportunity to express my profound gratitude to Zygmunt Bauman, Martin Bowles, Tobiasz Cwynar, Yiannis Gabriel, Mary Jo Hatch, Heather Höpfl, Henrietta Nilson, Stanisław Obirek, Przemek Piątkowski, Patrik Persson, and Diane and Tony Watson.

Kasia Korzeniecka, Joakim Larnö, Szymon Rogiński and Peter Tillström created artwork that inspired me and that I use a lot in my writings and as illustrations to my lectures and talks about organizational myths and archetypes. Some of the work is included in the current text. Thank you very much!

Jan-Erik Malte Andersson, Klara Nilson and Patrik Persson composed music, touching the topics of the current volumes, that I listened to during the writing and that gave me much joy. I regret that music cannot be attached to the final publication – it would indeed add a lot to the message. Nonetheless, it reverberates throughout the composition of these volumes, as it does in my mind when I think of mythologies.

I would also like to thank Keith Povey and his colleagues for their excellent work in the editing process, as well as Virginia Thorp and Emily Bown at Palgrave Macmillan for their kind help and support.

My deepest thanks go to my husband Jerzy Kociatkiewicz for all the greatly inspiring talks, for the help with the language editing, and for being there.

MONIKA KOSTERA

Notes on the Contributors

Iiris Aaltio is Professor at the University of Jyväskylä and Lappeenranta University of Technology, Finland. Her research work covers issues on organization culture, leadership and gender, and has been published in journals like *Organizational Change Management* and *Human Relations*. She has co-edited *Gender, Identity and the Culture of Organizations* and *Women Enterpreneurs: Constructing Social Capital in Business Life*.

Elena Antonacopoulou is Professor of Organizational Behaviour at the University of Liverpool Management School and Director of GNOSIS, a dynamic management research initiative. She is a Senior Fellow of the Advanced Institute of Management Research, UK. Her principal research interests include change and learning processes in organizations, social practice and dynamic capabilities.

Dorota Bourne has worked on research projects that address international knowledge transfer, the idea of the built-in quality, a difference between organizational image and identity, and the application of personal construct psychology in business. Her current research interests include cross-cultural reverse knowledge transfer and the notion of creativity in organizations.

Dirk Bunzel has studied in Germany and Australia and has researched the future of work in Scottish call centres and software firms. He has been lecturing at Keele University in England since 2001. His current research interests concern ethics at work in service industries and the management of diversity.

Małgorzata Ciesielska is a doctoral student at the Copenhagen Business School, Denmark. She graduated in management and marketing from the School of Management of Warsaw University (Poland) in 2003. Her current research interests include entrepreneurship in small and medium companies, institutional entrepreneurship, ethnography of organizations and critical management.

Yvonne Guerrier is Professor of Organization Studies and Dean of the School of Business and Social Sciences at Roehampton University, UK. Her recent research has focused on jobs in the tourism and hospitality industry. She has published in *Human Relations*, *Gender, Work and Organization*, and *Work, Employment and Society*. Her PhD was on managers' job changes and her chapter returns to this topic. Before joining Roehampton, she was at South Bank University and before that at Surrey University, UK.

Dariusz Jemielniak is Assistant Professor of Management at Kozminski Business School (Poland) and visiting researcher at Cornell University (2004–5), Harvard University (2007) and the University of California at Berkeley (2008). He is the co-editor of *Handbook of Research on Knowledge-Intensive Organizations* and *Management Practices in High-Tech Environments*, and a recipient of scholarships from the Fulbright Foundation, the Foundation for Polish Science, the Kosciuszko Foundation and Collegium Invisibile. His interests cover action research, organizational ethnography and knowledge-intensive work.

Joanna Jemielniak is Assistant Professor at Leon Kozminski Academy of Entrepreneurship and Management in Warsaw, Poland. She specializes in international business law and arbitration and in the theory of legal discourse. Her recent work is dedicated to legal interpretation and argumentation in international commercial arbitration.

Karin Jonnergård is Professor in Corporate Governance and Management Control at the University of Växjö and also connected to the University of Lund, Sweden. She is research leader at the Forum for Research on Professions, Växjö University, and is a member of the research group Corporate Entrepreneurship and Governance.

Mihaela Kelemen is Professor of Management Studies at Keele University, UK. Her research takes a critical approach to the management of quality in the UK service sector and to processes of economic transition in Eastern Europe. She is also interested in the production and consumption of organizational knowledge, postmodernism and American pragmatism. Her most recent book, *Managing Quality: Managerial and Critical Approaches*, was published in 2003.

Monika Kostera is Professor of Management at Växjö University, Sweden, and Warsaw University, Poland. She has published several books in Polish and in English, most recently *The Quest for the Self-Actualizing Organization*, and articles in *Organization, Organization Studies*, the *Scandinavian Journal of Management* and other journals. Her current research interests include organizational archetypes, organizational ethnography and narrative methods.

Marcus Lindahl is Assistant Professor at the Royal Institute of Technology in Stockholm, Sweden. He is also Research Director of the Centre for Industrial Entrepreneurship and Creativity in Sweden. His current research is focused on system deliveries within the area of translational education and especially aspects of unintentional organization in project management.

Sumohon Matilal is a doctoral student in the Department of Accounting, Finance and Management at the University of Essex, UK. He trained as an accountant and teaches on courses in both accounting and management. His paper is the result of a chance conversation with his mother on a day she was feeling particularly depressed and lonely.

Lena Olaison is a doctoral candidate in the Department of Management, Politics and Philosophy, Copenhagen Business School, Denmark, and in the Department of Accounting, Finance and Management, University of Essex, UK. Her research interests include new approaches in entrepreneurship research with emphasis on relationships with humanities and critical management studies.

Elżbieta Pakszys is Associate Professor in the Institute of Philosophy at Adam Mickiewicz University in Poznań, Poland. Her areas of interest are the philosophy of science and cognition, life sciences, feminism and epistemology. From the latter area she has co-edited several collections of papers and published her own book in Polish: *Between Nature and Culture: Sex/Gender Category in Cognition*.

Alf Rehn holds a Chair of Management and Organization at Åbo Akademi University, and is Professor of Entrepreneurship and Innovation at the Royal Institute of Technology in Stockholm, Sweden. He has written extensively on moralization and ideology in management and organization studies, and is a devoted fan of the divine Patsy Cline.

Marja Soila-Wadman is Assistant Professor at Växjö University School of Management, Växjö, Sweden. Her research focuses on aesthetics and relational processes, entrepreneurship and leadership in (art-creating) organizations.

Alexander Styhre is Professor in Technology Management, specializing in project management at Chalmers University, Gothenburg, Sweden. He is a Research Fellow at the Institute for Management and Innovation of Technology (IMIT) and member of the editorial board of the *Scandinavian Journal of Management* and the *International Journal of Knowledge Management Studies*.

Mats Sundgren is Principal Scientist, Clinical Development, at Astra Zeneca R&D Mölndal, Sweden. He has a PhD in Technology Management and Economics at the Chalmers University of Technology, Sweden, where he is also Senior Research Fellow in the Department of Project Management. He takes a special interest in R&D management, organizational creativity, and change management.

Tony Watson is Professor of Organisational Behaviour at Nottingham University Business School, UK. His interests cover industrial sociology, organizations, managerial and entrepreneurial work, and ethnography. His current work is on the relationship between the shaping of the 'whole lives' of managers and entrepreneurs and the shaping of the enterprises within which they work.

Katarzyna Wolanik Boström is Senior Lecturer in the Department of Culture and Media/Ethnology at Umeå University in Sweden. Her doctoral thesis *Berättade liv, berättat Polen* (*Narrated Lives, Narrated Poland*, 2005) is a narrative study of how well-educated Polish specialists create their identity, interwoven with images of history and society, in their life-stories.

Introduction to the Trilogy: Mythologies of Organizational Everyday Life

Monika Kostera

Myths about organizations and about organizational actors are powerful stories that touch something profound in the reader or listener. They can help us see and understand many important phenomena that are invisible to the rational instrumental mind. This is not universally acknowledged, perhaps due to a large extent to the dominance of that instrumental mind for the past decades and centuries. Furthermore, myths stem from the sacred realm of experience and many people consider business and work organizations as emphatically profane – for an exploration of the distinction between sacred and profane see Eliade (1961) and Armstrong (2005). However, there are times where these two realms meet, for example in ethnographic stories of organizations, where the actors draw on the realm of shared spiritual experience when referring to values and important events. Myths provide a language for these accounts, as well as ideas which people relate to when dealing with the most vital questions.

Myths are, however, not just a language that organizational actors sometimes invoke, but a frame of reference that can be discerned underneath many rationalistically minded organizations. Myths help people to see the whole not just as a sum of parts, and they socialize them and guide them throughout their lives (Bowles, 1989). This function was traditionally served by cults and religions; nowadays it is often left to work organizations: 'With the decline of the role of the Church, work organizations have become increasingly influential in their impact on peoples' thinking and behavior' (Bowles, 1989, p. 411).

Traditionally, myths describe creation, supernatural beings, heroic quests and adventures including the conquering of magical beasts (Campbell, 1949). Nowadays:

> Management and Organization myths can be seen to follow the traditional myths described above. Organizations, by virtue of their

competitive position in the marketplace, sometimes create images of quest and trial, struggling, like the hero, for survival against life-destroying forces. (Bowles, 1989, p. 413)

Why organizations strive to fulfil this role, and how they sometimes succeed, will be the topic of the present three volumes.

The trilogy is not a collection of texts assembled *ex post* as a result of a conference or seminar, but rather it consists of essays requested by the editor from various scholars on a specific theme: the way they see and use myth in their research of, and reflection on, organization.

Myths and human beings

For many people 'myth' brings to mind either something not true, a false belief or erroneous idea – or else, a tale of the religious domain (albeit other than one's own religion). In the first meaning, we often encounter derogative uses of the term in the popular media, in everyday talk, as well as in academic contexts (Bowles, 1989). If we hear of a narrative labelled 'the myth of success' we may suspect that the story is not very trustworthy or rational. In the second meaning, as sacred tale, it is encountered in academia (especially among anthropologists and ethnographers) as well as in day-to-day conversations, when we speak of origin myths or mythical heroes, usually thinking of exotic or glamorous tales from times or parts of the world where the magic is still alive. Rarely is myth spoken of as part-and-parcel of our everyday life, witnessed here and now. This is exactly how it is seen in the present trilogy. Here myths are

> telling us ... of matters fundamental to ourselves, enduring essential principles about which it would be good for us to know; about which, in fact, it will be necessary for us to know if our conscious minds are to be kept in touch with our own most secret, motivating depths. In short, these holy tales and their images are messages to the conscious mind from quarters of the spirit unknown to normal daylight consciousness, and if read as referring to events in the field of space and time – whether of the future, present, or past – they will have been misread and their force deflected, some secondary thing outside then taking to itself the reference of the symbol, some sanctified stick, stone, or animal, person, event, city, or social group. (Campbell, 1972/1988a, p. 24)[1]

The question whether a myth is true or not is irrelevant (Armstrong, 2005; Campbell, 2004). Myths merge outer and inner reality – the outer world provides images and the inner realm brings insights and awareness (Campbell, 1972/1988a). Myth is the fusion of these two and thus is 'true' from the point of view of human experience and consciousness and 'untrue' from the point of view of empirical history all at the same time.[2]

According to Martin Bowles (1993, p. 414), 'Myths express in ways that we are not able to articulate, our feelings, thoughts, consciousness, or sense of our own behavior.' It is a form of art, transforming the human psyche and the soul, not by means of persuasion but through experience (Armstrong, 2005). It inspires people to see life as a poem, consisting not of words but experiences (Campbell with Moyers, 1988).

Myths have accompanied humans from prehistoric times, providing guidance as how to live a more fulfilling life – humans are myth-creating beings (Armstrong, 2005). Mythology elicits and supports a sense of awe before the mystery of being; provides a set of ideas that enable humans to answer the most vital questions; socializes the individual; and guides him or her towards maturation (Campbell, 1976, as quoted in Bowles, 1989). Martin Bowles (1993) also emphasizes the role of myth in social life, one beyond the 'ego psychology', enabling understanding insights offered by the collective unconscious.

Myth enables the re-enacting of the ancient sacred past, making a personal and experiential connection to the mythical ancestors and 'the beginning' itself (Eliade, 1961). It carries the experience throughout time and provides participation for the current generation in something that happened long ago, disconnecting it from its actual historical occurrence (Armstrong, 2005). 'Time is what shuts you out from eternity. Eternity is now. It is the transcendent dimension of the now to which myth refers' (Campbell, 2004, p. xxii).

Myth fulfills four key roles (Campbell, 2004): namely it strives to 'reconcile consciousness to the preconditions of its own existence' (p. 3); elicit awe in the face of cosmos; 'validate and maintain a certain sociological system' (p. 8) with its norms and values; and guide the human being through the various stages of his or her life. The second and third functions, according to Campbell, nowadays have been taken over by secular orders. However, in the remaining two, myth is still irreplaceable. Yet in modern times humans have expelled myth from many areas of life, replacing it with science and rationality (Armstrong, 2005; Campbell, 2004). And so, the place of traditional myth and religion has been taken over by modern myths such as film and rock music and by popular heroes such as Princess Diana or Elvis Presley (Armstrong, 2005), or modern supernatural beings like The Invisible Hand of the Market (Kostera, 1995). Martin Bowles (1997) presents management as a modern myth. According to Bowles, the values central to the myth of management are competition, the imperative of growth and function rationality. The myth is quite limited in its ability to guide individuals toward maturation and give answers to life's important questions, which traditionally are the key roles of myth (Campbell, 2004). It fails to respond to the needs of the participants and thus turns out to be inadequate as contemporary myth. It is rather 'an attempt to fill in the "in-between" left by declining myth, expressed in Nietzsche's comment, "God is dead", and a new mythic path' (Campbell, 2004, p. 782). And yet it 'amounts to a religious fundamentalism in the way it has largely monopolized the goals and informed the understandings and mindset of (late) twentieth century societies' (p. 785).

Even though myth as such is intimately connected with human fate and history, it does not mean that it is always good and leads to a genuinely more fulfilling life for its creators and supporters. There are constructive and destructive myths, myths that connect and myths that demonize the Other, myths promoting empathy and myths that generate fear and egotism (Armstrong, 2005). The use of myths does not guarantee a better society or business, neither a more humane culture, nor better communication. In fact, it does not guarantee anything at all.

Organizational mythmaking

Myths are, then, rather an ambiguous organizational feature. However, being attentive to the mythical side of organizations can bring many good insights. They can be sought for directly in ethnographic material collected in organizations but they will not necessarily surface in the pure form. Contemporary life is to a high degree de-mythologized, and myths have often survived in culture in other narratives and art forms that reflect and try to fulfil the functions of myth, even though they remain different from it in many important respects (Eliade, 1963/1998). Some of their functions are being fulfilled by fairy tales (Bettelheim, 1976), psychological accounts of the human mind (Hillman, 1980; Miller, 1974), contemporary films, such as *Star Wars*, and books, such as *Lord of the Rings* (Trzciński, 2006), and tales of contemporary sociological phenomena (Gabriel, 2004a). This may be due to the fact that myth is vitally important as a guide to how to live one's life (Campbell, 1972/1988a) – or that, in fact, the myths never died but live on as a part of the human psyche

(Hillman, 1980) and/or human culture (Armstrong, 2005). Ernst Cassirer (1946) pointed out that engaging with myth leads storytellers and artists into mythological consciousness, which lies at the core of humanity and offers an alternative way of being in the world. Myth is, according to Cassirer, fundamental to language and storytelling, which are the main fabric of culture. Adopting this view on the role of myth as the foundation for the creation of culture, it is natural to see myth as potentially relevant for all kinds of culture, including the cultures of business and organizations.

The literature taking up mythical themes in connection to management and organization is not abundant but there are several high-quality, interesting texts dedicated to organizational mythmaking. I will now briefly introduce three of them that have made the strongest initial impression on the way I think of organizational mythmaking.

The first book on mythical themes and their relevance for organizing that I read was *Work, Death, and Life Itself* by Burkard Sievers (1994). The book depicts the meaning of work in the context of life and death. It criticizes mainstream and popular approaches to leadership, participation and motivation, and reveals the aspects of organizational life not envisaged in mainstream texts. Among the metaphors the text adopts to shed new light upon phenomena of organizational everyday life are the Greek myths of participation and immortality. The boundary between immortality and mortality in Greek mythology is imprecise and blurred. Hades is inhabited by the souls of dead people, but also by gods and goddesses. Gods are immortal, but they sometimes destroy and annihilate each other:

> What has become obvious in applying Greek mythology and its struggle with immortality as a metaphor for participation in contemporary work enterprises is the wide similarity of psycho-social processes operating to establish and sustain a limited access to immortality. (Sievers, 1994, p. 130)

The organization is often mythologized as immortal; leaders are deified and reified, while workers are reified. All participants are, thus, devoid of their mortality. In conclusion, the book proposes a *management of wisdom* – a way of using and framing managerial knowledge that avoids reification, a view of humans and relationships in organizations that acknowledges human dignity.

The second book I would like to briefly introduce here that takes up mythical themes is a study of popular management texts as a medium for the creation and dissemination of myths by Staffan Furusten (1992; see also Furusten, 1995). The book explores how popular management books, such as *In Search of Excellence* (Peters and Waterman, 1982), *Thriving on Chaos* (Peters, 1989), *Iacocca: An Autobiography* (Iacocca, 1984), and other bestsellers, serve as the guardians of the myth of leadership. The myth gives 'the manager healing and omnipotent abilities' (p. 71) and 'this myth is important as an inconsistent norm, never possible to realize practically, but when people talk about the manager in such terms, this norm will be satisfied mentally and then individuals to a certain extent are enabled to satisfy their searching for security and meaning in life' (pp. 71–2). The popular management books are tracts about virtues and ideals, their role in society is similar to that of antique mythological biographies of heroes and demigods or legends of saints. Staffan Furusten's study of managerial discourse (1995) concerns the creation and diffusion of popular management knowledge. The author explores the diffusion of popular management books of the 1980s in Sweden and analyses the ideas that they represent. This discourse 'propagates institutionalized myths, beliefs, institutions, and ideologies in the modern Western world' (p. 161). The myths disseminated by the books are then not only lived in organizational practice, but they serve as powerful sets of symbols to control reality. The texts are not unlike medieval Crusaders, advocating 'assent to a faith in North-American managerialism' (p. 168). I have commented in a similar way upon the role of Western management consultants in post-communist Poland (Kostera, 1995a).

The third book that I think of as having contributed in a major way to my desire to collect accounts on how organization scholars view and use myth is Yiannis Gabriel's edited book *Myths, Stories and Organizations* (2004), a collection of texts exploring the relevance of myths, legends, stories and fables for contemporary social and organizational settings. The chapters of Gabriel's book show that ancient stories are alive in the contemporary world and can be re-told and re-interpreted in ways that throw new light on how organizations work and what motivates people that populate them:

> Stories travel and stories stay. Stories cross boundaries and frontiers, settle in different places, and then migrate to or colonize other places. They resurface in different spaces and different times, preserving their ability to entertain, to enlighten, and to bewitch. (Gabriel, 2004b, p. 1)

With the narrative turn, there is a renewed interest in how they can help our understanding of social life, including the life in and of organizations. The chapters in Gabriel's book depart from a traditional tale to explore some aspect of organization, such as knowledge, crime, friendship and power. As Gabriel points out, engaging with stories means to engage with oneself, with the storyteller and with the outer world, touching the unknown and opening up new fields for exploration.

The three books have proven to me the relevance and importance of mythical thinking in organizational contexts and have made me want to see how different contemporary researchers view myths in their fieldwork as well as theorizing on matters related to organizing and organizations. Sievers' and Gabriel's books made me wonder about the relationship between mythology and social and organizational roles, as well as the role of organizations as such, that can be observed in the field or etymologically and philosophically interpreted. Organizational myth is a spontaneously emerging consciousness that bears many consequences on the individual and the collective domain. I wanted to find out how it is conceived by other scholars. Furusten's book caused me to think about the practical and often conscious uses of myth in managerial contexts and what purposes they serve. Myth can be a sort of a 'managerial tool', or a 'tool to manage' one's social and organizational role. I became interested in why and how do people use myth this way. In order to learn more, I decided to ask other researchers and sent out a call for contributions that resulted in the present collection of essays.

The three volumes present mythical thinking and consciousness in organizations, the use of myths in organizational storytelling, as well as different mythical characters present in the contemporary cultural context of organizing. The composition of this trilogy is based on the main themes and synergies of all the chapters. It is organized along three major themes/volumes that emerged from the collected material:

- *Organizational Olympians: Heroes and Heroines of Organizational Myths*, containing texts about individual characters and roles;
- *Organizational Epics and Sagas: Tales of Organizations*, dealing with stories of organizations and their mythical features; and
- *Mythical Inspirations for Organizational Realities*, taking up the role of myth and mythmaking in organizations and organizational discourse.

Notes

1. The way myth is seen in these volumes is thus different from definitions concentrating on the semiotic dimension, such as Roland Barthes's (1957), that

sees myth as a type of speech, a semiological system – the dominant ideology of its time serving to naturalize the social order in the interests of the bourgeoisie.
2. In Joseph Campbell's words, 'mythology is not a lie, mythology is poetry, it is metaphorical. It has been well said that mythology is the penultimate truth – penultimate because the ultimate cannot be put into words. It is beyond words, beyond images, beyond that bounding rim of the Buddhist Wheel of Becoming. Mythology pitches the mind beyond that rim, to what can be known but not told. So this is the penultimate truth' (Campbell with Moyers, 1988, p. 163).

Introduction to *Organizational Olympians: Heroes and Villains of Organizational Myths*

Monika Kostera

Myths are typically populated by heroes and villains. In fact, they are quite often two sides of the same coin, as the archetypes that they are based on are bipolar (Jung, 1966/1992). Bowles (1997, p. 796) points out that

> The negative expression of the hero archetype manifests where the hero acts in a self-interested egoic way where only narrower or particular interests or goals are served, perhaps to the detriment of the community at large. In idealizing the hero and projecting their own hero archetype onto the leader, which can make the leader appear larger than life, others can miss the fact that their own interests are perhaps not only not served, but in fact undermined.

Gods (and other mythical characters) 'represent the patron powers that support you in your field of action. And contemplating the deities, you're given a kind of steadying force that puts you in the role, as it were, that is represented by that particular deity' (Campbell, 2004, p. xv). These images of *true heroes* (or indeed true villains) have been built up over centuries and millennia and the models they offer have a special profundity and relevance for human life (Campbell, 2004; Gabriel, 2000). A hero is 'someone who has given his or her life to something bigger than oneself' (Campbell with Moyers, 1988, p. 123):

> Mythology begins where madness starts. A person who is truly gripped by a calling, by a dedication, by a belief, by a zeal, will sacrifice his security, will sacrifice even his life, will sacrifice personal relationships, will sacrifice prestige, and will think nothing of personal

development; he will give himself entirely to his myth. (Campbell, 2004, p. 89)

Heroes engage in heroic deeds, which may be twofold: physical and spiritual (Campbell with Moyers, 1988). The myth typically recounts the quest that the hero or heroine, or, in fact, villain, embarks on where such deeds are committed. This quest begins with leaving the familiar reality of everyday life. The protagonist moves out into the unknown, where s/he faces a series of trials, receives magical help and receives a number of key realizations, before s/he is able to return home but with all the insights and treasures gained during the quest (Campbell, 2004). The heroic quest is a manifestation of the hero's, heroine's or villain's character, everything that they encounter on their way somehow expresses their important attributes and abilities (Campbell with Moyers, 1988). In fact, heroes, heroines and villains of mythical tales can be seen as incarnations of life itself, which is why they represent that which is especially vital for human beings (Trzciński, 2006).

In the same way that not all stories are myths, not even all stories containing heroes are necessarily myths. In order to be myths, stories need to touch something very profound in the soul, not on the level of the plot but of the sacred experience. I quite agree with Yiannis Gabriel (2000), who discourages organizational theorists from an undiscerning use of the term *myth*. However, some stories become myths over time; for example, 'when a person becomes a model for other people's lives, [s]/he has moved into the sphere of being mythologized' (Campbell with Moyers, 1988, p. 15). This is what happens with certain media personalities or stars who move beyond celebrity status into the domain of cult and of being spiritual guides for others.

Leaders are perhaps the most commonly mythologized organizational actors. For example, Mary Jo Hatch, Monika Kostera, and Andrzej Koźmiński (2005) identified narrated characters present in the interviews with well known CEOs as having common archetypical traits as Greek gods. The mythical dimensions may not be obvious and are often hidden underneath a rationalistic rhetoric. However, managers draw intensively on a mythical consciousness when they engage in storytelling. By doing this, they were able actively to use their ability to manage meaning as well as act as symbols for the changes within the organization (Hatch, 1983). Silvia Gherardi (1995) shows, likewise, how female managers tend to be inspired by Greek goddesses in their leadership styles. The most popular role models are either the virgin goddesses (Artemis, Athena and Hestia) or the vulnerable goddesses (Hera, Demeter and Persephone).

Such a construction of their role enables them to use the links between power and gender to their advantage. Björn Rombach and Rolf Solli (2006) do not explicitly use the language of mythology, but rather, they describe mythologized characters as role models for modern leadership. They present nine films, such as *Elizabeth*, *The Godfather* and *The Life of Brian* with the aim of portraying certain themes connected with different aspects of leadership; as for example, decision making and accountability. The characters in the films are referred to as role models, fictional 'mentors' that may inspire and teach how to manage. People do not become like the characters they admire in a movie, but sometimes they just want to be influenced, the authors point out. That is why certain films may be so important for understanding our social reality and roles or, in my terms in this book, why they become mythologized.

Non-leaders are the theme of Jerzy Kociatkiewicz's (1997) study of the interactions between computers and professionals using them in Polish organizations. He analyzes the field material as a set of mythical themes, where the intercommunication between human actants and technology are portrayed as typical mythological plots. He also names some typical roles of computers in his interviewees' narratives: the computer is referred to as a demon, an angel, a trickster. The fundamental set of myths these narratives are rooted in concerns the idea of *progress*, which can be also recited as characteristic myths (of the Promised Land and paradise lost). Jerzy Kociatkiewicz concludes the study by reflecting on the role of these myths. It seems to appeal, first and foremost, to the sensemaking of people's experience, keeping the everyday reality real. The narrative aspect of the myths enables communication and reproduction of the socio-technical net and the actors' construction of reality. Myths are ambivalent and, therefore, they can be seen as a poetical form of expression, helping the actors to cope with the intransparence and paradoxicality of their everyday experience.

Martin Bowles (1993) shows organizational social life as underpinned by mythical characters that emerge from the psychological energies of the employees. For example, Zeus symbolizes the hierarchical order, based on personal power. Not just the leader but all of the organization based on a Zeus myth is immersed in a culture of power and emotional distance. In contrast, an Apollonian organization is bureaucratic and concerned with law and regulations. If Zeus consciousness creates emotional distance, the Apollo consciousness creates emotional coldness, the repression of feelings. Athena, concerned with pragmatism and rationality, is another consciousness type that is often present in contemporary organizations. All these mythical characters have their dark sides that can be represented by Poseidon, Aries and Hades, that can be destructive when they are repressed but also have a creative potential if made conscious. The realization that some gods and goddesses are conspicuously absent, such as Demeter, Aphrodite and Artemis, is equally important for the understanding of how organizations work and why they so often fail to meet important human needs. Bowles concludes that organizations are often dominated by mythical characters linked to power and manipulation. They fail to represent the vast spectrum of human feelings and values.

Ronny Ambjörnsson (1999) shows how the social roles played by men are influenced by mythical heroic figures, such as Don Juan, James Bond, Dracula and others. He has chosen myths deriving from our own world and time, rooted in modern history, since he believes that they resonate with how male roles are constructed in modern cultures. The stories he recounts in his book have all transcended their immediate context and started to live a kind of a narrative life of their own – a mythical life. The male characters are at the same time heroes and villains. For example, both Sherlock Holmes and James Bond, whose missions are to hunt down crooks and evildoers, often themselves operate on the boundaries of the law and even of the entire social order. The myths Ambjörnsson describes have an enormous potential for the inspiring of different enactments and interpretations of the male social role – as well as for the questioning of the patriarchal culture and masculinity. For example, Don Juan is the epitome of masculinity but at the same time he challenges it by his rejection of family and responsibility. He thus refuses to submit himself to power or to grasp it – he remains immature, approaching life as a permanent party where all the social roles collapse and fall out from their order.

What all these mythologized role models have in common is that they can be and, in fact, are practically used as material and inspiration for the role construction of contemporary social and organizational actors. People may not consciously imitate such role models but they often take up their own quests for identity starting from a character that influences them positively or negatively.

Structure of the book

Many uses of mythology pertain to individual actors: heroes and heroines. Most notably, they tell about roles people play in organizations (such as loners, leaders, subordinates), but also of how different types of social actors (women and people from Eastern Europe before 1989) play

Table I.1 Structure of this volume

Tale	Hero/Heroine	Author
Tales of mythical inspirations for various organizational roles	Loner	Iiris Aaltio
	Leader	Elena P. Antonacopoulou Dorota Bourne Alf Rehn and Marcus Lindahl
	Entrepreneur	Małgorzata Ciesielska
	Long-server	Yvonne Guerrier
	Client	Dariusz Jemielniak
Tales of how different actors play organizational roles	Women	Lena Olaison Elżbieta Pakszys Sumohon Matilal
	Actors from Eastern Europe	Mihaela Kelemen and Dirk Bunzel Katarzyna Wolanik Boström
Tales of attitudes and temperaments	Heroism	Tony Watson
Tales of different professions and their ethos	Architect	Alexander Styhre and Mats Sundgren
	Arbitrator	Joanna Jemielniak
	Film producer	Marja Soila-Wadman
	The professional	Karin Jonnergård

key roles in organizations, of how attitudes and temperaments can be made sense of mythically, and of professional ethos. Table I.1 shows the topics taken up in this book, as well as the names of the authors of the chapters dealing with each of the aspects of main theme.

The first part consists of tales of mythical inspirations for various organizational roles. Iiris Aaltio portrays the role model of the loner using the Finnish myth of Louhi, the hag of the North from the epos *Kalevala*. She is a powerful character and even if she does not prevail against the male gods, she is certainly their equal and does not fear to stand up to them all alone. Louhi is portrayed as an alternative archetype for female leaders, one not based on cooperation and support offered to male colleagues but on being a loner. Elena P. Antonacopoulou describes the leader in his or her transformative and engaged guise through the facets of Greek mythology. The chapter conceptualizes leadership virtues in terms of the virtues of the Olympic Athlete, such as for example fighting well (rather than winning) and everyday engagement in the world. Dorota Bourne reflects upon the relationship between organizational culture and leadership styles. She presents several leaders from a car manufacturing company (General Motors) that have been operating in two plants: one British and one Polish. Dramatically different leadership styles, rooted in deep archetypical values, had tremendous effects upon organizational performance as demonstrated in quality results.

Alf Rehn and Marcus Lindahl use the image of the superhero from comic books to portray the contemporary business leader. They show how closely related both archetypes are and how they influence one another. They both spring from older archetypical characters and play an important role in the contemporary cultural unconscious. Małgorzata Ciesielska tells the mythical tale of Polish entrepreneurs, corresponding in many interesting ways to the classical American myth of success: from rags to riches. Even if the Polish interviewees presented in the chapter are quite different from Benjamin Franklin or John Rockefeller, and so is their cultural context, they find inspiration and motivation in their version of the American dream.

The second part of this volume contains tales of how different actors play organizational roles. The long-server's role is the topic of Yvonne Guerrier's chapter. She presents the character of Ken Barlow from a popular TV series, *Coronation Street*, who has been in the show for almost 50 years. Nowadays the idea of a life-long career is not seen as fashionable or very impressive. However, it is still sometime seen as attractive and the role of Ken Barlow invokes an archetype that proves to be relevant for some people. Dariusz Jemielniak depicts the role of the client of IT firms and his or her encounter with IT specialists. The client is constructed by invoking various images of the Fool. He or she is seen as not very smart but exceedingly funny by the frontliners. While, at the one hand, this may lead to stigmatization, it is also true that the Fool inspires and provokes, and so often does the user of software. Lena Olaison draws from her ethnographic material of female entrepreneurs in Kosovo to consider the mythical roots of the role construction of the female entrepreneur. She portrays the emerging heroine archetype – whom she labels *femina curans*, the healing woman, the re-constructor of society. Elżbieta Pakszys studies the roots of gender roles themselves and reflects on how we think of women and why. She shows how the gender content of creation and foundation myths plays an important role in how social actors understand and construct their identities today. Sumohon Matilal links ancient Vedic characters to social behaviours of women in contemporary organizations. Indian goddesses, such as the maternal Durga and the chaste Sita, are important for how Indian women enact their social roles, channelling women's energy towards traditional ways rather than exploring new ones. East Europeans are another group of social actors described in two of the chapters. Mihaela Kelemen and Dirk Bunzel present an ethnographic portrait of Romanian managers and consider how the social role they have been playing under communism can be seen as rooted in traditional Romanian folktales. Heroism and trickery – traits eminent in these tales – helped them to deal with the difficult context of totalitarianism and the contradictory demands of the communist Party and their social roles as business leaders. Katarzyna Wolanik Boström takes up the inspirations for the typical social roles played by Polish professionals before 1989. They used archetypal characters such as The Donor or The Dark Force to find the material for the construction of a role model that simultaneously would be professionally and morally satisfying.

The third part of this volume, tales of attitudes and temperaments, contains a reflection on heroism itself by Tony Watson. The main protagonist, Mighty McManus, is a mythical photographer who allegedly worked on several publications. He was a hero and a villain at the same time: secretive, brilliant, unreliable and a womanizer, he would suddenly materialize with a scoop and then disappear again. The chapter considers the elusiveness of the protagonist as well as the ambiguity of the myth, positive or negative depending on organizational circumstances.

The fourth and last part of the book is dedicated to different professions and their ethos. The foundations for the role of the architect are presented by Alexander Styhre and Mats Sundgren. Mythical talent and charisma are part of the profession's symbolic capital. By means of ethnographic data, the chapter shows how this kind of capital can be used for the building up of prestige and approval of the stakeholders for the ideas of a successful Swedish architectural office. The mythical inspirations of the role and dilemmas of the arbitrator are discussed by Joanna Jemielniak. The impartiality of an arbitrator is based on a different archetype than the impartiality of the judge. The latter holds logocentric and transcendental authority, and the former uses power ascribed locally, not universally. The mythical role-model of the arbitrator needs to be relational, entrepreneurial and able to balance different cultural and legal elements. Marja Soila-Wadman ponders the consequences of different framings of the role of the film producer. The archetype now dominating in the field where she has been doing her ethnographic study is that of the scapegoat. The film producer, associated with the financial aspect, can be blamed for all difficulties and failures encountered by the film-making team. There is, however, an alternative archetype that the author finds more useful for collective creative endeavours: that of the mid-wife, someone assisting in the passage to life through death.

Karin Jonnergård reflects on the role of the professional in contemporary society. She presents four major ideal types of professionalism which are based in four different archetypes: the Witches, the Scientific Hero, the Organizational Man and the Caretaker. All of these ideal types have different bases of legitimacy, ethical codes and positions in society. Even if different times have a predilection for different archetypes, there is still space for all of them in the present, including the oldest one – the proud and independent Witches may inspire contemporary professionals as they did their ancestresses and ancestors.

1
Louhi, the Mistress of Northland: The Power of the Loner

Iiris Aaltio

Introduction

Myths, as sometimes defined, are the nourishing power of our inner lives. In national epics, myths are usually a retelling of ancient stories about gods and their deeds, and about heroes who make history, or what passes for history. This is seen also in the *Kalevala*, which is the epitome of national Finnish poetry. Myths can also be seen as the underlying structures of human culture, being both collective and temporal in their nature, appearing in archetypes, dreams and symbols (Jung, 1968). The origin of mythical creation springs from the human mind's search for interpretation and order in a world of chaos. That is why myths are not irrational stories, and why they are sometimes called 'sacred narratives' (*Kalevala*, 1999, p. xxxiii) in the sense that they embrace the ontological nature of the world.

In organizational study field myths, have been studied for around 20 years and their meaning for work organizations, their narrative construal of reality, their forming of organizational identities as well as their methodological nature are all referred in these approaches (Boje, 1991; Bowles, 1993; Czarniawska, 1997b; Gabriel, 2000). Myths bring into organizational studies a sense of drama, reveal the irrational sides of organizational life and show people's relatedness to wide spheres of life even within narrow organizational realities.

Northrop Frye (1990) has described mythical thinking in terms of 'primary' and 'secondary' reality. Primary reality does not involve consciousness; however, when this primary reality is lost, it is replaced by a secondary conscious reality, containing mythical structures, dynamics and oppositions. Myths, for their part, incorporate a reality in which subject and object are one and the same, inseparable. Mythical thinking means true participation in the reality narrated by the myth, experiencing that reality in a primal consciousness (Cassirer, 1955). Thus, the Finnish national epic, the *Kalevala*, tells its story more or less unselfconsciously, without straining for effect, and almost without abstraction or moralizing (*Kalevala*, 1999, p. xxxiv). Epic characters, on the other hand, consciously describe this reality and give readers some structure on which to base their thinking about the objective world.

One of the leading epic characters in the *Kalevala* is *Louhi*, a great woman of power. In Finland, the homeland of the *Kalevala*, Louhi is a character who has inspired a good deal of debate, speculation and research, in addition to numerous works of art. Her lone figure contrasts sharply with all the other women in national epics worldwide. Silvia Gherardi (1995) deals with organizational stories and myths, and discusses how female leaders tend to be motivated by certain archetypes that are found also in ancient Greek mythology. According to Gherardi (1995, pp. 71–83), the Greek female deities can be roughly divided into virgin goddesses and vulnerable goddesses. The former choose to live apart from men, as in the case of Artemis, or identify with them, as in the case of Athena, or are marginalized by them, as in the case of Hestia. The other three female deities – Hera, Demeter and Persephone – suffer from, but also rejoice in their relationships with men, and these relationships motivate them more profoundly than accomplishing an objective achieving autonomy or enjoying a pleasurable experience. Hera represents the desire to provide companionship, Demeter attention to household chores and Persephone dependence. All of them seek approval, love and attention. The *Kalevala* has other female characters besides Louhi who differs sharply from them. Moreover, if we compare Louhi with the Greek goddesses, we see a big difference. Louhi is a powerful woman, equal to the male gods, even persuading them to serve her by using her beautiful daughters as a trap. She communicates with them directly and does not need the help of her husband either publicly or privately.

The *Kalevala* as spoken tradition: the origins of Louhi

How do narratives get created? Although stories may be presented in the form of written texts, their roots still lie in spoken tradition. Storytelling occurs in all human cultures. As discussed by Hatch, Kostera and Koźmiński (2005, pp. 12–15), the repetition of stories to others builds up a collective memory, which is retained as cultural myths and sagas or, in contemporary times, as history, novels, films and 'poetic' forms. Stories are structured much like life itself, which is why people naturally find them attracting. As is known from identity research (*ibid.*), people easily view their own life as a story as well – they find themselves in the stories and their lives take on significance. Stories also reflect human history and culture. Their central themes even act as foundations for human self-understanding.

The *Kalevala* has both male and female characters. The three central male figures portrayed in the *Kalevala* are godlike mythical heroes, namely *Väinämöinen*, the sage, *Lemminkäinen*, also called 'wanton Loverboy', and *Ilmarinen*, the master smith. The long digressive poem narrates in detail the adventures of these heroic figures. Yet, as Caraker (1996) has pointed out, despite the abundance of the supernatural in the *Kalevala*, its verses also describe ordinary men and women as they lived their everyday lives in ancient times. The women in particular emerge as 'real' people with their own hopes, joys and sorrows, and with lives that are easy to understand even in today's cultural context.

But then there is *Louhi*, the Mistress of Northland, which is an unknown, frightening country far in the north. In modern organizational and feminist terms, Louhi can be said to have broken the 'glass ceiling' of high power within the community described in the *Kalevala*. Interestingly, she is not so much a divine goddess as a witch. The *Kalevala* has inspired artistic work and many compositions of Sibelius and it is still a source of many recent artistic pieces of work. Whereas the mythical male heroes tend to be depicted as godlike figures in the art and literature inspired by the *Kalevala* – as in the paintings of Akseli Gallén-Kallela – the Mistress of Northland is represented as an ugly old woman, a 'hag', a witch. Yet she could also be described as a charismatic leader, bearing in mind the argument that male and female forms of charisma differ from each other because of the cultural heritage of femaleness and maleness (Aaltio and Takala, 2003).

Louhi and the story of the Sampo

The scenes in the epic in which Louhi plays a central role are the forging, theft and destruction of the magic *Sampo*. In the literature there is no consensus about what the Sampo really is, but it seems to be a source of prosperity and richness, and hence desired by everyone. Louhi's Northland is the place where the Sampo is created. In fact, it is Louhi who devises the whole idea in the first place. She turns to Väinämöinen, persuading him by saying: 'Shrewd Väinämöinen / O everlasting wise man / I don't ask for your gold coins / nor do I want your silver: / gold coins are children's playthings / silver coins are horse-trinkets. / If you can forge the Sampo / beat out the bright-lid...' Väinämöinen himself is unable to forge the Sampo, but he recommends the smith Ilmarinen as someone able to do the job instead.

In the following excerpts from Forging the Sampo (*Kalevala*, 1999, pp. 105–19), Louhi persuades Ilmarinen to forge the Sampo:

> Louhi, the mistress of Northland
> the gap-toothed hag of the North
>   comes into the yard
>   and hastened to say;
> 'What kind of man may you be
>   what sort of fellow?
> You came here by the wind's road
>   by the gale's sledge path
> and the dogs don't bark at you
> nor do the fluffy-tails speak!'

—

> Then the mistress of Northland
> inquired of the newcomer:
>   'Have you come to see
>   hear and know about
> that Ilmarinen the smith
> the most skilful of craftsmen?
> He has long been waited for
> and ages been longed for, here
>   in furthest Northland
> to make up the new Sampo.'

Ilmarinen introduces himself, saying that he himself is the skilful craftsman. Louhi offers one of her beautiful daughters to Ilmarinen in return for forging the Sampo:

> My younger maiden
> my child, my smallest baby!
>   Put on your best now
> on your body the whitest
> the softest upon your hems

> the most splendid on your breasts
> around your neck the fairest
> the most blooming on your brows
>   put red on your cheeks
>   and show off your face
> for the smith Ilmarinen
> the everlasting craftsman
> has come to make the Sampo
> Brighten the bright-lid!'

—

>   Smith Ilmarinen
> O everlasting craftsman
> if you can forge the Sampo
>   brighten the bright-lid
>   from a swan's quill tip
>   a barren cow's milk
>   a small barley grain
>   a summer ewe's down
> you'll get the maid for your pay
> for your work the lovely girl.

Ilmarinen shows no hesitation. He no doubt sees that the daughter is beautiful and tempting and he embarks on the tasks needed to forge the Sampo:

> Then the smith Ilmarinen
> put this into words: 'I'll be
> able to forge the Sampo
>   beat out the bright-lid
>   from a swan's quill tip
>   a barren cow's milk
>   a small barley grain
>   a summer ewe's down
> because I have forged the sky
> beaten out the lid of heaven
> with nothing to start off from
> with not a shred ready made.'

And so Ilmarinen begins to forge the Sampo. He has to destroy it first because it does not turn out as he wanted; then finally, after another three days, the Sampo is ready. The Mistress of the North takes the great Sampo and hides it inside the hill:

> The hag of the North was pleased;
> then she took the great Sampo
> into Northland's rocky hill
> inside the slope of copper
> and behind nine locks.
> There she rooted roots
> to a depth of nine fathoms;
> sank one root in mother earth
> and one in a riverbank
> and a third in the home-hill.

Ilmarinen goes to beg the girl: 'Will you marry me, maid, now / that the Sampo is finished / and the bright-lid fair?' The maiden is not ready, for who 'would set the cuckoo calling, / set the birds singing' if she were to go with him. She says that she is not free and cannot leave her maiden days, she has 'jobs to be done / in the summer rush – / berries on the land unpicked / the bay shores unsung / untrodden by me the glades / the groves unplayed in by me.' It is interesting that Louhi does not force her daughter but gives her free choice. She helps Ilmarinen to return home to Kalevala, which is also the home of Väinämöinen and Lemminkäinen. She is the winner – the daughter stays with her to take care of her domestic duties and now she also possesses the Sampo:

> Then the mistress of Northland
> fed the man, gave him to drink
> sat him astern in a craft
> with a paddle of copper;
> told the wind to blow
> and the north wind to bluster.
> Then the smith Ilmarinen
> the everlasting craftsman
> made for his own lands
> over the blue sea.

But when the miraculous machine has been created and Northland has grown even more prosperous, the heroes Väinämöinen, Ilmarinen and

Lemminkäinen, the wanton Loverboy, set out to take this source of wealth away from Louhi. At first they propose to share the Sampo, perhaps half of it, but Louhi is not willing:

> 'What message do the men have
> what news the fellows?'
> Steady old Väinämöinen
>   this one answers that:
> 'The men's message concerns the Sampo
> the fellows' news the bright-lid:
> we've come to share the Sampo
> to look out for the bright-lid.'
> She, the mistress of Northland
> uttered a word and spoke thus:
> 'No grouse can be shared by two
> nor a squirrel by three men.
> 'Tis good that the Sampo hums
> and the bright-lid churns away
> within Northland's rocky hill
> and inside the copper slope;
> it is good too that I am
> keeper of the great Sampo.'

After this, Louhi 'called Northland together... out for Väinämöinen's head'. The three men try to get hold of the Sampo but it is difficult. We are told that wanton Lemminkäinen 'gripped the Sampo in his arms / strove with his knees on the ground / but the Sampo will not move / the bright-lid will not swivel / for its roots had been rooted / to a depth of nine fathoms.' What is needed now is a good ox to plough up the Sampo's roots and make it move. Väinämöinen is determined to bring the Sampo out of Northland to Kalevala, home of the three heroes. He plans to do this after a journey by sea and he begs the water powers to help him:

> O wind, lull the craft
> water, rock the boat
> give help to the oars
> ease to the tiller
> on these wide waters
> on these open expanses!

Louhi takes this badly and sees her power sinking, her authority failing. She prays to her daughter, Mist, to help her forestall the intentions of the three men:

> Mist-girl, fog-maiden
> sift mist with a sieve
> waft some fog about
> drop slime down from heaven
> let a haze down from the sky
> on the clear high seas
> upon the open expanse
> to cut Väinämöinen off
> stop the man of Calm Waters!

A battle at sea ensues, as Louhi and her men fight to regain the stolen Sampo. Väinämöinen drags his sword through the water and the mist rises up to the sky. Nor is the sea monster able to get the better of Väinämöinen. It looks as if Northland's armed host is helpless and powerless; Louhi does not seem to have personal contact with her armed host and so she is left alone in the battle. Only she herself can try to get the Sampo back from the three men. She runs on foot through the water and tries to lift up the ship with her supernatural powers but fails again:

> Louhi, mistress of Northland
> runs on foot in the water
> went to raise the craft
> to lift up the ship;
> but the boat will not come up
> nor will the craft budge:
> all its ribs had snapped
> all its rowlocks splintered too.
> She thinks, considers
> and she put this into words:
> 'What is the best plan?
> What is to be done?'

Louhi decides to pursue her quest by using her supernatural powers again, assuming another shape, and transforming herself into a giant bird of prey with huge wings. She changes her shape into that of an eagle, 'spreads her wings to fly / as an eagle lifted off / and she flaps along / heading for Väinämöinen / one wing flicked the clouds / and one swerved off the water'. She tries to get the Sampo out of the boat from the three men but again fails:

> Now she changed her shape
> dared to become someone else.
> She took up five scythes
> six hoes past their prime:
> she fashioned them into claws
> fitted them to be her feet;
> the shattered part of the craft
>   she put under her;
> the sides she slapped into wings
> the rudder to be her tail;
> put a hundred men under a wing
> a thousand at her tail tip –
>   the hundred swordsmen
> the thousand fellows who shot.
> And she spread her wings to fly
> as an eagle lifted off
>   and she flaps along
> heading for Väinämöinen:
>   one wing flicked the clouds
> and one swerved off the water.

Väinämöinen once more offers a deal: to share with Louhi this miraculous artefact created by the smith Ilmarinen, one of his fellow-men. But again Louhi refuses. This leads to a final confrontation between herself and Väinämöinen: 'No, I'll not share the Sampo / with you, mean one, not / with Väinämöinen!' In the struggle that follows the Sampo falls into the water and goes crashing into a thousand pieces. In the end, no one gets it:

> As for old Väinämöinen
> Steady old Väinämöinen
> the everlasting wise man
>   saw that it was time
> knew the moment had come. He
> drew his paddle from the sea
> the oak sliver from the wave:
> with it he bashed the woman.
> He struck the claws off the eagle;

> the other claws fell to bits;
> but there was one talon left.
> And the boys fell from the wings
> the men went splosh in the sea –
> a hundred men from under a wing
> and a thousand fellows from the tail.
> The eagle herself plumped down
> clattered upon the rib beams
> like a capercaillie from a tree
> a squirrel from a spruce bough.
> Then she reached for the Sampo
> with her ring finger: she dropped
> the Sampo in the water
>   felled all the bright-lid
> down over the red craft's side
> in the midst of the blue sea;
> there the Sampo came to bits
> and the bright-lid to pieces.

These verses describe how the great Mistress of Northland loses her power. She is left on her own and she gets no support from any peers; she is without friends, without networks, without anyone to back her up. Louhi has invested her confidence in the Sampo, which is now in splinters: 'Now the power has drained from me, / my authority has failed:/ my property has foundered / the Sampo smashed in the waves!'

The loneliness of Louhi

Louhi, the Mistress of Northland, is a loner in the *Kalevala* story, but she does not look to suffer from that. She rises into a central role in the stories, a powerful woman figure in her mighty land – probably a reference to Lapland in the far north of Finland. Although Louhi is a married woman, her husband remains a distant figure in the stories. But Louhi is a mother as well; her daughters are called by name and Louhi appears to take good care of them, although they are not portrayed as particularly close. Louhi is also the figure originally behind the creation of the Sampo, the magic artefact, the source of riches and wealth. She persuades Ilmarinen to forge it but in the end she is also involved in its destruction. The male heroes steal the Sampo from Louhi, ultimately the miraculous machine falls to pieces and no-one gets it. Without cooperation between the powerful woman character, Louhi, and the men, the struggle ends to a lose–lose situation. Throughout the epic, Louhi comes across as an equal among her male 'colleagues', the three gods. Nevertheless, she remains a loner, a figure who does not seem to receive any real support from any quarter, whether from her weak husband, or her evil sons, or from the heroes of *Kalevala*. Neither does she seem to have the backing of any female characters. All in all, her relationships with the other figures in the epic are intriguing: her aloneness sets her apart, and she remains something unique, a question mark.

Ultimately, Louhi emerges as a human figure, even if she does exhibit some witch-like traits. Nevertheless, she is a skilful social negotiator and capable of long-sighted strategic thinking, as shown in the Sampo creation. Her relationships with the other characters of the *Kalevala* can be summarized as follows:

- *Louhi vs. Ilmarinen and Lemminkäinen*: Louhi is an equal colleague and a rival; she is also the one who persuades the smith Ilmarinen to forge the Sampo.
- *Louhi vs. her husband*: Louhi's husband is a weak figure with not much power either in Northland or in his own family.
- *Louhi vs. her daughters*: Louhi is a caring mother and she wants to make sure that her daughters marry worthy brave men; at the same time she seems distant and does not show much close emotion to her daughters.
- *Louhi vs. Väinämöinen*: Louhi respects Väinämöinen; they talk to each other on equal terms and also negotiate as equals. In fact, Väinämöinen is the only figure in the story with whom Louhi communicates showing empathy and closeness. She also communicates with the smith Ilmarinen, who is an artisan and thus not a fully fledged divinity. She also shows empathy towards Väinämöinen. At the beginning of the story, when Väinämöinen weeps because he is lost in Northland and yearns for home, she says: 'Do not weep, Väinämöinen / don't whine, man of Calm Waters! / 'Tis good for you to be here / sweet for you to tarry here / to eat salmon off the plate / and pork beside it'. Later she tempts Väinämöinen to forge the Sampo as a recompense for her aid in helping him to return home; thus she does not help him merely out of kindness: she wants something in return.

Most of the other female characters in the *Kalevala* are young maidens, unsure figures, beautiful and idealized women, but also subject to other people's control. Lemminkäinen's mother is a notable exception: she is an unselfish and respected older woman, deeply devoted to her son (Aaltio and Hiillos, 2003, pp. 27–46). Yet what is noteworthy about her is that she is valued solely for her son's heroic deeds (Sawin, 1990, pp. 45–69). Louhi, in contrast, is a woman in her own right, a wise elderly woman, maliciously referred to as a 'gap-toothed hag'. She does not derive her power from beauty – one source of female power – having earned it for other reasons. Louhi also possesses mystical powers, as described in the episode of the battle at sea. For example, she can transform herself, take on the shape of a bird.

All in all, the Mistress of Northland comes across as a mature and mighty woman, a strategic thinker and planner, someone who is able to maintain her powerful position and ward off her male rivals' attempts to conquer Northland. The male characters, on the other hand, are in a different position. They are friends among themselves, they have networks, whereas Louhi is on her own. Although she wields a great deal of power, she has no truly supportive friends or colleagues; she is 'a token' in the world of powerful men. Her emotional relations with her family appear quite limited; for instance, there is no mention of warm relations between Louhi and her daughters.

Many women researchers have noted the predominantly masculine viewpoint of the *Kalevala*. Its heroic narrative is masculine. Similarly, the many works of art inspired by and drawing their themes from the *Kalevala* have usually been hero-oriented and created by male artists. Moreover, the cultural milieu behind the story appears to be reflected in the way the character Louhi is described: overall she is portrayed as evil and bad, despite the fact that what she does is defend her own land and her own rightful property.

Yet in spite of the above, the Mistress of Northland herself exhibits many contradictory features. She crosses boundaries and refuses to fit into given categories. She does not match the image of a woman, and especially that of a benevolent elderly woman. She is a 'gap-toothed hag' rather than a self-sacrificing mother figure; and she is also more of a witch than a divine hero. Louhi is free to flee from Northland, free to move into areas usually dominated by men, and free to make decisions and to govern both her land and her own destiny (Vakimo, 1999, p. 71).

Final words

As in other ancient epics, the heroes in the *Kalevala* also represent gendered stereotypes. Epic structuring is, by nature, a human and also a gendered process. We can, therefore, also study the figure of Louhi as representing an image of a woman of her times. Her relationships with the epic's other characters reveal how a mighty woman like her was able to attain an important position in society. If we compare the story of this powerful woman with the findings of gender research, it is amazing how many resemblances there are: these are women without supportive networks; their decision-making is representative of their own sex; they are mediators; they face strong rivalry from their male counterparts; and they know the worlds of life and death.

It is also noticed that the *Kalevala* is the only known national epic which displays a woman, middle-aged or elderly, fighting against a whole group of male heroes. Other cultural epics have heroes fighting either against monsters or gods or, in the case of women heroes, against other women. This aspect opens up a somewhat different view of the *Kalevala* from the one sometimes taken. In feminist analyses the *Kalevala* has been criticized for misogyny and a hatred of women (Sawin, 1990, pp. 45–69), which is shown especially in the story of the Sampo as described earlier.

What can be claimed is that Louhi, the Mistress of Northland, gives dynamics to the narrative, gives it adventure and contrasts. Yet although she is mighty and powerful, she has to accept a loser's role in the end. And why does she lose? Because she lacks the supportive networks of her male rivals. She is a lonely figure in the male world of the *Kalevala*. In terms of charisma, she is undoubtedly charismatic, but not in the same way as her male rivals. Hers is a dangerous charisma, bordering on the evil and the demonic. More than a goddess she is a witch, she even transforms herself to an eagle. The male heroes remain unchanged throughout the epic. The *Kalevala* epic sees the creative but also dangerous forces of transformation and metamorphosis as belonging to female nature and as embodied within the female principle.

2
Engaged Leadership: Living the Myth and Embodying the Legend of the Olympian Athlete

Elena P. Antonacopoulou

Introduction

Leadership is one of the concepts in our language that maintains a mythical tone. It describes those – so-called 'leaders' – who are extraordinary and demonstrate qualities that are unique akin to super-humans. The legendary image with which leaders are being presented positions them in a league of their own. Leaders are heroes and in the management and organization studies literature in particular, their unique status in history is earned by their success – most frequently their success in delivering financial prosperity to the business. Therefore, it is not uncommon for leadership to be associated with winning and celebrating achievements of extraordinary proportion. Ironically, reaching the pinnacle of success is often presented with little account for any struggle, pain and suffering. It almost seems that leaders emerge to their status miraculously as if they were meant to be that way. This adds to the mystique that leadership entails, which on the one hand, makes narratives of leaders create a promising world of possibility that everyone could envision and on the other hand, a promising world of possibility that very few can be part of and only a handful can deliver.

The debate on leadership may have gone a long way to account for the vulnerability implicit in not knowing, the need for openness to engage with the insecurity of the unknown rather than clinging to the comforting security of false competence. Yet, the myth of becoming a leader has not fully accounted for the level of engagement necessary in the pursuit of leadership. It has not fully revealed the virtues of leading. It has not fully captured leadership as a practice reflecting beyond its social character, the very personal commitment requiring complete devotion, persistence and perseverance, courage and idealism. These qualities reveal that leadership is not only about purposeful action. Leadership is also about forging powerful connections through action towards making the impossible possible and mythical alive. It is also a process of practising in search of perfection where failure and disappointment are just as integral to the pursuit of leadership as the achievement of becoming a leader ought to be itself. It is these avenues for expanding the concept of leadership and the possibilities for a pragmatic understanding of what leading entails that this chapter will seek to introduce using the Olympian athlete as an illustrative example of how a myth can become a living reality. Olympism offers a useful avenue for extending the leadership debate.

The discussion begins by drawing attention to the virtues of engaged leadership. The nature of engaged leadership is illustrated in the qualities of Olympian athletes. They are chosen as a living example of mythical and legendary beings who demonstrate how extra-ordinary accomplishments are possible. The chapter concludes with some wider reflections about the place of Olympic ideals in the world of business and the leadership implications if the Olympics of organizing were to be positioned as the agenda to which leadership research and practice were to speak.

The virtues of engaged leadership

Leadership is increasingly acknowledged for being a process of learning, a process of becoming, a way of living in the search for meaning (Vail, 1996). Antonacopoulou and Bento (2003) make the case for 'Learning Leadership' as an avenue for rethinking and redefining leadership. Learning leadership is not simply about facilitating other's learning, or indeed being a skillful learner, as previously argued by proponents of the notion of learning leadership (Garratt, 1990; Schein, 1992). Learning leadership is about acknowledging that *leading is learning*.

Leadership understood as a learning practice emphasizes the importance of participation as a learner in collective leadership, as well as, the importance of participation as a leader in collective learning. In other words, confronting the dilemmas and tensions that learning and leadership present is central to also addressing the paradoxical nature of what being an engaged leader is about. This means that learning and leadership both require focus as well as flexibility. They require structure as well as agency. This fundamentally captures what engaged leadership is all about – allowing one's self to be vulnerable and to have the humility and willingness to learn things that one often does not want to learn (Hodgson, 1999). The flexibility and ability to move freely between apparently contradictory polarities requires an open mind and an open heart, but above all the ability to make practical judgements. These dimensions reveal some of the virtues of leadership and help explain why engagement is key to leadership.

The virtues of leadership

The intensions and tensions underpinning learning leadership bring attention to the embodied nature of action (Dourish, 2001). The actions of leaders are not only a matter of choice and the responsibility and accountability entailed. It is also a reflection of what they care about, what they may have a passion for. Beyond desire and passion, action also entails the very personal commitment to a goal. This personal commitment forms the orientation of leadership in relation to the human power of leaders who strive for excellence, growing through their leadership as a person and discovering their humanity.

The choices leaders make are both a reflection of their identity and self-image as well as their motivations and virtues. They are what Carlsen (2006, p. 134) calls 'life enrichments' in the search for higher purpose and in the process of improvization and imagination. To understand learning leadership is not simply a case of seeking meaningfulness in human behaviour (see Harré and Secord, 1972; Holland et al., 1998). For if we only focus on observable behaviours we will fail to see what lies beneath and what the essence of leadership is: *phronesis* (practical judgement).

The Aristotelian notion of *phronesis* as a virtue attests to the power of practical judgement in agency. *Phronesis* provides access to the ways leaders negotiate competing priorities and the internal conflict they may often encounter forms the basis of their power to excel in what they do by virtue of being who they are – individual, different. *Phronesis* is a means of making a difference not only through choice, but through application of actionable knowledge to define leadership at different points in time. *Phronesis* defines the standards of performance. It guides the leader embodying leadership in their conduct. It defines purposeful action by sensitizing leaders to be more aware of their intentions and the processes of trying, deciding, believing that an intention exists and will be pursued. Moreover, *phronesis* connects intention to actions, events and language as manifestations of intention (Hampshire, 1965). Intentionality, therefore, is not only praxis and telos; it is also *phronesis* as it reflects virtues like justice, trustworthiness, courage and honesty (McIntyre, 1985). As Beckett (2004, p. 6) reminds us 'phronesis enhances intentionality because it adds to action decisionality (the "making" of judgments) ... The making of judgments is embodied, it is constituted in *what we try*' [emphasis added]. This very point is also echoed by Sophocles (Trachiiae 415 BC) when he said that: 'One must learn by doing the thing; for though you think you know it you have no certainty until you try.'

Engagement in leadership

The ethos and virtues of leadership, coupled with the importance of intensions, actions and judgements reveal only more clearly that we cannot talk about leadership without understanding the engagement that it demands. Engagement etymologically is as much about commitment and connectivity as it is about something being under pledge. Engaging in leadership is, therefore, a promise and a vow to pursue a goal honourably beyond simply achieving desirable results. This point draws an important distinction between process (pursuing a goal) and outcome (achieving a result). The former draws more attention to the ongoing effort, the doing that any action entails. The latter draws attention to the result and mostly to positive results – success. The process of pursuing a goal involves persistently and systematically trying things out *practising*.

Practising reflects a process of becoming that is tentative and ongoing. It is not merely a process punctuated by events or activities; it is a movement that develops and unfolds through the intensity of connections that drive the process of becoming. This means that practising entails rehearsing, refining, learning, unlearning and changing actions and the relationships between different elements of an action (intension, ethos, internal and external goods, phronesis etc). Practising is as much a process of repetition as it is a space embracing the multiplicity of possibilities as different (new) dimensions are (re)discovered in a moving horizon where past, present and future meet. Antonacopoulou (2004a; 2006) defines practising as the *deliberate, habitual and spontaneous repetition* reflective of the dynamic and emergent nature of action.

Repetition in the context of practising is not a mechanistic process of replication. *Replication* implies institutionalization in the process of re-presentation and re-production. *Repetition* on the other hand, implies transgression, perfection and integration (Deleuze, 1994). Repetition forms a condition of movement, a means of producing something new in history.

Practising applied to leaders and leadership reveals that at the core of practising leadership is not simply a case of learning to rely on routines of habit. Instead, it is about unlearning and discovering different ways of embodying leadership through engagement with the process of leading. Such engaged leadership employs practising as reflexive critique (Antonacopoulou, 2004b). This means that practising must not be confused with improvizing. Researchers who have studied improvization and its application in a range of contexts (Crossan *et al.*, 1996; Hatch, 1998; Moorman and Miner, 1998) explain that improvization is about the engagement of a leader in leadership through active participation and listening as well as openness to ideas and possibilities. While all these qualities are important in practising they are not sufficient. Practising also entails visualization and immense concentration in rehearsing again and again aspects of leadership differently. It also involves a process of loosing the structure once in the act. This means that the practices of leading becomes second nature for the leader to the extent that they *are* their leadership. Practising engaged leadership, therefore, is about learning leadership that is founded not on the promise of success but on the promise of participation. Such leadership can be identified among Olympian athletes and Olympian ideals, who attest to the virtues of leadership discussed so far.

Olympian ideals and Olympic athletes as vision for leadership

In the Olympic Charter (2004) of the International Olympic Committee (IOC), the principles of Olympism are defined and are expected to guide the actions of Athletes throughout their lives and not simply during the Olympic Games:

> Olympism is a philosophy of life, exalting and combining in a balanced whole the qualities of body, will and mind. Blending sport with culture and education, Olympism seeks to create a way of life based on the joy found in effort, the educational value of good example and respect for universal fundamental ethical principles. The goal of the Olympic Movement is to contribute to building a peaceful and better world by educating youth through sport practiced without discrimination of any kind and in the Olympic spirit, [and] requires mutual understanding with a spirit of friendship, solidarity and fair play. (Olympic Charter, 2004, p. 9)

Another articulation of those principles could be summarized in one sentence by Pierre de Coubertin (the founder of modern Olympic Games): 'the most important thing in life is not to have won, but to have fought well.' In other words, the essence of achievement, which is inextricably linked with acting and performing for Olympian athletes, is not on any material stakes. Rather, the stakes are of different kind and of different qualitative value; they are underpinned by the notion of 'fighting well' and not of 'winning'. 'Fighting well' means that, athletes compete on equal terms and with will-power as the differentiating characteristic of their efforts (Owens, 1969). The embodiment of the Olympic spirit in the life of Olympian athletes is incarnated in the harmonious practising of their eternal attempts to act and perform for the sake of achievement. The most important functions of Olympian athletes are not solely training and physical practising; the educational and philosophical dimensions need be harmoniously embedded in any achieving attempt as well. Tziotis (2001) explains further that athletics, education, harmonious development of intellectual, spiritual, and bodily virtues are central to becoming an Olympian athlete and considered the highest achievement in one's life. Olympic athletes are embodying the ultimate for the society ideals of freedom, peace, equality, religion, self and mutual respect (Palelogos, 1964).

In essence, the attainment of Olympic 'goals' is the ultimate value in Olympic athletes' everyday practice and engagement with the world. Olympism is, therefore, something of a 'practical' value. Olympian athletes become the embodiments of questions not only about the relationship between physical form, mind, personality and soul, but also about cultural and historical traditions. They serve as popular educators. To be an 'Olympian' is to hold a status that is instantly recognizable and one that can never be taken away. Justifiably Jesse Owens (1969) argues that Olympic athletes are ambassadors of goodwill and are a reflection of what the Olympic Games are.

The life of truly Olympian athletes, i.e. those athletes who participate in the Olympic Games and fight neither for the glory nor for the any material gain, but for the spectacle, could be described as an 'active fighting accomplishment' (Lenk, 1982). The Olympian athlete maintains a mythical stature for the spectators akin to a Herculean man. In other words, Olympian athletes and their acting in the field of Olympic Games cannot be understood without appreciating the mythical aspect of that acting. The self-confirmation in aspiring to achievement, the dream of mastering nature and under control, with enhanced vitality and risk taking, as well as surpassing existing achievements can only be understood under the prism of the 'mythical principle' (Lenk, 1982). Ideally, the athlete dares to enter a new field of human achievement behaviour, namely the field of symbolic demonstration of strength, not over others but over himself. In essence, the Olympian athlete illustrates the Herculean myth of culturally exceptional achievement, i.e. of action essentially unnecessary for life's sustenance that is nevertheless highly valued and arises from complete devotion to striving to attain a difficult goal (Lenk, 1982).

Olympian athletes not only orient themselves and their lives to act in the world, but mainly they try to materialize goals to perform better and better, and achieve higher and higher goals. It is important to note that, by goal we mean the mythical goods of participating and of outperforming oneself. That sacred goal drives the actions of the Olympian athlete and 'creates' a passionate mind and most importantly a passionate spirit. It is the latter which defines the genuine Olympian personality. In short, the Olympian athlete acts in the world and performs in the world in order to achieve something of 'higher' value; as Lenk instrumentally puts it, Olympian athletes are 'achieving beings' that afford us to see idealism in action.

The Olympics of organizing: living the myth and embodying the legend of the Olympian athlete

The preceding sections have presented some of the virtues of leadership and illustrated these in relation to Olympian ideals and the ways in which Olympic athletes reflect these in the ways they engage with their practice. Perhaps most significantly, these virtues coupled with the standards and goals underlying the pursuit of 'excellence' reveals the achievement orientation through their participation in the games rather than the winning itself. These principles promote new ways of understanding leadership beyond the myth of success. They suggest that leadership is something of higher value and its attainment is not what defines a leader. Instead, leaders are defined by the Herculian, undefiant commitment to take up a challenge and honourably fight to excel in the goal of exceeding the challenge. This means that the goal is no longer a target to be met but an embodiment of an ideal that provides freedom and purposefulness to action.

Conceptualizing leadership in these terms is not intended to provide another metaphor for leaders as Olympic athletes nor generate another story/narrative about leadership behaviour. The objective here is to use this alternative image of leadership as a method of learning to discover leadership. In doing so, the aim is to broaden the scope of revisiting not only leadership but some of the boundaries around which leadership can be manifested. The Olympic ideals may not sit comfortably with the realities of contemporary business organizations in which leadership tends to be examined. Justifiably it could also be argued that the Olympic ideals detailed here are neglecting the political nature of Olympism at least in the way it has been commercialized. Moreover, malpractice such as doping undermines its professional orientation. These issues stand in opposition to the amateurism that has been one of the founding principles of Olympism. Unquestionably, it would be naïve to suggest that the Olympic ideals have remained intact throughout time, from the Classical Greek society where these ideas were founded to the wider global world where they have been interpreted and currently 'protected' by committees and other governing bodies that are meant to preserve them. These structures are much in evidence in the Olympic Games where clear, fixed and public rules of qualification and evaluation of play shape the arena in which Olympism manifests itself. Perhaps, the transcience of these ideals throughout time lies more in their generality. This does not mean that the concept of Olympism is unclear but that the meanings it comprises of admit to possibly contesting interpretations. This point is succinctly made by Macaloon (1982, p. 139) when he stated that the Olympic Movement strives essentially to educate humanity to 'experiment with the possible relations between conflict and cooperation elsewhere in social life, to contest "for the best representations" of how things are, might be and ought to be.'

Thus, naturally, the concept of Olympism will find different expressions in time and place, history and geography. There will be differing conceptions of Olympism, which will interpret the general concept in such a way as to bring it to real life in a particular context. Taken together, the promotion of these values will be seen to be the educative task, and sport will be seen as a means. The Olympic ideas are, therefore, offered here as a basis for a framework that opens up new possibilities for conceptualizing the myth of leadership as an accomplishment worth making sacrifices for. It is also intended to provide an illustration of how a myth can become alive in action. If business leaders were to entertain the possibility that their objective is to strive towards the Olympics of organizing instead of the bottom line. If business leaders were to become living Herculian legends in their embodiment of leadership virtues; if business leaders were to embrace leadership as an arena for learning, practising and performing, what might the consequence of this be? It would certainly be worth exploring all these 'what ifs' because they widen the scope of leadership to become a mastering of business action entailing so much more than current leadership theory and research allows it to be.

These questions and possibilities open up a new chapter in leadership theory and research. They provide a different platform from which to understand the nature of organizing, the challenges of leading and the opportunities for leadership. Fundamentally, the Olympic perspective encourages further inquiry into the concept of leadership to embrace learning and engagement as two very significant dimensions. It also encourages reflexive critique in the myths that our current dominant paradigms limit us in contructing. By exploring the Olympic ideals we do not seek to replace one metaphor for another. Instead, we look beyond the ideal to the real, to provide new meanings and greater alighnment between theory and practice.

This point reminds us that in contructing the leadership myth we have a number of unexplored arenas in which to extend our investigation, and the study of Olympic athletes may well be one arena worth investing in capturing examples of leaders. These examples of leaders may in fact be more relevant to business practitioners as they will be less bounded by specific cultural, historical and economic forces of a particular organizational context. These examples would have wider generality to encourage them to reframe their paradigms and governing practices in relation to leadership by discovering beyond the contextual forces what their personal level of commitment is, what goals define their actions and with what level of engagement they seek to pursue the Olympics of organizing. In short, how genuine can their leadership be taken to be, if beyond their professional conduct one was also looking to unravel the true amateurism (love for) leading?

Conclusions

The analysis in this chapter has sought to extend the transformational paradigm of leadership research by revisiting the notion of 'learning leadership' to reveal the important leadership virtues that shape how leadership is pursued in action. This view challenges the myth of leadership and its relationship to short-term/bottom line success. It invites researchers and practitioners instead more fully to appreciate the richness of pursuing leadership with an achievement orientation that does not focus on the winning but on the fighting. The latter, embraces not only virtues of humility, perseverence, courage, care and passion. It also places the emphasis on trying things out, practising in an engaged way, taking failure as a necessary basis for achieving a better performance next time. The beauty of embracing leadership as the pursued of the Olympics of organizing is that it transforms a myth into a living reality and a legend into an embodied manifestation of what leading is, could be, and ought to be.

Acknowledgement

The author would like to acknowledge the support of the ESRC/EPSRC Advanced Institute of Management Research under grant number RES-331-25-0024 for this research. Mr Emmanuel Gheredakis was employed to gather some of the material on the Olympics and his research assistance is acknowledged.

3
From Managers to Artists and Priests: On Transformation and Development of Organizational Leaders

Dorota Bourne

Introduction

The collapse of the Soviet bloc in 1989 and the opening up of the boundaries in Eastern Europe created an opportunity to stimulate the transfer of knowledge between Western and Eastern Europe, which had been restricted since the end of World War II. According to Zaleska (1998), the process of cultural change and the learning of Polish leaders in foreign companies in the early 1990s were inhibited due to the relations of dominance embedded in the processes and structures of multinationals. The learning and development of Polish managers often lacked opportunities for the development of key management skills in market economies: for example, leadership and strategic expertise (Koźmiński, 1993; Zaleska, 1998). The roles of Polish managers were subordinate and executive as the creative decision-making took place in multinational central headquarters. However, according to many authors (see Kostera, 1995a; Koźmiński, 1995; Zaleska, 1998), some aspects of Polish culture also contributed to a new, emerging dependency structure. As they argued, the behaviour of Eastern European managers involved such elements as unrealistic expectations and feelings of inferiority and was, therefore, partly to blame for the imperialistic behaviour of Western managers and the impediment of knowledge transfer between these parties.

According to Koźmiński (1995), there are two kinds of expatriate manager coming to Eastern Europe: 'mercenaries' and 'crusaders'. The former are expatriates who bring with them Western ideas of management in a simplified and standardized form that does not take into account local culture and context. They tend to operate on the basis of having knowledge of a specific 'one best way' of management. The latter type of expatriate, the 'crusaders', take an approach targeted at the sensitive promotion of cultural change by engaging in culture-clash management and the implementation of new management techniques (Koźmiński, 1995, pp. 98–9).

Hatch *et al.* (2005) discussed the role of leaders in business by introducing three types of leaders:

- *Manager* – characterized by a disciplined, rational approach to work, organized, controlling, focused on strategic vision and decision-making. This type of a leader helps employees develop their skills and relies on his/her expertise as a source of power.
- *Artist* – characterized by a curious and independent approach to work, able to create and provoke others. This type of artist helps employees develop their imaginations, focused on artistic vision, innovation and originality.
- *Priest* – characterized by an emphatic and ethical approach to work, offering inspiration, comfort and faith to the employees. His/her vision is transcendent (metaphysical), and its purity a source of power.

This typology brings out the importance of inspiration and innovation in the relationship between leaders and their followers. It could be argued that in order for expatriate managers to become 'crusaders' they need to engage in behaviours and actions characteristic of 'artists' and 'priests'. Their reliance on managerial functions without elements of creative contribution on the part of the employees limits the potential for organizational learning as well as the ability of the company to engage in a transformationalist type of knowledge transfer and globalization as defined by Giddens (1996; 1999). By developing their leaders beyond managerial functions and creating 'artists' and 'priests', multinationals can create an environment where the learning and development of their employees can go beyond basic training and enable them to reach a higher level of expertise and self-fulfillment. This in turn can enable more equal power relationships and some decentralization of strategic decision-making on an international level.

Research design

This study looks at the function of leadership within General Motors (GM) during the process of transferring managerial ideas and know-how between different GM plants. I focus on the role of expatriate managers as being a necessary medium for the transfer of knowledge. Their role involved transferring and maintaining ideas that were required for the successful implementation of know-how in several GM plants. The ideas they brought consisted of concepts related to manufacturing processes, Total Quality Management (TQM), people management and General Motors' corporate philosophy.

The research used the ethnographic techniques derived from anthropology, which represents the most distinctive methodological approach in the study of knowledge transfer (Rogers, 1962/1995). The incorporation of the ethnographic interview and non-participant observation enabled the study of two cultures between which the process of ideas transfer took place.

The empirical study was conducted at the Vauxhall Luton Plant in England and Opel Polska in Gliwice, Poland. It consisted of 30 in-depth, key-informant interviews and non-participant observation in both locations.

Two locations, two different pasts

The Vauxhall plant in the UK has a very long and rich history. It used to be one of the biggest and best employers in the Luton area. It was an independent plant, planning and assembling all of its products (e.g. engines, exhausts) or getting them made locally. After GM acquired the plant, the majority of UK operations were shifted abroad. The company became centrally governed by GM and started operating as all other GM's plants. From massive production, it changed the system into lean manufacturing. Many local suppliers have been swapped for other foreign suppliers from the GM network. Vauxhall became part of the GM Family and was transformed into a lean manufacturing plant. This transformation happened after the plant had already existed for 22 years and had had a well-established culture, workforce and facilities.

In the early 1990s, GM decided to build four new plants in order to keep up with the emerging markets of Eastern and Central Europe. Poland was among the potentially cheap producers with low labour costs and a convenient Central European location, enabling a reduction in the transportation costs of cars sent to Western Europe (Opel Polska exports cars to Germany and England, among other countries). The Polish market, with its quickly developing economy, was itself a very important target for Opel cars.

GM chose Gliwice as a location for their Polish plant. It is a small town in the South of Poland, situated in the region where local employment used to be largely dependent on coal mining. It was strongly affected by the mining crisis of the 1990s with the local employment rate dropping below the national average (GUS, 1998).

The selection process set up by GM was targeted entirely at young, inexperienced people who were willing to learn and accept the new ideas brought by GM as the way in which cars were going to be produced. The selection of employees that fitted this profile was also enabled by a very high number of applicants and the high unemployment rate in the Silesia region.

Leaders in General Motors

International Service Personnel (ISP) is an institution developed by GM to enable knowledge transfer to new plants on an international level. Those at the top of the organizational mountain are often ISPs who call themselves 'the founding fathers' of the company.

For the creation of the Opel Polska plant a group of approximately 25 people was chosen, in which there were candidates predominantly from Great Britain, but also from Germany and Canada. They were all experts in their fields with considerable lean manufacturing experience as long as 38 years for some. Most people in this group were ex-employees of Japanese car companies (mainly Toyota and Nissan), the majority of which had also worked in Japan. The ISP can be perceived as a medium enabling effective knowledge transfer. Despite being very expensive, the ISP network is deemed essential and remains a very important institution in the GM world.

Leaders as managers

The most traditional and basic role adopted by organizational leaders relates to managerial responsibilities and tasks. The core of this role consists of a decision-making, rational, analytical approach to work and training, and the development of specific skills among the employees.

The managerial function was dominant at the Vauxhall Luton plant, which also had a history of this style of leadership being favoured by past leaders:

> When I first came here, it was full of autocratic, dictatorial managers, who dictated the daily events. And it was with people who literally did what they were told to do. Today, it's much more dynamic, it's much faster. It's much more stressful but there is a greater involvement and it's not the arrogant kind of 'big boss' syndrome in all environments. The hierarchical structure, if you like, is a kind of plateau, more of a flatter, natural environment where generally people can interact together. And when I started here, you would not

talk to your boss unless your boss spoke to you. You just didn't. If you were asked the question and you answered it wrong, it was absolutely career limiting, much more intimidating, much more the fear factor, and stressful for the wrong reasons, it was just stressful for fear whereas now it's faster, it's much more interactive. It's stressful but it's a stress that could be adrenaline. You know, it's a buzz. It's a much more business-orientated place. (English Manager 7, Vauxhall Luton)

Vauxhall went through an enormous change in the 1990s. The managerial style and way of conducting business became less 'archaic' following the company's new philosophy of people management inspired by the Japanese philosophy of organization. However, the plant never progressed to a more transformational style of leadership that would stimulate change at a deeper level of culture. Organizational leaders in Vauxhall remained in their managerial roles not being able to unleash the creative potential that lay in them as well as in their workforce. The plant was plagued by low motivation and involvement of the employees on the production level. Poor quality and financial results over several consecutive years lead to the plant's closure in 2001. Some ISPs admitted that Vauxhall's long history contributed to their inability to engage in a different leadership style:

> In the green field, we just told people, 'This is what you do. This is what you check. This is where we check it. If you find the problem this is whom you tell.' Now, if you are trying to do that in a brown field site, where people have had long experience with another system, you will struggle because they will say, 'Well, we don't need to do that. Why do we do that?' So, you change the mindset. And that's the most difficult challenge anybody has to have, to take a brown field workforce, a brown field culture, and try to change it. That is very difficult and very frustrating. I spent two and a half years trying to do it and let me tell you, all the hard work of this green field was nothing compared to the frustration of trying to change an old, traditional group of people. (English Manager 1, Nissan UK, GME, Opel Polska)

The attitudes towards the learning of new managerial and lean production practices in Poland were in stark contract with those in the UK. The Polish workforce was selected on the basis of their young age and openness to learn. Therefore, it is not surprising that they approached their organizational training with eagerness and ambition. Additionally, their lack of previous experience in car manufacturing made them less critical of the techniques and principles of car production introduced by the expatriate managers:

> I'm particularly impressed by their [the ISP's] systematic approach to their job. That they really can think, react, divide and connect, analyse and partition, allocate work, collect results and come to conclusions, all in a deliberate and measured way. Sure, it reflects an enormously well developed training background; at the same time, those people really must believe in what they're doing, otherwise they couldn't possibly keep it up on a day-by-day basis. That's what we lacked in the old days. (Polish Manager 3, Opel Polska)

It took only three years for Opel Polska to become a fully developed, mature car plant. In 2000 the plant's excellent quality results gave it the first place in GM's European rating. The English managers call it 'the best plant GM has got', a benchmark for Europe.

Leaders as artists

The changes that Opel Polska has gone through since 1998 are enormous – from a green field to the leading GM car manufacturer in Europe. Considering the lack of success in the Polish car manufacture in the past this is a very significant achievement:

> I firmly believe that if you treat people with respect, if you train them properly and you clearly tell them what you're trying to achieve, they will do it. And where this business has gone wrong in the past is where management has not stepped out clearly set objectives, clearly explained what is expected, and management not knowing what's going on in their plant ... We need to listen to them and take into account their opinion, which traditionally in a lot of the older industries, you know, they're just workers, we don't need to talk to them, which is crazy. (English Manager 1, Nissan UK, GME, Opel Polska)

Leaders in Opel Polska adopted a role that went beyond managerial responsibilities and reliance on expertise. They engaged in a dialogue with the local workforce that enabled both parties to be creative and innovative. By creating a platform where people could express their ideas in a non-threatening environment they used a potential of the Polish employees that may have otherwise remained hidden. This also stimulated a development of the ISPs who had to develop their role and become 'artists' of the company:

> I must say that managing this sort of team is, on the one hand, a great treat since these are people who really do have lots of ideas, they're very creative, and they're self-starters. There's no hard done-by attitude of the kind you sometimes see where the only thing that's talked about is remuneration. Here, they take their satisfaction from the quality of their work and the innovations they might introduce to it, as much as from their pay. And there's some internal competitiveness as well, healthy competitiveness I'd say. But, on the other hand, managing this sort of team is a great challenge because you simply can't cover up uncertainty or inability with some sort of facade of self-confidence, because these people will see through it very easily. Simply stated, they're very demanding subordinates. (Polish Manager 5, Opel Polska)

The development of Opel Polska employees as well as ISPs enabled some changes in the organizational structure of the plant. During the initial few years of the Opel Polska operation, there was no first line management, only first line supervision by 'ex-pat' managers, which created a deliberate gap in the management structure. The creation of this gap enabled the best people from the local teams to be promoted and fill these positions. Those who were promoted were high calibre people with excellent communication skills who replaced many ISPs who had left Opel Polska. This change in the structure lowers costs for the plant, and those ISPs who have stayed have taken up roles as coaches to their Polish colleagues:

> It no longer needs to be an ISP company. Now it needs to be a Polish company. And I can already see that this change has already started to happen ... And actually, all that you will eventually have, maybe it will take another five years, but eventually, there will only be two or three positions like plant director, maybe manufacturing director and finance director. Eventually, those will be the only, how can I say, non-local positions. Just like they are in IBC. Just like they are in Vauxhall. They will always be ISPs in Opel Polska because there are ISPs everywhere, you know, specific skills gaps or to identify them, other people are brought in. So what I want for Opel Polska now is that as fast as possible it becomes a company run by the local people

and that the ISPs take a side role, which is guidance and coaching, rather than directing and managing. (English Manager 4, Nissan UK, Vauxhall Luton, Opel Polska)

Leaders as priests

The process of ideas translation in Opel Polska proved to be creative and led to the full institutionalization of the managerial concepts brought by General Motors. The centralization of decision-making present in GM was accepted by the staff and perceived by them as relatively loose and enabled them sufficient degrees of freedom. Standardization and other organizational rituals were hardly ever questioned and were welcomed as a refreshing novelty. Many of these ideas were new in Poland and were received by the local staff as a factor in making them members of the GM world:

> These people may have excessive expectations of the company. Their parents' generation looked on the General Motors or Opel brand as an impossible dream, a magical token of life elsewhere; and now this dream has been realized here. (Polish Manager 7, Opel Polska)

This willingness to belong to this organization was further enhanced by the strong sense of ownership the Poles gained from their participation in building the plant, and also from their national ambition to succeed within the global car manufacturing arena. This success symbolizes the Polish transformation from a centrally planned to a market economy – from the membership of the Eastern block to the membership of Western Europe:

> Opel Polska is almost a bit evangelical. Do you know what I mean when I say that? It's almost like a religion. You know, our management team tends to be a fairly outgoing, passionate group of people that strongly believe in what they are trying to do. We have a lot of team and leadership-type activities ... And it's tooling mechanisms like this that drive the culture of Opel Polska, which is really very strong. (English Manager 4, Nissan UK, Vauxhall Luton, Opel Polska)

Opel Polska is not a typical Polish factory. The introduction of Western concepts of management resulted in the creation of a highly distinctive plant. There is a stark contrast between the ways in which

Opel Polska operates and develops its employees and that of other Polish companies:

> And this kind of development is a huge responsibility for the company management. Some would call it brainwashing, but taken in good faith, it's simply a form of training in various work practices. And you can tell just by looking at people. Some have got so involved and have changed so much that even their nearest and dearest don't recognize them. They don't recognize what's happened to them in a good way; but also, it may be, in a way which is problematic for their environment. (Polish Manager 3, Opel Polska)

Conclusions

Organizational theory literature analyzing leadership and factors impacting on the effectiveness of leaders usually focuses on the behaviours and actions of leaders. However, as this chapter shows, leadership style and its effectiveness are closely linked to the organizational culture and the values shared by all organizational members. Therefore, it is important to consider leadership as a process which is not only embedded in organizational culture but is also shared by leaders as well as their followers.

As described in the example of the General Motors, leadership is a two-way process where both parties can have significant impact upon the style of leadership that will develop in a particular context as well as the roles that will be adopted by the employees. Using the example of Vauxhall Motors in the UK one could argue that strong resistance to change and willingness to maintain status quo on the part of employees will stimulate a managerial style of leadership. It can also potentially hinder the development of organizational leaders into 'artists' and 'priests' as defined by Hatch *et al.* (2005).

The example of Opel Polska illustrates that the presence of shared values such as willingness to change and learning and progress in the organization can create a platform for further development of leaders. The type of environment where both parties engage in creative effort and organizational learning stimulates leaders to advance to the roles of 'artists' and 'priests'. Moreover, when both parties are actively engaged in this process, a higher level of organizational creativity and innovation can be achieved.

Following Kostera (2005), I argue that organizations can provide a meaningful platform for identity formation and self-actualization. This study portrays the journey that organizational actors took along with their leaders. The Vauxhall Luton and Opel Polska plants, despite having very similar management traditions, developed contrasting cultures and platforms for the development of their employees as well as leaders. While Vauxhall remained plagued by problems with control, poor quality and motivation, Opel Polska people embraced General Motors leaders as well as the philosophy they brought with them. This enabled both parties to create an organization where training and culture management enhanced the development of leaders as well as other employees. It also positively contributed to the identity formation of both parties and actualization of some important collective ambitions.

4
The Uncanny Organization Man: Superhero Myths and Contemporary Management Discourse

Alf 'Orgspawn' Rehn and Marcus 'Analysator' Lindahl

Introduction

Mythology, as a concept, is commonly thought to refer to a system of stories of ancient gods or similar archaic religious phenomena, a template adhered to even in more modern mythologies, such as the powerful *Cthulhu Mythos* (*Iä! Iä! Cthulhu fhtagn!*). However, we can in popular culture find elaborate mythological systems not strictly tied to religious structures, and more akin to the often less studied hero-myth tradition. One specific such, which we'll argue has an influence on contemporary management discourse, is that of superhero comics. Starting from the first issue of Action Comics (June 1938), superhero comics have been at the forefront of analyzing the prevailing cultural unconscious, and no other form of cultural expression can measure up to comics in sheer popular culture referencing value. Even if we restrict ourselves to the two main Western mythologies – DC and Marvel – the collected storylines in these 'universes' (as comic book mythologies are nowadays commonly known) contain an almost limitless amount of potential for story-telling and iconic referencing, and one which is oft-used across cultural forms – including the form we know as management.

The focus of this chapter is dual: on one hand, it discusses how management tropes have been used in the art of the comic book; on the other, it analyses the ways in which business leaders have been compared with, and likened to, superheroes. The chapter thus discusses a dialectic of sorts – whereas superheroes are used as icons through which one can describe and idolize business leaders (and other organizational figures), our understanding of managers and CEOs is in part affected and filtered through how these are portrayed in comics. A dual figure such as Batman/Bruce Wayne or Ironman/Tony Stark shows this duality well – the hero as a tycoon with multiple masks and identities, and an internalized notion of the business leader as a potential superhero. Working from a cultural studies perspective, the chapter thus studies this duality by discussing superhero-managers, both real/ascribed and fictional.

The chapter suggests a need for a broader approach to the study of both myths in organizations and the cultural analysis of management and organization. Rather than seeing the relation between myths and management as a unilinear process, it works from a perspective that sees this as a complex sequence of iterative effects, where a separation between the mythology and the manager becomes untenable. In a very real sense, business leaders can be superheroes and comics management manuals. But the chapter also argues for a broader perspective on the notion of mythology within management studies, one which sees the former as something beyond a metaphoric grab-bag.

On universes

If we assume that a mythology cannot simply be any story with mythic elements, but must instead form a system of differing mythical beings, several narratives, and a notion of connections between the differing parts of the selfsame, we will see that a study of mythology must extend beyond simple metaphoric comparisons between different kinds of actors, and instead focus on the way in which mythological narration builds on the existence of a system. Often, when mythological aspects have been explored within the field of management and organization studies, this fact has been ignored, and one has instead been content with making simple one-to-one comparisons to a solitary mythical figure, ignoring the cultural and ideological context within which this figure exists. In this vein we can find, for instance in the ever-popular 'Leadership Secrets of ...'-category of books, comparisons between a CEO and a defunct deity without any sense for the cult of said deity, or the way in which s/he occupied a specific place in a pantheon and so on and so forth. A central aspect of any mythology is a notion that in comic-book universes have been referred to as 'continuity'; that is, that the intermingled and connected web of narratives that a mythology consists of must be consistent over time and that paradoxes must be solved somehow.

The way this has been done in comic-dom is by introducing the notion of a shared universe. This emerged as a kind of necessity, driven by the desire to do so-called 'cross-overs'. When Superman and Batman met, this obviously was only possible if Metropolis and Gotham City existed in the same physical universe (even though both cities are New York, thinly veiled). Over time, such visits became more frequent, and in some cases even affected story-lines. As the world of superhero-comics is dominated by two companies, Marvel and DC, these developed into a kind of parallel universes, so that it became natural to assume that the Justice League lived in a universe where what happened to Superman could well affect the life of the Green Lantern, whereas this would have no impact on; for example, Hawkeye, who as a member of Marvel's the Avengers occupies an entirely different universe. Arguably this was taken furthest by Marvel, where a character might turn up in just a single frame of another character's adventure, yet still affect the happenings in the universe as a whole.

This might seem like a fairly marginal observation regarding storytelling, but it has some bearing as to how we are to engage in the study of mythologies. This text is built on the assumption that these should be studied as wholes with their own internal but fairly complete logic. Whereas the notion of continuity and universes was first brought in to explain how it was possible for different heroes to meet and interact, it has also served to explain things which were earlier taken for granted. For instance, whereas the question as to how a hero or a group of heroes could afford their suits and equipment (not to mention their hideouts) used to be ignored or explained away in an off-hand manner, the later development in comic-book storytelling put almost as much focus on backstories and explanations than on the action itself. This has also led to comics becoming a complex form of cultural expression, one which can be used to understand society and societal change.

Where the assumption has often been that comics and similar popular culture forms are less interesting than more highfalutin cultural products, due to associations to low-brow entertainment and juvenile amusement, we would contend that the opposite is in fact true. Whereas the dramas of an Ibsen or a Shakespeare may carry more cachet among academics who like to see themselves as cultured and sophisticated, popular culture is in fact a much more potent form when it comes to disseminating ideas in society. Whether we are talking about leadership, management, entrepreneurship or plain old capitalism, chances are that the first place we encountered these was in children's culture and specifically in comics. The myth of management is not born in organizations, nor is it carried by tales of Ulysses. Instead, it comes to us first with a SOCK! and a POW! in magnificent colour, panel for panel. And what tales they tell ...

Tales of capes and champagne

No one, not even the eponymous Superman, has managed to become as iconic superhero as Batman. As one of the world's most recognized brands, and as one of the two linchpins of the DC universe (with Superman, a friend and frequent collaborator, as the other), Batman is the pre-eminent example of both the 'human' superhero and the dark and complex category of superheroes. He might even be seen as a partial inspiration to how Marvel re-cast heroes as capable of human foibles and ordinary problems. The figure of Batman has been analyzed in depth, both as a psycho-sexual wonderland of traumas and as a symbol of vigilante justice and urban decay, and one might wonder how this relates to the field of management. Still there is a side to Batman that is closer to the boardroom than it is to the back-alley.

The aspect that is most pertinent to this chapter is his 'real' identity as Bruce Wayne and the vast family fortune and corporation that is tied to this. As owner and (occasionally) manager of Wayne Enterprises, Bruce Wayne has access to a number of things such as advanced technology and otherwise hard-to-get information, and in addition a handy way of replenishing the wealth he so happily squanders on crime-fighting. In the early days, Bruce Wayne was simply a playboy millionaire, where his wealth served mainly as a *deus ex machina* for the various (and often lavish) expenditures his escapades as Batman necessarily led to. As children, we realized that the Batcave, the Batcopter, the Batmobile, and the envy-inducing utility belt were major investments and that we couldn't afford them. We accepted the fact that Bruce Wayne was born into money and that he, therefore, could. However, this little fact might be more central to the story of Batman than it originally seems. Batman has no real superhuman abilities, even though he is one of the world's most accomplished hand-to-hand fighters, a fantastic acrobat, and has a genius-level intelligence with technical aptitude to boot. Still, he is 'merely human', whereas many of his friends and foes have *bona fide* super-powers. Most of his powers in fact stem from his wealth and his position in society, which have enabled him to develop into the Batman and equip himself with some of the finest gadgets in the DC universe. (Interestingly, this makes Batman rather similar to one of Marvel's major villains – the aristocratic psychopath Dr. Doom.)

Although Bruce Wayne was originally more of a cover-story for Batman, the dual role of being both a tycoon and a hero has become increasingly important for understanding his nature. In the early stories, Wayne Enterprises was barely mentioned and not seen as particularly important. In the contemporary storyline(s), Bruce Wayne is an active (if a little *blasé*) manager of a major corporation, and it is implied that his skills in sleuthing and crime-fighting actually support his management activities. In the latest movie incarnation, *Batman Begins*, the corporation and the intrigue therein even become an integral part of the storyline. What can be learnt from this change, the way in which Bruce Wayne is slowly morphing from a playboy to a manager? Obviously, one of the things this shows is a change in society. While readers in the 1940s and 1950s would have been comfortable with the thought of an idle millionaire fighting crime, such a figure would seem rather odd today. In the contemporary era, where economy is no longer merely a specialized interest for a small group of people, but rather a sphere that encompasses all aspects of society, and all individuals therein, it is natural that the economy and its relations become fodder for popular culture. Another thing is the fact that managers are no longer the faceless men of the organization. Whereas a manager in the 1960s was a boring and rather faceless figure, the swashbuckling 1980s brought in the idea that management and economy could be dramatic and populated by colourful figures. Even though public discourse had the tendency to portray managers as villains more than heroes, the possibility for a more rounded and ever super-human manager was established both through figures such as Ivan Boesky (who probably could have carried off both a pretty good evil laugh and a cape) and more embraced icons such as Lee Iacocca.

If we look for the character in the Marvel universe who most closely resembles the Batman/Bruce Wayne duality, the obvious choice would be Iron Man/Tony Stark. Whereas Bruce Wayne even in later incarnations is portrayed as aristocratic and part of 'old money', Tony Stark is cast more as a plucky entrepreneur who develops into an industrialist. Although he also inherited in part his father's company, Stark Industries, the saga makes much of the way in which he develops it into a major global corporation, Stark International, later Stark Enterprises. At one point, having battled with alcoholism and losing his company, he even starts a completely new company, Circuits Maximus. Just like Batman, Tony Stark lacks real super-powers – he is just a man, with a heart condition (later cured), occasional neurological damage, and alcohol-dependency issues. However, his skills as a manager and a technologist have enabled him to construct a form of armour which he can don and become one of the more powerful heroes in the Marvel universe. None of this would have been possible without the help of a corporation (or at least the framework of such has helped a whole lot). The fortunes of the Stark conglomerate has been a continuous presence in the Iron Man storyline. It is often implied that it is the same set of talents that enable Tony Stark to run his company that help Iron Man save the world. This intermingling of the manager and superhero is part of what makes both Batman and Iron Man so intriguing.

Management, get ready to Rrrrumble!

We can now think about what this might mean for those who read comic books. While the literature on leadership and management often bemoans that culture tends to cast managers as soulless and evil, we can see quite a different logic in superhero comics. Here, instead of assuming that accountants are boring, photographers geeks, and jocks heroes, comic books turn the tables on most other cultures, transforming clichés and traditional images into both novel interpretations and turning them upside down. For a reader of comic books, the notion of a manager can mean both 'normality', heroics, and villainy, often amplified to extremes. Arguably this is true of literature in general as well, but at stake are not the benefits and sublime dimensions of literature, but the question why comics have been ignored in the analysis of management. Working from the assumption that cultural impressions acquired at an early age will strongly affect how we view a phenomenon (i.e. sticking with one of the basic assumptions shared by sociology, anthropology, social psychology and developmental theories), this would go to show that comics are one of the places where we acquire the mythology of management. Further, by casting managers in a number of roles – good, evil and beyond – comics create early templates and position contemporary capitalism as a place where both drama and heroism can take place.

A critical case for doing this could be the tale where Tony Stark is almost crushed by his rival Obadiah Stane. Stark's alcoholism has at times been critical. In this storyline, he is pushed to a point where he starts drinking on such a scale that he eventually finds himself losing everything, including Stark International. This narrative, which might resonate with entrepreneurship researchers, leads to our hero finding himself a homeless derelict and his friend, Jim Rhodes, stepping up as the new Iron Man. When Stark finally bounces back, he founds a new company (the aforementioned Circuits Maximus) and starts developing an even better version of his armour. As he succeeds as a businessman, Obadiah Stane feels it necessary to retaliate through the usual approach of comic-book villains – sending henchmen. After all else has failed, Stane equips himself with an alternate Iron Man suit (called 'The Iron Monger', which goes to show that even super-villains struggle with branding issues) in order to fight Tony Stark/Iron Man to the death. In the end, the new, more entrepreneurial version of both the armour and the man prove themselves and Stark defeats Stane. The latter then swiftly commits suicide.

What does this little story, which took place over a number of issues of *The Invincible Iron Man* (Stane is first seen in issue no. 163 and dies in issue no. 200), tell us about how management can be understood? To begin, it shows that business dealings can be understood and presented as life-and-death issues and that the machinations of managers can be seen as having drastic consequences. Stark's descent into alcoholism is shown as a direct consequence of how Stane tried to manipulate him as a business rival, and the ascent of the new Stark as an entrepreneur is told in a way that would make Schumpeter proud. But it also presents the mythological character of 'the manager' as a template that can be filled in different ways. Stark and Stane are both shown as being hard and capable businessmen, demanding managers and exceedingly smart. Both are consummate professionals, driven and highly intelligent. The only real difference is that one is (mostly) good and the other is (assumedly) evil. This duality, with two managers representing both good and evil, big business and entrepreneurship, winners and (potential) losers, and so on, is one of the main driving forces behind comic mythologies, but it also serves an interesting ideological function. From this position, it might not even be particularly important who wins their internal battle as in both cases it will be management that comes out on top. Now, the kind of simplified narrative that's presented here might not necessarily affect an adult, professional reader who has his or her ideological framework in place, but for the main audience of such tales it presents a potent figure of how corporations (personified in their CEOs) can be powerful and moral agents, and that management can be seen as just as mythological as ever the jousting between the *Theoi Olympioi* and the *Theoi Khthonioi*.

'Chainsaw', 'Neutron' and the rest of the boys

In 1986, John Byrne created a complete re-imagining of the Superman *mythos* in a mini-series called 'The Man of Steel'. This altered the character in many ways as well as introducing new elements to the mythology. The most radical change, however, was the way in which this retelling cast Superman's arch-nemesis, Lex Luthor. Whereas Luthor was originally presented as an evil scientist in the tradition of pulp detective comics, a megalomaniacal genius with a penchant for phantasmagorical gadgets, he was now presented as a major tycoon who ran his business enterprises through ruthlessness as well as illegality and malfeasance.

Much has been made of how this was a way to make Luthor a more believable villain in our modern age. A contemporary reader is less likely to fear corrupt scientists than evil businessmen and the new Luthor would be both more realistic and easier to fit into the DC universe. However, we have a slightly different reading of this change. Whereas most commentators have focused on the fact that a manager now made a good villain, we're more interested in the fact that a CEO now could be seen as a worthy adversary to an almost infinitely powerful being, almost Superman's equal. Whereas Marvel's Kingpin was a powerful criminal businessman, his main adversary was Daredevil, a hero with acute superhuman senses and admirable martial art skills but in no way a match for a Superman. The new Lex Luthor was something much more, ending up as the president of the United States and coming very close to killing Superman.

Whereas the caricature of the businessman as a scoundrel and a conman might well be as old as trade itself and has existed in various racist and xenophobic versions throughout history, one might look to other social changes in the 1980s to try to grasp why Lex Luthor became a businessman, Tony Stark more clearly an industrialist, and Bruce Wayne started noticing his businesses. Obviously, the 1980s were the age where businessmen and financiers became larger-than-life. Jack Welch took over General Electric, and his management style afforded him the decidedly superhero-like nickname 'Neutron' Jack (because after him, houses still stood but all the people were gone). Michael Milken became something like Marvel's Dr. Strange, a sorcerer supreme of the financial world who could make billions appear out of thin air. 'Chainsaw' Al Dunlap had yet to make it to the headlines (his story, worthy of any Stan Lee comic, took place in the late 1990s), but a young nerd by the name of Bill Gates become increasingly visible (he appeared on the cover of *TIME Magazine* in 1984). Carl Icahn helped create the notion of a corporate raider (interestingly, he later tried to take over Marvel, although without an Iron Man suit). The dealings around RJR Nabisco were setting the stage for one of the most public leveraged buy-outs in history. In other words, it wasn't necessarily the fact that 1986 was a good year to launch a crooked businessman (many of the aforementioned hadn't fallen from grace yet), but rather that it was a great year to state that a businessman could truly be a Master of the Universe (Tom Wolfe's *The Bonfire of the Vanities*, which popularizes the term, was published in 1987). It wasn't a question of comics creating a management mythology or the real world of business turning into a cartoon, but rather a both/and. Both management and comics are potent reagents to the Zeitgeist. The study of these two in conjunction can highlight dynamic characteristics in how our culture creates and recreates images of management.

What we've tried to illuminate in our discussion is that the study of both management and mythology must rid itself of cultural bias. Much of the study of how culture portrays themes from the business world is done in/on cultural forms that represent elitist interests and narrow niches. One often feels these are written primarily to highlight the cultural know-how and sophistication of the author rather than illustrate any salient point. (Luckily, the authors of this chapter have no sophistication at all.) However, this has by 'mainstream' business studies been seen as proof positive that the cultural analysis of management is marginal and unnecessary, which is also missing the point completely. We're arguing for the study of popular culture not for amusement purposes, but because the way in which these capture the times and feed these back to us is an important aspect of how ideas are transmitted in society. Ask a teen today whether Benthesikyme was related to Zeus and you'll get a blank stare. Ask about Spiderman's aunt and chances are they'll at least venture a guess (it's May Reilly Parker, by the way). Similarly, the mythology of management one can find in comic books will in all likelihood be much better known, much more efficiently spread, and have much more of an impact than any retelling of ancient gods. Rather than giving us fragmented and metaphorical connections, the study of popular culture mythologies can present actual and current analyses of the state of the world. Further, the sometimes obsessive approach to universes is important on an epistemological level, as it shows us the necessity of continuity, logic and relationships in the study of mythologies. Superhero comics might not be the most complex form of entertainment or thinking, but neither is it as simplistic as we sometimes assume. And, regardless, they exist and show us things about our world.

Comics might be childish and immature, trivial and overblown. But so is the world, and scholars are supposed to study it in all its guises: villains and heroes, crooked businessmen and heroic managers – both the Bruce Waynes and the Lex Luthors, with capes or without.

References

Did you ever see a list of references in a comic? We thought not.

Orgspawn and Analysator Away!

5
From Rags to Riches: A Fairy Tale or Living Ethos? Stories of Polish Entrepreneurship during and after the Transformation of 1989

Małgorzata Ciesielska

Prologue

The American dream is 'an ideal of a happy and successful life to which all may aspire' (*The American Heritage Dictionary*, 2007). Adams (1931, quoted in Cullen, 2003, p. 4) wrote that the 'American dream is better, richer, and happier life for all our citizens of every rank'. A powerful symbol and continuous feature of the American life is an 'active, individual, self-sufficient, competitive, tough ... and poor (at least at the beginning) entrepreneur' (Bellah *et al.*, 1985/1996). The self-made man is a role model of a person that is independent, entrepreneurial and hard working. It can be personified both by biographies of industrialists and successful managers. The best-known examples of self-made men that actually went *from rags to riches* within a single lifetime are: Benjamin Franklin – an early capitalist and statesman (Meyer, 1941/1955) – and John D. Rockefeller – a 'robber baron' (Josephson, 1934). Those two Americans are icons of the American dream, a proof that hard-working people can elevate their social status and become rich.

The breakthrough of 1989 began a new political era in Poland. It was also a trigger for social and economic changes. As Kociatkiewicz and Kostera (2002, pp. 217–18) describe:

> We were facing the impossible – the immortal institutions imprisoning individual initiative and belief have died before our eyes. Together with the rest of reality, the world of enterprises changed as well – lots of new private companies, small and large ones, appeared, the big state-owned enterprises were privatized, divided or significantly changed

their role; the planned economy was replaced by the free market; many people's jobs were dramatically transformed, administrative cadre [*kadra kierownicza*] became managers [*menedzerowie*].

The early 1990s exist in my memories (of an 11-year-old girl) as the period when open-air markets started to bloom and blue jeans from Turkey flooded the market. Due to the lack of intellectual property rights, semi-illegally copied video and audio tapes were widely available. The graduates of New Management and Economics got a golden ticket to their careers in multinational corporations which were desperately seeking employees. Finally, it was a time when small and medium businesses started to grow like mushrooms after rain. It seemed that anyone could take his/her chances. My mother planned to open a bakery and my father thought about establishing a transport company. They are far from the risky businesses that are found nowadays. In the new millennium, making business seems to be much harder than in '89 when many Poles took practical lessons in market economy.

Grzeszczyk (2003) argues that in the 1990s the image of the American self-made man was promoted by Polish media, training companies, book-guides, big corporations and became 'an imperative of the current époque' (Grzeszczyk, 2003, p. 158). The ethos from rags to riches seemed to inspire many Poles who, at the beginning of the transformation processes in 1989, decided to start their own businesses. Having worked only in state-owned companies and with no experience of or knowledge about market mechanisms, they tried to make their dream come true. Apparently without the awareness of dangers, 'everything was much easier' [Janek][1] – and one could take or reject the opportunity. Many did fail, but others succeeded. In 1990 there was no training or study programme for owners of SMEs. The entrepreneurs based their decisions on intuition, imagination and luck.

As the transformation was in progress, Western advisors came to Poland to sell their knowledge. At first, managers of newly privatized or state-owned enterprises, as the only large companies in the market, were the focus. But even then, training was of rather poor quality (Kostera, 1995a) as the consultants showed no understanding of cultural context and semantic problems (Jankowicz, 1994, 1999). The interest in Polish state-owned enterprises and their managers resulted in some studies of the period of transformation or Western influences after 1989 (see, for example, Dobosz and Jankowicz, 2002; Kostera, 1995b; 1996; 2003; Kostera and Wicha, 1995; 1996). The beginning of the 1990s was also a time when people started to build their fortunes, totally on their own, by opening small grocery shops or assembling computers in a garage.

This chapter tells the story of one of those start-ups. The company was established in Poland in 1989 as an outgoing entrepreneurial process, common among early transformational movements in Poland. I compare those early entrepreneurial experiences with some insights from the tales of two young Warsaw companies. Even though they were set up just a few years ago, in new economic realities by people who hadn't worked in the communist era, they still have some similarities with the '89 business.

I use anthropological interviews conducted in Poland to show how the rags to riches scenario (or 'from waiter to entrepreneur' [Waldek]) occurred in Poland. Finally, I discuss the status of the American dream in entrepreneurs' narratives about creating and running their companies. Is it still a living ethos or just a fairy tale comparable to the popular American television series *Dynasty* (1981).

In this chapter an ethnographic narrative mode is applied, which incorporates quotations from the interviewees. The field material, which constitutes the basis for this text, is a part of a larger research project among the owners of small and medium enterprises in Poland. The interviews took place in 2005 and 2006. At the same time I had several informal meetings (non-recorded) with some of my informants and the outcomes of those appointments are also reflected in this chapter, mostly in the interpretation and conclusion sections.

I have worked with the full transcripts of seven interviews, but mainly with the one about business launched in 1989. In this chapter, I will retell the story of business creation and development, an entrepreneurial tale (e-tale) (Smith and Anderson, 2004) to juxtapose it with the rags to riches secenario. In order to do so, I will reflect on the characteristics of the self-made man, especially individualism, diligence, thrift, planning, methodological self-improvement, and goal-orientation (Franklin, 1960, quoted in Grzeszczyk, 2003, p. 30) and their relevance for Polish e-tales.

The study is rooted in the interpretative paradigm and social constructivist epistemology (Berger and Luckmann, 1966/1991; Burrell and Morgan, 1979/1994) and uses methods inspired by the ethnographical approach (Hammersley and Atkinson, 1995/2000; Kostera, 2003/2005, Van Maanen, 1988). I consider ethnography a method for presenting different experiences, which directly corresponds to the narrative mode of knowing (Czarniawska, 2004a). As Johansson (2004) claims, the fastest way from experience to knowledge goes through storytelling. Narratives enacted or told in communities are 'a main device for making sense of social action' (Czarniawska, 2004a, p. 11). Human actions acquire meaning when they are narrated.

Storytelling is the starting point for this chapter. First, I will introduce the 1989 start-up story. Second, I will compare Janek's e-tale with narratives told to me by entrepreneurs operating in Poland in the new millennium and discuss their relations to the rags to riches dream.

The 1989 business begins

Janek, just after graduating from SGPiS,[2] was called into compulsory military service. He had left it just before martial law was declared in Poland on 13 December 1981. After a short period of working at an educational institution, he was offered a job in one of the *Centrala Handlu Zagranicznego* (CHZ, The Center for Foreign Trade), which represented Western companies in Poland and which had a licence to perform internal export.[3] In CHZ Janek sold paints and paint enamels to craftsmen, small traders, and car remodelers. In the second half of the 1980s he decided to move to another company where he became a director of an internal export department. The scope of activities was similar to his previous experiences, except for goods, which were at that time mostly cloth, especially denim.

In February 1989 Janek, his co-worker from CHZ and a female attorney quit their jobs to establish a partnership. All three of them wanted to use their experiences and personal relationships with clients and suppliers from their previous employers.

The decision to start a business brought them more rags than riches:

> We came to the conclusion that in fact in the place we were working, they were using our knowledge and enthusiasm but nobody was willing to really pay for it. For me it was a great risk in terms of finances, because in [company name] I had earned decent money with high commission on sales. And then, for several months I did not get any income from our new business, because we were spinning it off. It could have failed, but ... we had enough [of our previous employment] and we wanted to try. (Janek)

The seed money for the business was US$300, provided by Janek and the other colleague: 'Miss Attorney did not have at her disposal *that* kind of money at the time' [Janek]. Her role and activities are absent from Janek's tale. He just mentions that she quit their business after two years to start her own law firm.

Jeans, cassettes and paints

From the beginning, Janek and his partner decided to trade in denim and cassettes. It was easy as Janek knew the cloth import business and the people working in it. The partners were very receptive to other opportunities. They started to improvise. Very soon they were also selling other popular goods, such as shoes or video and audio cassettes:

> It was the best business at that time. We were selling cassettes in shipping containers... In Poland the copying business was blooming. Those cassettes were used both in private homes and also, I think, that other companies – were using them for illegal copying. It flourished. We, of course, made use of our previous relationships and contacts. One container of those cassettes cost us 20,000 dollars. We of course have never had that much cash. We were getting [goods] on credit, being considered as trustworthy by our suppliers. (Janek)

Janek and his partner quickly realized that it is not always profitable for the company to trade the products that the client wants to buy. It was a lesson on economies of scale and cash flow problems connected with high turnover. They thought of changing the assortment of products. The new direction was an obvious choice. Both Janek and his partner did work with paint producers and trades. Moreover at the same time their previous employer stopped importing the products from the Danish producer with whom they had worked. The gap on the market was spotted:

> At the end of 1989 we decided to make use of my contacts with [company's name] and to sell wood preparation products. We did as we decided. I went to Copenhagen with the [company's name] representative, who resided in Poland. I knew people from [company's name], the whole sales department for European markets, and their boss, when I was working for Centrala Handlu Zagranicznego. Those negotiations went fairly fast and smoothly and we got *very good* conditions for the first delivery. (Janek)

The partners agreed that they had to learn a lot about their new product line. They spent a lot of time on self-education. They visited factories to get to know the production process. They also learned how to use the products properly. Janek called themselves 'the little chemists'.

During those site visits, Janek tried to learn how their Western partners worked, and how the foreign markets functioned. Thanks to this benchmarking, a term that they had never even heard before, Janek and a partner tried to introduce marketing to their business. Although they knew little about it, Janek says that:

> We decided, basing our decision on our insights into our Western partners' businesses, to take care of the marketing side of our enterprise. In the Polish market those activities were an absolute novelty. We issued very decent leaflets ... We placed fairly attractive ads in prestigious journals like *Murator*.[4] We were even awarded a prize for the most interesting advertisement. (Janek)

They also tried other channels of marketing communications: radio, regional TV and trade fairs. The business grew fast and the distribution chain grew with it. Paints became the main source of income for the company and the main reason for its existence. Investments were necessary to provide superior service and be able to fill all orders:

> Very fast we came to the conclusion that it was a right development direction. In fact, we dropped all other product groups. We stayed only with paints. We added car paints; we also introduced a variety of paints so that we offered not only products for wood but also for walls and metal. We signed new contracts with German producers, and in two years we managed to become a fairly big selling chain. We were selling in our own shops. I guess, we had five of them at that time ... We gained over 100 business partners, both big wholesalers, which were distributing paints in Poland, and the smaller ones, individual companies, which were operating in wholesale and retail markets. It was Poznań, Wrocław, Rzeszów... Łódź and many other smaller towns. [Danish producer] had a very good reputation so our business was smoothly developing. In the next year we managed to reach a turnover of 1.5 million dollars. (Janek)

The business was going great. In the best year they employed 50 people, who worked in the offices, shops and in logistics. As Janek describes, decisions were taken instantly, without much consideration. An impulse, an idea, an opportunity were driving forces. For instance, it took only four to six weeks to open a new shop. It was important for the company to continuously spin off: 'We were very satisfied with our work, although we were never greedy, we didn't want to collect a big capital. We were taking a risk' (Janek).

In the meantime they planned to create their own logistic structures. They bought a parcel of land on which to build a warehouse. The parcel was perfect, situated near Warsaw. Unfortunately, administrative problems forced them to suspend that project for two years. Nevertheless they finalized their investment and purchased three trucks: 'The company flourished. [Danish producer] was extremely pleased with our activities. I must admit that we were an exclusive distributor of their products in Poland, therefore we felt safe' (Janek).

In the second half of the 1990s some worrying information got to Janek. On the one hand, foreign corporations were preparing to enter the Polish market. On the other, their main supplier had been taken over:

> We did know about the infiltration of the Polish market by big paint producers, but we did not think it could touch us. All the time we thought, that our exclusive distributor's rights would protect us. And if they [Danish producer] decided to do something else [against their agreement], we of course would find a way to get appropriate compensation for that. (Janek)

Finally Janek had to face new market realities:

> In the meantime [Danish producer] was bought by a tycoon in a paint branch [Tycoon name]. [Tycoon name] had specific plans about their future expansion into central European markets, including Poland. Rather fast, they came to the idea that they have to buy a factory in Poland. And he [the tycoon] made an extremely smart business move by buying for a ridiculous price a [Polish factory name], which had been ranked number three among the biggest Polish producers of paints. They had a significant market share, in different sectors of the paint market ... That changed the realities of our activities, because [Tycoon name] came to the conclusion that their Polish subsidiary will distribute [Danish producer's] products, which are such good-sellers and are popular among clients. (Janek)

Suddenly it appeared that having exclusive rights would not help them stay in business:

> We had several talks, which were supposed to lead to a solution that was acceptable to both parties. We had this exclusive distribution agreement, so the compensation was an option, but those proposals

of [Tycoon name] were just ridiculous. Therefore we rejected them. Then [Tycoon name] had an idea that they could offer us a cooperation agreement within a newly created division which was supposed to deal with professionals – building companies, craftsman, which offered services both for Kowalskich[5] as well as for refurbishing or interior design companies [as a subcontractor]. We were to supply them with paints and give advice on those products, but it soon appeared to be just a trick. We had never made it. (Janek)

Epilogue

When they lost the exclusivity rights, their business 'burst like a bubble'. [Janek] Their paints became available in many shops, including super- and hypermarkets. The prices dropped 10–15 per cent. Janek's customers couldn't sell their stocks, and so neither could Janek. Nor was he paid for the deliveries to the wholesalers who started to go bankrupt. The dominos were starting to fall. Janek and his partner were stuck with goods they couldn't sell and a lot of insolvent debtors.

The attempts to save the business from bankruptcy did not work. The money earned on the sale of their warehouse was not enough to cover all their liabilities. Without sufficient cash, they could not finance the other business ideas they had kept 'for later'. No profits, a lot of debts, and a rising disagreement between partners resulted in a split:

> We parted in 1998. He had left with this bigos.[6] We split what had been left but [laugh] what was left was almost nothing. I left with two cars. We also split what was left of our business structures. I took over two shops – the small one in Warszawa, the other in Łódź... but soon I realized, that running this business, when DIY markets are developing, makes no sense. Those shops were not profitable at all, so I had to close them. And that is how my business career came to an end. (Janek)

'It was like on a stupid film on business:'[7] reflections on Polish e-tales after the transformation of 1989

The rhetoric presented by Janek is very similar to that of the other interviewees – co-owners of small businesses that were established in the late 1990s or at the beginning of the new millennium. It may be considered as a macho talk, even patronizing at times. The self-centred, verbalized use of the pronouns: 'I' and 'we' in the meaning 'my partner(s) and I', indicate a strong conviction that they are the company. As Louis XIV used to say, 'I am the state.' Employees are controlled almost all the time, directly or indirectly and they are not interesting topics for them to discuss. The same is true of women; Janek mentioned his female partner only is passing. Although she worked with them for two years, he says nothing about her tasks or her role in their successes. She seems to have been a very salient participant in the male business processes.

I do not consider their way of self-presentation as surprising or worthy of blame. In a way it is understandable. Their accounts must be seen in the light of Polish socio-economic and political realities.

Nowadays, it is a common opinion that 'the Polish State torpedoes entrepreneurship in Poland and chokes it down' (Radek) and that 'from one day to another the political situation in Poland changes' (Marcin). It is said that the first serious tax audit may end up in a company's closure. Janek mentioned that this kind of problem also existed in the early 1990s.

At the same time, business owners must always be careful with partners who may try to cheat them. In Janek's case the unfair play on the part of his contractor was a direct cause of bankruptcy. Unfortunately, those kinds of problems are (often painfully) familiar to the other entrepreneurs I interviewed. My interviewees, after all, had stayed in the business for some years. Being tough survivors makes them a bit more likely to present themselves as macho knights.

Grzeszczyk's (2003) study of success as a social phenomenon argues that a self-made man was promoted in the 1990s as a role model of a successful person. Mass media played an important role in this depiction of success. Janek once said that his company's story 'was like a stupid film on business'. It implies that certain programmes (mostly American, like *Dynasty* or *Dallas*) broadcast on Polish television persuaded people to start their own businesses, especially by showing images of what a business is and what one can expect it to bring. The role of television might be especially important because no training was offered to small and medium enterprises:

> It was difficult to get to the sources of information. There were some books. But even so they weren't that good, because those were mostly on business events and ideas for running business and mostly American, and very out of date. So they were useless ... I guess, the training market was poor too. Several times we had approached it ...

> A few times we did those trainings, but they were just ridiculous. (Janek)

The business life had appeared to be much harder than the Carringtons' life, and none of my interviews considered themselves to be Blake, who '[has] a great talent for knowing where oil is and how to get it out' (*Memorable Quotes from 'Dynasty'* 1981, n.d.).

However, the philosophy of the self-made man is consistent with 'the mammoth's complex' (Grzeszczyk, 2003), a warrior instinct that makes the Polish man act macho in order to be seen as a real man. In Poland, men's emancipation is yet to come. Grzeszczyk (2003) makes the interesting observation that Poles are very critical of the role model but they use it to present themselves to the stakeholders because they have no alternative. The successful man should be self-centred, self-confident, patronizing and macho. And that brings us to the American robber barons. This image may be a reason for the Polish dislike of private entrepreneurs. Surveys show that 'small' entrepreneurs have a very low social status. Since 1995, small entrepreneurs and unskilled workers have been at the bottom of statistical tables (CBOS, 1999; CfK, 2006).

Some final remarks

There was a strong sense of individualism that emanated from the interviewees' stories. The entrepreneurs-owners are the main experts in their companies and they seem to like this or at least consider it as inevitable. They are the front-men with the right connections and, as soldiers (one of interviewees [Waldek] used terms like 'the general' and 'the sergeant'), fight against all adversities. The 'conscious[ness] that you can rely only on yourself and what you do' [Janek] is always present. Then, responsibility and information enter an organization through the entrepreneur. For a new millennium entrepreneur it is a source of stress. Such sentiments were present in all my interviews with entrepreneurs who are currently running their businesses. Janek, an 1989 entrepreneur, was much more positive and joyful. When I asked him about the emotions connected to his business:

> From absolute apathy to unspeakable euphoria. When business spins off and you can see clients entering through doors and windows, your soul is delighted. Of course we were anxious that suddenly everything would blow up, or somebody in authority would change the law and make it [our business] impossible. Quite often those things happened,

but probably both of us were a bit abnormal or too optimistic, because I cannot say I was very stressed about that. (Janek)

It seems that 1989 entrepreneurs were more optimistic and more prone to accept risk. According to Janek, it was a time of unrealistic, non-market business conditions. It was fairly easy to get extended payment even for your first delivery. One could trade without having any capital. At the same time, people were very positive toward new possibilities. Sometimes they were too naïve. The naiveté and belief that anyone can succeed in business made some people very rich:

> Once we cooperated with Zbigniew Jakubas[8] who is today fiftieth in the *Wprost* ranking.[9] He was a guy who started by running a boutique. He cooperated with us on cloth selling, but he had more capital. He also established a company [name], which was a sewing subcontractor for German partners, for BOSS... It slowed down a bit when the German partners went more East, but then he bought a mineral water spring... In the meantime he also started taking over all kinds of factories. Nowadays he is, I guess, the main shareholder of the Mint of Poland [*Mennica Panstwowa*]. (Janek)

... and the others very poor:

> It was easy. There was such a model – everything that was imported to Poland, was sold instantly. However, we had a lot of friends who got carried away by the wave. People went bankrupt within a week, because they had invested their assets, their savings. They had an idea, for instance, that they would sell 10 trucks of melons, but it turned out that they had not bought watermelons and they did not sell anything and that killed the business. We had also friends who got involved in a shoe business and lost everything. (Janek)

In that sense, the American dream was actually present in a form of business naiveté, faith that it is worth investing all available recourses in (at least one) golden shot. However possibilities of fast money and vast fortunes are nowadays approached in terms of a fairy tale. Polish entrepreneurs, in the new millennium, seem to be more concerned about limitations and the probability of failure. The Polish understanding of the American dream is that it may occur but is neither for everyone nor sure. None of the entrepreneurs I talked started from scratch. Their businesses are created on the basis of market knowledge and relations to important players. What Polish entrepreneurs had also learned is that even though the rags to riches scenario can be realized, it is just as easy to go from riches to rags.

Notes

1. The names of all interviewees in this chapter have been changed to those in brackets, such as [Janek].
2. *Szkoła Główna Planowania i Statystyki* (Main School of Planning and Statistics) offered a master programme for future administrative and state-owned companies' managers.
3. As Janek explained, internal export was fairly popular trading praxis in the 1980s. It enabled the sale of imported Western goods for foreign currency in Poland.
4. A name made from a Polish word for bricklayer (*murarz*) with an English noun (profession) suffix.
5. Kowalski is one of the most popular surnames in Poland and is often used as a metaphor for 'everybody' or 'anybody' (like Brown in English – any individual).
6. *Bigos* is a Polish dish made of sauerkraut. In a colloquial Polish it also means 'a problem', 'a mess', 'pretty kettle of fish'.
7. Janek.
8. A well-known Polish businessman.
9. *Wprost* is a Polish weekly magazine that presents every year a list of Poland's wealthiest people.

6
'I Could Have Been Like Lou Barlow, But I'm More Like Ken Barlow'[1]: Long-Stayers as Heroes or Failures

Yvonne Guerrier

In the long-running British TV soap *Coronation Street*, there is one character, Ken Barlow, who has been there from the beginning. He was seen in the first episode in 1960 as a new university graduate, the first in the street, returning to his family in Weatherfield a fictional working-class region in North-East England; 46 years later he is still a fixture in the show. Ken Barlow has a popular reputation as being rather boring although, in the way of soaps, his fictional life has not been uneventful. He has been married four times (twice to the same woman), widowed twice and divorced once in addition to having 27 girl-friends. He has had three children and one step-daughter who have drifted in and out of the series and had a long-running feud with another long-serving character, Mike Baldwin. The show has changed around him from the grainy black and white live show in the 1960s, which was influenced by the working class 'kitchen sink' plays and films of the late fifties to the more glamorous and youth oriented show now, which remains, even in this digital age, one of the most watched shows on British television. The actor who plays Ken, William Roache, has also achieved a remarkable feat in a transient and insecure profession of only ever having played the one role in his career and, indeed, being so typecast in this role, it would be impossible to imagine him playing anything else. He has been well rewarded, of course, but it seems to be an odd accolade just to be rewarded and recognized for 'being there' longer than anyone else.

  Last year I attended the leaving party of a colleague, who I will call David, who was retiring from a university where he had progressed into a top management role after over 30 years' service. Another colleague who had joined the university at about the same time gave an entertaining speech in his honour showing photographs of them both as young lecturers in the English department in the 1970s looking like typical long-haired radicals. Like the Ken Barlow of the 1960s, the David of the 1970s would certainly not have expected to follow the career path that he did. 'I only wanted to teach English literature', he commented. As someone who was ideologically uncomfortable with notions of management, his 'success' in reaching a senior management role was arguably tinged with some ambiguity. As in the song quoted in the title, he wanted to be Lou Barlow (the 'indie' musician) and turned into Ken Barlow. But like Ken Barlow, his stay in the same organization had not been uneventful, both from a career and a personal perspective (as he had met his wife through the university). For me, with only a recent familiarity with this university, it was a little like watching a very old episode of a soap one has only followed recently. It emphasized how different this university is now to the institution that David joined and, by revealing past and long-lasting connections of which I had been unaware, it threw a new light on the present. It marked the end of an era, not least because, when David left, the longest-serving member of the senior management team of the university had worked there less than five years. It also raised questions about the appropriate way to mark the leaving of someone who had given so much of their life to one organization.

It is these questions that I will explore in this chapter. How are long-serving staff members seen in a liquid modern society in which, according to Bauman (2005), 'loyalty is a cause of shame not pride' (p. 9) and which has 'degraded duration and elevated transience' (p. 83)? How does their memory and knowledge of an organization's history impinge on its present? What are the issues associated with leaving as, and celebrating the leaving of, a long standing member. In exploring these questions, I will make use of the character of Ken Barlow as an archetype for those who stay in the same organization while others move on.

Staying put is not normally regarded as a heroic act. Our archetypal heroes are men on the move. It is easier to find women in mythology who are renowned for staying put and remaining loyal: Penelope in the *Odyssey*, for example. Men who stay put tend to have supporting roles in myths: the notion of the loyal servant or retainer is a common one. One of the Greek gods who may be imbued with some of the characteristics I am discussing here is Vulcan-Hephaestus, the forger to the gods who stays in his smithy at the bottom of craters tirelessly working away at objects for the other gods and he is not one of the best known or most immediately appealing of the gods.

The changing history of careers and attitudes to staying and leaving

> Haven't you read the obits? The job for life is dead. The marriage contract between employer and employee lies in shreds. Our solemn vow to honor and cherish until retirement, forgotten. (Wiley, 2006, p. 7)

> The modern culture of risk is peculiar in that failure to move is taken as a sign of failure, stability seen as almost a living death. The destination therefore matters less than the act of departure ... To stay put is to be left out. (Sennett, 1998, p. 87)

As the two quotes above show, it is accepted thinking by both popular and academic commentators that, in the Anglo-Saxon Western world at least, the life-long career has disappeared. Waves of organizational restructuring from the 1980s onwards have dismantled the old-style predictable bureaucracies. The risk and responsibility for managing one's career has been shifted from the organization to the employee. Long service within one organization is not always feasible: your job may disappear, your skills may no longer be relevant, the organization itself may disappear. Even if you can remain with the same employer, long service does not bring the rewards that it once did. Indeed, the long-server may have little external marketability and so be stuck with an employer that does not value or reciprocate their loyalty with little choice but to focus their main attention on their life outside work (Cascio, 1993; Scase and Goffee, 1989; Wajcman and Martin, 2001). These changes have affected traditional working class careers in public transport, the steel industry and the post office (Grimshaw *et al.*, 2001) as well as white-collar and managerial roles (Kniveton, 2004; Wajcman and Martin, 2001).

The dominant management orthodoxy is that these changes have been liberating. We are expected to embrace rather then resist more flexible career patterns because they free us from a childlike dependence on bureaucratic organizations and allowed us to pursue our own goals and ambitions. Nevertheless, change and constant risk also builds anxiety and apprehension (Sennett, 1999). The British management guru, Charles Handy, has been one of the proponents of the portfolio career rather than the traditional bureaucratic career. Even so he eloquently expresses the anxieties involved in leaving the safety of a secure job within a large organization and adopting a portfolio career:

> in 1981 it was time for me to leave [the] safety [of an organizational career] and try my fortunes outside, before I became too fossilized to survive there ... Life was going to be a trifle uncertain, I could see ... Maybe I had been unduly rash ... to leave the world of the elephants and the big battalions and join the fleas, the lone warriors who, I was predicting, would be the growing population of the future. (Handy, 2002, p. 7)

While Handy successfully managed the transition to a portfolio career and felt liberated by this change of lifestyle, he recognized some of the dangers of a society where no-one commits to a job for long: that the divide between those who can cope and those who cannot will increase; that in an increasingly individualized society the ties that bind us as a community will decrease. Research on those who have moved from stable organizational jobs to portfolio careers suggests that responses to this change are often ambiguous at best (Cohen and Mallon, 1999; Platman, 2004): people may value the new freedom they gain but still regret losing some of the privileges and security of a stable career.

In fact, both in practice and as an ideal, the job-for-life may not be as dead as commentators claim. British labour statistics reveal a sizable minority of long-stayers within the workforce. In 2002, 10 per cent of the workforce had over 20 years length of service and a further 19 per cent between 10 and 20 years of service (Office of National Statistics, 2003). This is marginally up on the proportions in 1986 when 9 per cent had over 20 years employment service. There are also many examples of highly successful managers who have remained loyal to one company for substantial periods of time. Lord Browne, chief executive of the oil giant BP, stepped down after 41 years with the company in May 2007, but was succeeded by another BP lifer, Tony Hayward (Teather, 2007). In the fast-moving retail fashion business, Jane Shepherdson recently resigned from her role as brand director of Topshop, the brand she has been credited as transforming. She had joined the brand after college and stayed for 20 years.

Ng and Feldman (2007), building on Mitchell *et al.* (2001), use the term 'organizational embeddedness' to explore the reasons why people may choose to stay in the same organization even when there are opportunities available elsewhere. They identify three sets of forces that encourage people to stay. 'Fit' is the extent to which a person's skills and abilities meet organizational requirements. 'Links' relate to the ties of friendship and activities that the employee has within his/her organization.

Finally, 'sacrifice' relates to the losses that an employee would incur by leaving the organization. As Ng and Feldman demonstrate, how these forces work depend on the life-stage of the individual. At the early 'establishment' stage of a person's career, there may be very positive reasons for staying. The person enjoys the work, is progressing and developing his/her skills, likes the people he/she is working with and feels that he/she would sacrifice the investment the organization is making in him/her if he/she moved on. But at the later, maintenance, stage in the career the reasons for staying may be less positive, at least as far as the company is concerned. People in this stage may have reached a plateau in their careers, have reconciled themselves to lower and different career aspirations from their initial goals and be as concerned about life outside work as within work. They may stay because it is comfortable and they increasingly have too much to lose by moving on. The disinclination to change jobs becomes stronger as people move into the 'disengagement' stage of their careers.

William Roache's decision to stay in Coronation Street can be interpreted in this rather pessimistic way. Certainly this is the way that some bloggers on the Coronation Street fan sites interpret it. Roache, according to the following fan, was initially reluctant to commit to even a three month contract:

> How many of you know Coronation Street was only supposed to run for 13 weeks and how many of you know that William Roache never wanted the role of Ken Barlow in the first place. William was talked into it and said o.k., but I am only doing the 13 weeks and here he is 46 years later. (anniewalker, 2006)

Having made a success of the role, Roache then, according to the same blogger, did not have the courage to move on and test his acting skills in a wide range of roles, which is what a 'proper' acting career requires. Instead, he settled for a safe career in a medium (acting in a soap), which is low in the hierarchy of acting work:

> Anne Reid who played Valerie Barlow, Ken's first wife had got the right idea. Anne got out of Coronation Street in 1971 and got herself a proper acting career. The writers would have been better writing Ken out of the show as well as Valerie in 1971 ... However, the writers decided to keep Ken Barlow in the show, which is why Valerie had to die unfortunately. (anniewalker, 2006)

The narrative of failure is transferred from Roache to Barlow. Because Roache stayed on, Barlow stayed behind on Coronation Street. Yet, as the 'educated' working-class lad, he would not have been expected to end up still living in a small terraced house in a working-class area. Boring Barlow, the 'nerd' who still could not escape, is elided with boring Roache, the actor who did not risk moving on.

There is an alternative narrative to this interpretation. Within a traditional bureaucratic structure where life-time careers are rewarded and expected, staying with the same company is the safe option. But within an organization that does not normally offer life time careers, those who want to stay have to work at ensuring their skills remain valued by their employer. Wajcman and Martin (2001; 2002), in a study of Australian managers, discovered that many of their respondents still wanted to pursue quite lengthy careers within one organization and many companies were still willing and able to sustain quite long careers even if they no longer offered life-time opportunities. But they noted a shift from a bureaucratic narrative to a market narrative. Within the bureaucratic narrative, people remain within one company because of strong norms that support the notion that this is what one should do. Within the market narrative, people are 'choosing selves'. They stay because they feel this is the best for them at the present time. The decision to stay, within this narrative, is always provisional and to be constantly reviewed. The 'best' situation is to be able to say 'I want to stay at the moment but if I needed to move on I would still be highly marketable.' Peiperl and Baruch (1997) offer similar advice to managers who want to remain with the same employer. To paraphrase, they say: 'Make yourself indispensable but at the same time cultivate relationships with other organizations so you could find another job if you need to and make sure you have enough savings so you could survive if you lost your job.'

Soap stars, even in long running soaps, are not indispensable. Soaps are ensemble dramas never totally dependent on any one character or actor (Butler, 1991). Stars, however iconic, may always be written out or played down with poor or marginal storylines. Within this narrative, Roache's survival in the same part for 46 years is heroic, not just a passive failure to move on. While he has not tested himself across a range of acting parts, he has been part of a show which is an iconic part of British television and has figured in some of its most memorable storylines. There is no guarantee that he would have had a more interesting and more successful acting career if he had left the soap. The case for moving on as against staying put is not an obvious one, even for an actor. It can offer its own rewards and successes. But what do long-servers contribute to the organizations in which they work?

What do they know?

> One of the most important consequences of immobility in the work careers of British management is what Thorstein Veblen once labeled 'trained incapacity' For non-mobile British executives 'trained incapacity' is the inability to conceive of, or utilize, new ideas. (Dubin, 1970, p. 193)

As far back as the 1970s, the story was being spread, as the quotation above shows, that an organization that relied too much on long serving employees was being held back. Indeed, Dubin, in the article quoted above, even suggested that British industry was held back since British managers were less mobile than their American colleagues. As individuals have been re-evaluating the notion that the ideal career is to join one company and stay with them for life, organizations have been re-evaluating the notion that the best type of workforce to cultivate is one committed for the long-term.

One of the reasons why the large bureaucratic 'elephant-like' organizations that Charles Handy railed against encouraged employees to commit to life-time careers was to create a cadre of 'organization men' (and occasionally women), who understood the organization's culture, had time to build up company-specific skills (King *et al.*, 2005), and would do what they were told. But one of the unintended consequences of this type of career structure may be to create a group of people who are subversive, resistant to direction, and committed to the organization as it was rather than as newer managers might want it to be. Indeed this has not always been an *unintended* consequence. One of the arguments in favour of life-long careers in the civil service and tenure for academics is about ensuring job holders can resist corruption and say what they believe without worrying about their job security.

'I used to enjoy winding up new directors and watch the look of terror on their faces when I said "I don't do this, I don't do that"', said Wendy Richard, who played Pauline Fowler for over 20 years in the long running soap *EastEnders* (*Woman's Hour*, 2007). For managers, particularly those new to an organization (like the young directors that Wendy Richard wound up), those who have stayed can be threatening. They may be difficult to control, particularly if they have 'plateaued' and there is little that they can be offered. Further, they come with baggage: both knowledge of the history of the organization and its relationships.

Pauline Fowler had the same iconic status within the BBC soap *EastEnders* as Ken Barlow has on *Coronation Street*. Wendy Richard had played this part from the first episode of the programme: her character was the matriarch within the central family and she had been part of its most memorable storylines. On Christmas Day 2006, she was written out. She collapsed and died alone next to her husband's grave having previously been hit by her daughter-in-law during a row. Although press reports emphasized that Richard's decision to leave the soap was not due to any disagreement, the radio interview quoted above suggested some tensions. Richard complained that scriptwriters had made Pauline Fowler behave in ways that her character, who she felt she understood better than anyone else, would not have done. 'I gave up fighting in the end ... I couldn't believe in it any more' (*Woman's Hour*, 2007). The work ceased to be fun, she had no mortgage and had other work to go on to. So she resigned. Wendy Richard's experience would seem to confirm that no character is indispensable in a soap opera. Finally she did not have enough power to shape, or even veto, her character's storyline and the only solution for her was to leave.

However, knowledge of where an organization has come from can be used positively. In 2004, Stuart Rose returned to the retail company, Marks and Spencer, as chief executive. Marks & Spencer, is perhaps the *Coronation Street* of British retailing: a company which more than another retail chain has its place in British cultural history but one which has been going through some difficult times. Rose had spent 17 years working for the company in the early years of his career and represents a rather different archetype in this discussion of people who forge long careers within one company: the person who comes back. In Rose's case, the highly successful career he had built in other retail companies since leaving Marks & Spencer the first time belied the notion that he could not take risks or 'hack it' elsewhere, while his decision to come back emphasized his commitment and loyalty to the company. It is interesting that his initial observations were not that Marks & Spencer had been unable to change but that it needed to rediscover its roots. In an interview in 2004 just after he had taken over Rose claimed:

> M&S has definitely changed. I think there is an element from what I have seen so far that people have forgotten their roots ... There has been a little bit of danger of late that we have said 'bugger that, it doesn't stand for much, we are going to reinvent this business and make it something else.' It isn't. It's Marks and bloody Spencer. (Pratley, 2004)

Rose has since been credited with turning round the company.

The end

Liquid life is a succession of new beginnings – yet precisely because of this reason it is the swift and painless endings without which new beginnings would be unthinkable that tend to be the most challenging moments and most upsetting headaches. (Bauman, 2005, p. 2)

In soap world, writing out a major character is an opportunity for a plot spectacular. The event is trailed for weeks in advance. Suspension is built up. Will the character be killed off or allowed a 'happy ending'? Will it be final parting or will the door be left open for the character to come back (although there can sometimes be comebacks even after the most 'final' of departures)? Often, as was the case with Pauline Fowler, the departure is timed to capture the largest audience: in this case at Christmas. These spectaculars belie Bauman's claim that departures in liquid modern life should be without ostentatious gravestones (2005, p. 3). Similarly, within modern work environments, the correct way to mark the departure of a long-standing employee is with a 'spectacular': an opportunity usually at a party to celebrate and reflect on the person's contribution.

But yet that is easy to get wrong. There may be a disagreement or scandal that means the actor is removed immediately from the programme with no opportunity for the 'final' exit to be planned into the plot. (I remember an employee with over 25 years service leaving suddenly from an organization I used to work in. He departed over the summer period and there was no chance even to say goodbye.) Some soap stars may attempt to avoid the final 'exit' altogether and just stay on. (There are actors in *Coronation Street* who are aged well over 80). But they may then lose the opportunity for a really memorable exit as their appearances gradually become less frequent, and they may no longer have the stamina to act out a dramatic storyline or worse still die in real life before they are granted a screen death, so they have to be killed off ignominiously and unsatisfactorily off-screen.

What will be the final fate of Ken Barlow/William Roache? Roache is reported as saying, 'I don't even think about retiring' (Corrie Blog, 2006), so there are no signs of the last act just yet. For all that liquid modern life encourages new beginnings and frequent endings, the story of Barlow/Roache is a reminder that it is still possible to avoid endings altogether until, of course, the final ending from which even soap stars cannot return.

Note

1. From *Lark Descending* by Half Man Half Biscuit, 2001.

7
Little Johnny and the Wizard of OS: The PC User as a Fool Hero

Dariusz Jemielniak

'When you look into the abyss, the abyss looks back into you.' (Nietzsche, 1966, p. 89)

There are only 10 types of people in the world: those who understand binary and those who don't. This pun has made a career as a status message in IMs, emails, forum signature notes, and on a T-Shirt in a ThinkGeek.com online store. It has been indexed by Google half a million times. Still, it is only one of millions of similar jokes that deprecate those who are not adept at technology and mathematics.

Users ('users-losers', as they are sometimes called by IT specialists) are depicted in these anecdotes as imbeciles, stupid beyond imagination. Certainly, support specialists often have to deal with problems that appear trivial to them, and they get over the frustration by sharing these archetypical stories. Some stories are obviously made up, some are urban legends, and some are pranks that geeks play upon each other. After all, computer work can be very demanding, since software companies often foster an atmosphere of distrust (Latusek, 2007) and of high time pressure (Jemielniak, 2005). However, such stereotypes shared by the group are also reenactments of their professional roles and help define their workplace (Berger and Luckman, 1966; Boje, 1991; Feldman and Skölberg, 2002; Weick, 1969/1979). In this sense, they do not describe the truth in a historical, factual sense. Rather, they are much more significant, because they reveal the symbolism that constitutes the actor's script, the underlying assumptions of what is and what is not important (Czarniawska and Calás, 1998).

The production of the roles in the relationship between the software engineer and the PC user is also conducted also through storytelling, including 'real' and mythical tales. Just as in the construction of organizational reality (Czarniawska, 1997a), the occupational community and professional identity are created through narration (Czarniawska, 1997b). The heroes appearing in the narratives, the archetypes recurring in the stories, and the returning symbolic characters all play a crucial role in perceptions and expectations of organizational actors (Gabriel, 2004a). They are important devices used to make sense of the organizational reality (Gabriel, 2000; Kostera, 2005).

Therefore, the analysis of occupational myths, even though certainly under the influence of group stereotypes and biases (Gill, 2003), is nevertheless useful for enhancing our knowledge of how social institutions are being +constructed (Czarniawska, 1997a). Such narratives, coming from a natural environment, are among the most common ways of communication and of creating social reality (Barthes, 1978; Czarniawska, 2004b; Fisher, 1987; MacIntyre, 1981). They are not always chronological. Indeed, in some instances only a single event is described. Yet, even in those instances, they are sometimes considered narrations (Corvellec, 2006), stories from the field that hugely impact role enactment.

Therefore, researching heroes of software engineer jokes and anecdotal stories may shed new light on IT projects and on the 'configuration' of the model user of a computer by software engineers (Grint and Woolgar, 1997). In preparing this chapter, I analyzed 1,177 statements, mostly anecdotal, from a portal entitled slashdot.org, a popular site for engineers and 'geeks', posted in a discussion entitled *Favorite Support Story* (ScuttleMonkey, 2005), and 360 posts from a portal entitled b3ta.com, a popular message board, under the heading of *Clients are Stupid* (Rob, 2003). Due to obvious spatial limitations, only a careful selection of the stories can be presented. Those cited were selected as particularly representative or particularly impinging.

The method of interpreting fiction in order to reach deeper archetypes is similar to methods used by other organization theorists (Czarniawska and de Monthoux, 1994; Kostera, 2005), with the exception that these particular stories were collected by Internet portals. As a result, the authors were quite probably unaware that anybody would bother to analyze their works and consequently may have been more open and candid in addressing their peers within the confines of the Internet medium.

The research process follows Czarniawska's (2004b) advice to collect, interpret and analyze the stories, and then deconstruct their selection with the author's own view, resulting in yet another story.

ID10T

Surprisingly, reading the dozens of posts about *Favorite Support Story* revealed numerous comments about the lack of competence among less experienced users:

> People (like my wife) who grew up using typewriters, and so insist on hitting the Enter key *at the end of every line* when typing a document.
>
> Oh, and the Enter key is good for spacing down to the start of the next page, too.

The same view was shared by many others:

> People who use the spacebar instead of the tab key (or, even better, 'style' tagging) in MSWord, WordPerfect, or other good word-processors, shouldn't be given remedial training: they should be taken out back and shot, to the benefit of all humanity.

The support specialists were apparently so engrossed in the reality of electronic word-processing that they did not consider that paragraph alignment and adjustment with the support of a computer is not really the 'natural' way of typing. One even made a facetious suggestion that people who have traditional typewriter habits should be executed. The ignorance of an arbitrary convention was quite often pointed to as an example of stupidity:

> My old roommate, Dan, went to get a programming certificate at the local college. All students (whether in computers or not) have to take an 'Intro to Desktop Systems', AKA, intro to Windows.
>
> In the first class, the instructor asked everyone to double-click on some icon to load up the tutorial program.
>
> The girl beside Dan clicked BOTH mouse buttons once, simultaneously. That's a 'double-click', right?

Again, being unaware of a particular term was perceived as ridiculous and funny. Polite and rather understandable questions from beginners were perceived or characterized as absurd, as in another post about mouse clicking: 'I could not believe the questions I had. "How do I do a right button click?"' The reaction of another support specialist in a similar situation was even more extreme:

> Many moons ago, I worked as a lab instructor at NCSU for, amongst other things, 'Introduction to the Computing Environment'. At the

time, it was a network of DEC workstations running Ultrix, but it was a lab about how to use the keyboard, mouse, word processor, etc. So it's early in the semester and I'm telling this one freshman how to do something (I don't remember what now), and I tell her to point at a particular button. So, she removes her hand from the mouse and physically points to the button on the monitor. So I say 'No. I mean with the mouse.' To which she responds 'Oh!', picks up the mouse and presses it against the glass. I was forced to simply turn around and leave.

The teacher, who should show patience and understanding for somebody else's inexperience, was so perplexed by the girl's ignorance that, instead of explaining what he meant, he left the classroom. This story, apart from involving an interesting gender note, is a clear admission of pedagogical failure presented openly and anecdotally about a lame user.

What was quite striking was the fact that women were heroines of many of the stories. Usually they were depicted as totally incompetent, carriers of the 'stupid blonde' stereotype. If there was any potential sexual innuendo or bawdy misunderstanding, the specialists perceived the story automatically as even funnier:

But a relative of a friend of mine ran a computer company in the DOS and Windows 3.1 days. One afternoon a customer who had bought a computer, phoned in. The conversation went as follows:

Techy: How can I help?
Woman: My computer won't work!
Techy: Can you be more specific please?
Woman: I don't know what's wrong, it's being weird and it won't do what I want!
Techy: Are there any messages on the screen saying what the problem might be?
Woman: Well, it says my himen has been broken or something.

The phone was subsequently slammed down, and the techy burst into fits of laughter, he barely managed to relay the story to his co-workers, at which point they all burst out laughing too. Moments later the phone rang, they manage to gain composure and answer. The same woman was on the phone 'Hello? I think we got disconnected, can you help me with my broken himen please?'

She was helped in the end, but I could never look at himen errors in the same light again.

The whole group of co-workers had a good laugh at the user's mispronunciation and her sounding as if calling for help with 'her broken hymen'. Many other misunderstandings and calls involving porn were cherished:

> Some wife called tech support complaining that her web browser was getting pornographic: the 'location' drop-down menu was full of porn-site addresses. The tech guy explained that those only appear if the user has typed them in before. Having a clue, she figured it out and very politely hung up...

Apart from women, another archetypically group of incompetent users were parents and particularly mums:

> A half a year ago, I went home for the holidays and fixed my parent's Windows machine for them.
> Not more than two weeks later my mom called me up saying it had a blue screen of death whenever it tried to boot up. I asked her what the error said and she started reading to me the hex from the screen.
> She said my *older* sister had been using the computer last so I told her to put her on the line and asked her what had happened. She told me her friend in college had sent her an attachment in an email named 'ms... blast... worm... 32.exe or something' but when she clicked on it, the machine started acting funny.

The user reporting the error was a mom, but, as we learn from the description, the family member who had really been at fault was another women: the older sister. In some sophisticated myths, the topoi of sex and parents intertwined, possibly in an ultimate fool-user pattern:

> I helped my mother learn how to use a computer... I went back a week later for Sunday dinner and asked if everything was ok with the computer. 'Fine', my dad replied. My mum just gave me a sheepish look. Later that afternoon I logged on to their computer to check my emails and was flabbergasted to see that their Internet history was full of gay porn sites.
>
> 'Er, why are all these sites in your history?' I asked – visions of my dad, a gimp and a family tragedy filling my head.
> 'That's your fault!', piped up my mum indignantly. 'You said if I typed "Hot male" into the search engine it would take me to the email login'.
> 'That would be m-a-i-l, mum.'

'Oh.'

Thing is there were loads of sites. She'd obviously tried dozens of links.

Another recurring theme involved clients who were obviously a bit slow on the uptake, especially in understanding how machines work. Some showed that they are a bit technically challenged and made history in Internet myths: 'One customer I heard of years ago was having a problem with diskettes becoming unreadable every night. Turns out the swing shift was leaving them for the night shift stuck to the side of a file cabinet with a refrigerator magnet.'

Dozens of other stories described users who inserted unintended objects into their CD-ROM disc drives, such as credit cards, coffee cups, etc. Some stories sounded really amazing, as if their heroes had skipped the electric era, too: 'How about finding a 5¼" disc in a 3½" drive? The client said he didn't have the bigger drive, so he figured if he folded the disc over and shoved it in. Oh, and then I had to explain that the extremely important data on this disc he just folded was likely no longer in existence.' Some users seemingly treated their computers as they would other kitchen appliances: 'I had a client trim their 5¼" discs with scissors so they'd fit in their new 3½" drive, then complained the drive was faulty.' A couple of other heroes used angle grinders to adjust unfitting ink-printer cartridges, recover CDs from 5¼" floppy drives, etc. One heroine managed something even more difficult: 'We talk for a while and I figure I'd just go over there since she's such a retard. I get over there and sure enough, it's plugged in the ethernet port on her laptop instead of the usb port. Don't ask me how it fit...' Again, it was 'she' who proved to be very incompetent, even referred to by the engineer as 'a retard,' although she put a plug into an incorrect, though quite seemingly unfitting, as we have to admit, port.

In some cases, the need for help was possibly more for reassurance in dealing with the unknown, rather than for anything else:

> I have defined what tech support does. The job of tech support is to read to the user any error messages that they see on their screen:
>
> *User*: I have a message on my screen
> *Tech*: Ok – what does it say?
> *User*: It says my password is wrong.
> *Tech*: Ahh right – that means your password is wrong.
> *User*: Ahhh great – thanks!

In a number of stories, the figure was referring not to reluctance to immerse into computer reality, but quite the opposite: an excessive identification of 'virtuality' with the physical world:

> Built him a brand new computer and as it was Christmas, installed Microsoft Flight Sim 2000 on there. He was made up. Until the point he phoned me up in a blind panic.
>
> *Him*: Chris you know on that Microsoft?
> *Me*: What, Windows?
> *Him*: No, the game...
> *Me*: Ah, OK. Yeah?
> *Him*: I've just crashed it
> *Me*: The game crashed?
> *Him*: I crashed the plane into a mountain...
> *Me*: Yeeeees?
> *Him*: Look, that won't have damaged the screen will it?

Some users were 'funny' just because they understood pictograms differently than the support specialist:

> *Me*: type in dir *.dat
> *Meat*: eh?
> *Me*: type in d i r star dot d a t
> *Meat*: star?
> *Me*: asterisk
> *Meat*: eh?
> *Me*: hold down the shift key and press 8
> *Meat*: oh right! you mean cabbage
> *Me*: eh?

In the cited story, the inept client was referred to by a derogatory term, 'meat'.

Perhaps the most unusual were the anecdotes where the user was literally following the instructions of the 'tech person':

> *Tech*: Insert the first floppy disk.
> *User*: Okay. done.
> *Tech*: When the computer tells you, insert the second floppy disk.
> *User*: Okay. Er... Damn! Done.

Tech: When the computer tells you, insert the third floppy disk.
User: NO WAY will a third disk ever fit into that slot! I can't get the first two out, either.

In the story, the support technician did not advise removing one disk before inserting the next. Yet, he nevertheless found the situation bizarre and considered the user dull.

Probably the most irritating were the users who considered themselves competent, although, in the view of the support team, they obviously were not:

1. Talking to a customer who is unable to get her DSL connection to work because she had inserted the network cable in the CD-ROM drive. 2. Talking to another customer having the same problem as the one above, but this one has not been able to locate anyplace on his computer where a network cable might fit. When I asked him if he had a network card installed I got the answer (in a very annoyed tone of voice) 'Of course I have a network card, do you think I'm an idiot?! The card is right here in the box from the store.' 3. Realizing that this will be a long and very painful day.

A client who denies being an idiot, while quite clearly behaving like one, is definitely a reason for a headache.

Only a few stories were partially non-depreciative. As one of the engineers put it:

Customers ARE everything you've heard about them. Every outlandish, unbelievable story you've ever heard is true, and odds are good I can provide at least one example of whatever incredible behavior you've ever doubted when you read it.

On the other hand, some customers, the ones that will act this way, actually DO know they are babbling and don't know what they're talking about, and it's a very rewarding thing to have them admit to being a pain and thanking you for being very patient with them. It doesn't happen all that often, but it's nice, and I try to keep it in mind the next time one of our 'high maintenance' customers strolls in the door (and then I usually consider finding somewhere to hide anyway).

As the specialist put it, although customers are often incompetent and cause 'horrors', occasionally they realize it and are at least thankful for assistance. The only positive feature of a client, as pointed out by the specialist, is that the client sometimes knows he or she is not really apt and 'babbles'. Still, this could be a serious merit when contrasted with the legendary customers who angrily deny their ignorance.

Interpretation and conclusions

The computer users are described anecdotally, but quite univocally, as idiots. One of the specialists, whenever encountering an inexperienced user, would report it to his colleagues by spelling out an 'ID10T' problem. The figure of the user was depicted mostly by referring to incompetence. 'Favorite support stories' were virtually filled only by images of lame creatures, requesting help in mostly trivial and obvious situations.

The hero that immediately comes to mind after reading all the stories is The Fool from Tarot. The Fool is one of the Major Arcana in the Tarot deck. (See Figure 7.1.)

The Fool in one of the most popular Tarot card sets is shown as walking toward the brink of a precipice with a rose in one hand and his head pointed to the sky. A small dog seems to accompany him, perhaps trying to warn him, as he seems to be just about to step over the edge.

This hero strikingly resembles the typical user as perceived by computer specialists. The traditional character exemplifies recklessness, light-heartedness and mental darkness. Fools do not realize their stupidity. This is what makes them difficult to deal with. Fools do not hear the warnings, but nevertheless expect help. After all as Ronell (2002, pp. 17–18) says:

> [t]he stupid are unable to make breaks or breakaways; they are hampered even on the rhetorical level, for they cannot run with grammatical leaps or metonymical discontinuities. They are incapable of referring allegorically or embracing deferral ... The stupid cannot see themselves.

In the game of Tarot, The Fool has another unique role. Playing The Fool temporarily exempts the player from having to follow the rules. Following this analogy, perhaps the PC user may be understood a liminal role then (Turner, 1967) in the sense that it deprives the person of all labels, apart from ignorance. When being helped, the users leave all of their identities behind and rely fully upon the IT expert supporter. The users cannot outsmart the high-tech specialist by accepting his or her rules. The users can, however, as the stories show, outfox the expert by literally following all advice. In this sense, computer user perception may be a replication of yet another icon of Western culture, namely Till Eulenspiegel (also known as Eugenspiegel). (See Figure 7.2.)

Figure 7.1 The Fool in the *Rider-Waite Tarot Deck*
Source: Smith (1909)

Till Eulenspiegel[1] is a hero of Northern German folklore, described in a story anonymously published in 1510 under the title *Ein kurtzweilig Lesen von Dyl Ulenspiegel, geboren uß dem Land zu Brunßwick, wie er sein leben volbracht hat*....[2] Some ascribe the authorship of this story to Hermann Bote. Till Eulenspiegel was later portrayed in a tone poem by Richard Strauss. According to the tale, while traveling in the fourteenth century across the Holy Roman Empire, Till Eulenspiegel played practical jokes on the people he met. In 95 tales, he played pranks on the noble, beguiling all, including doctors, monks, dentists and others in

Figure 7.2 Till Eulenspiegel
Source: Deutsche Literaturgesischte (1905)

respected professions. In his farcical and often scatological jests, he kept playing a fool. As a result, he was able in the end to outfox everyone by relying upon the underlying assumptions of society (condescension, pretentiousness, piousness, etc.). His most common ploy was what we now would probably refer to as a deconstruction or misreading of what he heard by taking a literal understanding of all figurative statements. This method is still popular today as evidenced by the success of the movie *Borat: Cultural Learnings of America for Make Benefit Glorious Nation of Kazakhstan*.[3]

The PC users in the stories about specialists were in some cases described in the same manner as Till Eulenspiegel. They personified the common wisdom and, by following the expert's advice verbatim, they played the fool. The situation with the three disks in a drive is an example. Another example involves a specialist consulted on the phone on how to remove coffee stains from the boss's keyboard. The specialist suggested washing the keyboard with tap water and drying it. Unaware that the 'keyboard' belonged to a laptop, the consultant had to deal with a furious boss. In these instances, the experts were not emphasizing the skillfulness of the users in tricking them by playing incompetent. Nevertheless, they replicated a formula resembling Till Eulenspiegel's trick: the specialists admitted being fooled by seemingly doltish clients.

Both archetypes (of The Fool and of Till Eulenspiegel) are built on one motif though: the stupidity of the user in one real case and in one fabricated case. Nearly all of the approximately two thousand stories read involved idiots, freaks, or clowns. These taken for granted, easily recognizable icons may be very powerful. For example, Elizabeth B. Silva (2000) showed how the user-figures in instructions for cookers and ovens over the past century helped to reinstate the gender and power roles ascribed to women. Kociatkiewicz (1997) used mythical metaphors to shed new light on the interaction between computers and their users. Similarly, the speciously indifferent language shift in describing people as 'alcoholics' rather than as 'drunkards' had a huge impact on the social reception of drinking and resulted in, among other effects, an authority shift from priests to doctors as the problem was transferred from a moral to a medical dictionary (Brown, 1998).

Therefore, such a common description of a client should not be underestimated, even if given in a frivolous Internet forum discussion. The fact that help desk consultants perceive their clients as idiots may have major consequences with regard to their relationships. Use of such recurring archetypes can have a deeply stigmatizing effect (Goffman, 1986). The reinstatement of the perception of the user also defines the role that is offered to computer users by specialists. We become what we think we are: if the users are repeatedly, and not always verbally, put in the position of a fool or Till Eulenspiegel, eventually they will become one (Rothenbuhler, 1998). As has been shown, however, some do not need much encouragement.

Notes

1. Literally in High German, the phrase means 'owls mirror', but the original in Low German is believed to be *ul'n Spegel*, which means 'wipe the arse' or 'kiss my ass' (Oppenheimer, 1995).
2. The title is sometimes translated into English as *An Entertaining Book about Till Eulenspiegel from the Land of Brunswick*.
3. I would like to thank Joanna Jemielniak for this trope.

8
An Emerging Legend of a Kosovar Heroine: Narrating Female Entrepreneurs

Lena Olaison

In search of female entrepreneurs in Kosovo/a

While walking around in the city of Pristina, Martin Bowles's words 'When the gods dethroned, and with the State and work organizations failing, to create meaning, where can people find inspiration and direction for their lives?' (Bowles, 1989, p. 418) came to my mind, helping me to organize my feelings and thoughts. This was in October 2005 when I had come to Kosovo/a to find female entrepreneurs. Not having any clear connections to organizations in the region or any key persons to extract information from, I started to ask people I met if they knew of any female entrepreneurs I could talk to.

After a while it felt like I was told the same story over and over again. Often, the person I asked could not name a female entrepreneur, but they had heard a story about one. I was not surprised to find stories of successful women: It was the pattern or rhythm of the stories that did it. They were stories of personal struggle and success – struggle for survival during the war as well as struggle with their personal career – through personal achievement and devotion to the cause. The stories were far more celebrative, however – avoiding descriptions of victims and injustices – than I had expected. Soon enough I started to characterize them as hero(ine) tales.

I am not the first one to ponder into the mythical hero-like tale of stories of entrepreneurs. On the contrary, the entrepreneur as a hero is perhaps the most common image in business tales (Ahl, 2002; Bruni *et al.*, 2005; Gabriel, 2004a; Hatch *et al.*, 2005; Pettersson, 2002). Hatch *et al.* (2005, p. 40), when analyzing business stories, conclude that 'any culture needs its heroes and constructs them according to its key values. The values of the epic form are heroism and achievement in spite of the odds. Success stories or stories of achievement ... are epics.'

Myths and legends have played and still play an important role for people in the Balkans; to narrate history, to create identity and to claim the right to space and place (Ditchev, 2002). Western countries, not the least, narrate Kosovo/a – and the Balkans in general – in mythical terms (Goldsworthy, 2002). However, it has been argued that it is mainly men and male experience that have been narrated and, further, when women are included in these stories – in the Balkans primarily war-stories – women are present as bodies and further as victims: 'women refugees carrying the remnants of their belongings in plastic bags; women dragging frightened and exhausted children; weeping women, angry women, women impregnated by rape, traumatized women. Whatever happens, women are depicted as bodies' (Kesić, 2002, p. 311).

In organization theory, as mentioned above, it has also been shown that women are primarily portrayed as the 'Other'; the one that the male or male experience is not (Ahl, 2002; Bruni *et al.*, 2005; Gherardi, 1995; Pettersson, 2002). In this chapter I want to contribute to the imaginary of women (as heroines) rather than building on the exclusion of gender and on gender blindness (Gherardi, 1995). We need role models to be put forward on their own, and we need to avoid the convention to 'portray women's organizations as "the other", or "the alter", and sustain social expectations of their difference, thereby implicitly reproducing the normative value of male experience' (Bruni *et al.*, 2005, p. 11). Here we will meet The Intrapreneur, the Spirit, the Controller and the Peacemaker. I narrate the stories from and about the women through writing them as an emerging legend of a Kosovar Heroine; a legend I see as creating space for new stories; embodying the tension between reproducing the past (male experience) and producing the future (female experience).

Emerging myths and legends

We will now return to the initial quote by Bowles (1989). Bowles argues that myths and legends are important in 'structuring peoples' experience and in providing meaning' (Bowles, 1989, p. 406) and when the traditional mythologies, predominantly our religions, are losing their power, there is need for new, or 'creative' mythologies.

The emergence of myths has also been problematized by Laclau (e.g., 1990). While Bowles is problematizing the importance of creative myths primarily in the context of Western societies, and their relation to organizing, Laclau is writing on (dramatic) political or social change – in his recent works (Laclau, 2005) using the case of Kosovo/a. For Laclau myth is not at all primitive, not contributing to irrational behaviour: '[M]yth is constitutive of any possible society ... Any space formed as a principle for the reordering of a dislocated structure's element is mythical. Its mythical character is given by its radical discontinuity with the dislocations of the dominant structural forms' (Laclau, 1990, p. 67). Further, the greater the 'dislocation' (change) is – as Laclau puts it – the greater is the need for the emergence of myths and mythical spaces in order to reorganize social life. However, and this is an important point for Laclau and for this chapter, although these ('creative') myths that emerge are indeed 'new', no dislocation is total, and myths will always echo the struggle between the before and the now. Myths are constituted by the interviewing processes of alteration and repetition. The structure as well as the content of the myth will resemble the local context and its (hi)stories as well as the break with these (Laclau, 1990). Listening to Laclau when making an analysis of emerging myths – in this case female entrepreneurs in Kosovo/a – one could gain from not rejecting the old stories, but making use of them. They are an important part of the emerging story, as the past is for the future.

Writing up an emerging legend

I use material from my field study in Kosovo/a. I asked people I met if they knew any female entrepreneurs; I also found and collected these stories in the written form; finally, I interviewed the women themselves. This is my interpretation of, and contribution to, the stories about female entrepreneurs. This is not an attempt to represent, or write, the true story of these women. I am as much a storyteller as anyone I talked to, and I have chosen to use the style and voice of a storyteller, rather than trying to repeat what I was told by quoting. In order to write up the emerging legend, I will use the model of primary story types as described by Hatch *et al.* (2005, p. 24). I use the epic drama – or the hero legend – to analyze my stories and hence start to trace the emerging legend: how is a female entrepreneur portrayed in Kosovo/a? What is the plot focus? What are the main achievements and challenges? Who is the villain, the assistant, and who is being rescued? What emotions are provoked by the stories? How are the stories being used?

Narrating female entrepreneurs in Kosovo/a

The Intrapreneur: making use of existing structures

She starts to talk even before we shake hands. She turns to my interpreter and says (in English) 'I don't speak English', and then she immediately, in Albanian, starts to describe everything we see (we meet at her farm). Repeatedly during our conversation, when she thinks that the translation is not good enough, or losing her point, she translates that part herself, impatiently. To make her point she often compares herself, and her farm, with other dairy producers, nationally and internationally, and she often goes into detailed, technical descriptions.

After the war she had started to work for a dairy production reconstruction project, run by an international aid organization whose goal was to give 'one cow to every household'. By the end of the project she was given the chance to buy 36 cows from the project, and she was also given machinery and a tractor. She says, with pride, that now, just a few years later she is the third biggest dairy producer in Kosovo/a. She might lose the farm nonetheless, she tells me: she owns the buildings and the machinery, but the property is not hers. It is one of the former state-owned farms and it is now in the process of privatization.

During my visit there are two men at the farm and I understand that one of them is her husband. I do not get introduced to him, not even when he drives us into Pristina. In fact, we do not discuss her family at all; we talk about her firm and the projects she is leading in connection with the firm. Her main project is to help others to set up and start dairy production. She believes that it is from the countryside that Kosovo/a can be rebuilt: the land is there and will always be there, now people just have to learn how to run a modern business, she says. Her strategy is simple, yet surprising: when people come to her asking for help, she offers them a chance to work at her farm. When she feels that their commitment is sincere she gives them, for free, 1–3 cows. At first they can keep the animals at her firm and use her machinery; gradually they move to a place of their own.

The Spirit: anything is possible and life should be beautiful

The spontaneous suggestion: 'Why don't you open your own florist shop if you like flowers' started it all. This was in 2003, during a visit to London. She had gone to London to celebrate her birthday and she was given a beautiful bouquet of flowers; not plastic, but fresh roses. She thought to herself 'why not' and two years later I meet her in her florist boutique. There is also a small counter with chocolate pralines in the shop. The Spirit explains that making this difference – bringing joy into people's lives – has inspired her to introduce other products in Kosovo/a, such as chocolate (*real* chocolate, as she calls it).

The Spirit is the youngest of my interviewees. It is clear that her independence is very important to her. As an example, when I ask her what people are important for her and her firm, at first she answers no one. Then she tells me that if she needs help she finds it at her job as an IT engineer; they are all professionals there, she says. Then she reveals that she has a mentor in Skopje and that it was her family that helped her financially when she started.

The Spirit has two degrees, and she thinks it is important that women go to university and at the moment there are two young women – both of them studying at the university – working in the florist shop. The Spirit admits that it is not the most efficient strategy; florists need training, and since her staff only stay as long as they study, she will spend more money on training than necessary, but she thinks it is worth it. First of all it is her way of contributing, she tells me, and second, young people bring new ideas and energy to the firm.

The Controller: this is a one (wo)man show

She has eight women employed in the bakery. The Controller tells me that her husband also works at the bakery sometimes, driving the van – I can see her husband behind a curtain, watching us, but we do not get introduced to each other.

Before we start to talk she insists on providing me with a selection of cakes from the bakery and a coffee from the café next door. Her story is told in short sequences, because as soon as she sits down she runs off again: to the kitchen to make sure that everything is proceeding accordingly; she is the only one allowed to answer the phone, which is constantly ringing; she opens the back door if there is a delivery, and takes care of the customers. The other women mix ingredients and bake the cakes, but when it comes to the final part – the decorations – the Controller makes them all. Her specialty is birthday cakes (or cakes for any other special occasions): She shows me pictures she has collected in an album – more than 70 by now. The album works as inspiration for her customers when they order cakes.

When I ask her what makes her successful she answers straightaway that it is the quality of the cakes: They are home-made. Her mother gave her the recipes, and she tells me over and over that there are no cakes in Kosovo/a like her cakes: She is the most expensive and the best you can find. Then there is some noise from the kitchen and she is gone again.

Once returned to the table, she gives me some background to her choice of career. She had supported her family, during the occupation, through selling doughnuts in the street. After the war she started to work for a women's NGO, in a project providing work training for women.

Through the project she got funding – on the premise to train women – and started the bakery. When the project came to an end she continued to train women, and several of them are now working for her. She also helped four women to start their own bakeries; they came to her for training, she helped them with equipment and gave them advice during the start-up phase. She tells me that she has no spare time, but that her greatest joy, and what she appreciates most about her firm, is to see her family and the families she has met through her bakery grow up.

The Peacemaker: live and let live

The first time I hear about the Peacemaker is at a women's NGO. She lives in the village of Obilic, an important place historically and culturally for Kosovo/a, and one of the few places where people of different ethnicities live side by side. The Swedish K-for escort me to the Peacemaker; not because it is dangerous for me to go there, but it makes the Peacemaker less nervous if they are there. She is a Bosniak, one of the minority groups in Kosovo/a, and although she speaks Albanian almost perfectly her accent can cause her problems sometimes.

The Peacemaker started the firm – manufacturing plastic bags – as a way to help women in her community. She is a Bosniak, but her partner, a woman working at the municipality, is Kosovo/a-Albanian, and the women working in the factory are of different ethnic heritages, too. They have been multi-ethnic from the beginning, she says, but they always find a way to communicate; they do not need language.

Before and after work, and also during breaks, she goes to the factory. The Peacemaker's partner never works there, but her husband does, more or less full time, without payment. Like the other men I (almost) meet he does not say a word during my visit to the factory. I notice that all the texts on the plastic bags are printed in German. The Peacemaker tells me that the plastic bags sell better in this format – people are suspicious of domestic products.

During my visit to the factory there is a power cut, and there is no one else at the factory. The Peacemaker explains that when there is no power they can't use the machines and it makes no sense for the women to stay in the factory. Therefore, the women go home to take care of the household. When the power returns they come back and start to work.

Discussion: tracing the legend(s) of a Kosovar heroine

The emergence of female entrepreneurs in Kosovo/a provides a novel situation for studying a myth-in-the-making. There are of course a

Table 8.1 Tracing an emerging legend of a Kosovar heroine.

Aspects of story	Epic drama	A Kosovar heroine
Protagonist	Heroines	Female entrepreneurs
Other characters	Rescue object	Creating heroines
	Assistant	Husband
	Villain	The past
Plot focus	Struggle and success	Bravery
Predicament	Challenge and mission	Tension between reconstructing Kosovo/a and business success
Emotions	Nostalgia and admiration	The woman before and after the war
Role in business	Inspiration	Creating market economy and a place for women in it

Source: Hatch et al. (2005) p. 24.

thousand faces of the Hero (Campbell, 1949, quoted in Bowles, 1989) and this is not an attempt to write them as ONE, neither to reject the old hero myths and legends. The aim is rather to resituate the Hero myth – a play in the structure – thus giving voice to silent parts of the story and a potential to alternatives – in this case women's experience in Kosovo/a.

My analysis is summarized in Table 8.1. The *plot focus* is struggle and achievement: if one tries hard enough, one can succeed and create life for oneself, for the becoming-nation and for the people. The stories avoid traumas, misfortune – which clearly breaks with the stereotype images of women in Kosovo/a – and details about the family. Further, there is a tension in the setting of the stories, in the *predicament*. The mission these women emphasize is the reconstruction of Kosovo/a and the creation of a joint future. The challenge for the women is connected to their firms; how to create and run a business successfully, how to find customers, suppliers and material; similar to challenges every person running a business struggles with. However, in the context of Kosovo/a this struggle becomes a tension, since some decisions – like the Spirit who enables women to study at the university – are irrational in the economic profit context.

My *protagonists* seem to be somewhere inbetween the 'independent-minded entrepreneurs who struck out alone, building empires and revolutionizing social and economic life, overcoming crisis and leaving lasting legacies' (Gabriel, 2004a, p. 82) and entrepreneurs as driving-forces of social change and entrepreneurship as forms of social creativity (Steyaert and Hjorth, 2006). They seem to be driven not primarily by an economic rationale, *homo oeconomicus,* but by creating, or re-creating – the firm, families, the nation, the people, as well as themselves and their career (cf. Hjorth and Johannisson, 2003) – so perhaps we can understand them as representatives of *femina curans.*[1] However, this analysis is dangerously close to seeing them as 'mothers'; caring about mother earth – an image they themselves carefully avoid. Therefore, through a discussion of the context of *other characters*, where, or with whom, these women operate, I hope to reach a more multi-faced image by the end of this chapter.

Kosovo/a – the heart of Europe's most complex transitional region – seems to be trapped on the threshold between the past and the future: its people cannot continue without dealing with the past; neither can they continue without carrying the past with them. Here, according to Laclau (1990), mythical spaces and emerging myths will be visible, and during my interviews people did refer to mythical events to explain Kosovo/a: 'It all started in 1389' (the answer to 'What year did the war begin'); 'People trust "The Canon"[2] more than the law' (explanation of why the implementation of laws is difficult); and the conflict during the 1990s produced new/reproduced old heroes, images used in public as well as private debates. Kosovo/a itself is in this sense the *villain*; the tension between being haunted by the past on one hand and the reconstruction of Kosovo/a on the other. This tension is also present in the stories, The Peacemaker is an explicit example of that, and so is the Intrapreneur, albeit more implicitly.

Physically present in the stories, but still excluded, were the men – my protagonists ignored them completely when I was visiting. However, when describing the day-to-day activities of their firms, it appeared that the men clearly had a role to play – as *assistants* – as a person close to the hero. I cannot know whether I did not get introduced to the men because it is indeed the women that run the show, or if this is a joint strategy (i.e., the international organizations promote women and gender equality, and, therefore, a female business owner can sometimes get funding where a male cannot).

Either way, it is interesting that my protagonists choose to reconstruct society. However, the women seem to be more than a means to reach a goal. On a micro level they are the *rescue objects*; the entrepreneurs are saving them from the villain – the situation in Kosovo/a – making them into heroines of their own. This also means that they are creating their own competition, but during discussions they avoid this topic; The Intrapreneur says that Kosovo/a needs more people working, and The Controller quickly adds that no one is as good as she is anyway, and hence there is no real competition. There are many interpretations of this: perhaps they need competitors for their own business to work better; or perhaps the 'social dimension' is something that others (men) can relate to without getting jealous. Further, as in the case of the Controller, she got funding to train women. However, no one forced the Controller to provide means for others to set up their own firm.

When I talk to people in Kosovo/a, their stories always start with 'before the war . . . after the war . . .' I interpret the war as marking the 'dislocation', using Laclau's framework that provokes a mythical space which is both connected and disconnected with the past. The women start their stories by telling me what they did before the war, what they were working with, and, more importantly, how they used this experience after the war to create their success, i.e. creating a professional career (having a professional career seems very important). It is as if they use this strategy to cross the threshold from the past into the future: using the scars from the past – often ethnic and/or cultural heritage – evoking *nostalgia and admiration* rather than melancholia.

Organizational storytelling, according to Hatch *et al.* (2005), 'is an act involving others, it has the power to engage and thereby the possibility to motivate and inspire' (Hatch *et al.*, 2005, pp. 15–16). As *inspiration*, the stories travel beyond the way they are used by the narrators themselves; they are, through the creative, or emerging, legends creating a space for women in the Kosovo/a that is emerging. Further, re-reading my heroine tales I interpret them as performing the image (they have) of the Western male entrepreneur hero in the (functioning) market economy. In a place without property rights; without laws and regulation; without social security and a functioning market, this needs to be created. Even competition, an important feature of a functioning market, needs to be created. In emerging companies, Gartner *et al.* (1992) argue, people are acting as if they had a stable organization, and this is how the firm eventually becomes a firm. In Kosovo/a these women are acting as if there were a market economy; as if there were property rights; as if minorities could live in peace; and as if the status were already solved. When thinking of the stories as 'acting as if', the tension in the stories starts to make sense. I rather understand the social dimension as an economic necessity than as 'motherhood'. The heroines are creating, by performing, a market (economy); indeed the turn of *femina curans* is creative.

Final remarks

One important question to raise is whether I am not making the mistake Bruni *et al.* (2005) are warning about. Am I not just 'implicitly reproducing the normative value of male experience' (Bruni *et al.*, 2005, p. 11) rather than contributing to the imaginary of women by using the hero tale and by calling them entrepreneurs, two labels connected to male experience? So it might be. At the same time every story has its intertextuality and, listening to Laclau (1990), any emerging myth will carry a trace of its local history. Therefore, I believe that using the same structure and storytelling provides an opportunity to resituate the story and listen to other versions. This also seems to be the strategy of the women I met: by using the same storytelling, or myths, perhaps the women are seen as less alien and frightening. By drawing on specific values, such as contributing to the rebuilding of society, helping others and being professional they seem to be recreating a market, a world, for themselves and others (cf. Spinosa *et al.*, 1997). Therefore, I do not believe that I am just repeating the male experience, pushing these women into a story they will not recognize or belong to. On the contrary, it is their turn now.

Acknowledgement

This chapter is a result of a project funded by FSF (Swedish Foundation for Small Business Research). I want to thank FSF and especially Bengt Johannisson for (personal) support.

Notes

1. *Femina curans* is inspired by Monika Kostera, and her discussion on *femina imaginas* (see Kostera, 1996) and by *homo curans*, a discussion initiated by Bengt Johannisson and Elisabeth Sundin (see Johannisson and Olaison, 2006).
2. 'Kanuni I Leke Dukagjinit' [The Code of Leke Dukagjini].

9
Gender-Content Myths and their Role in Nation Forming

Elżbieta Pakszys

All advanced thinking is immersed and grows from mythical soil, since myth and legendary stories in many respects proceed intuitive as well as discursive reasoning (Armstrong, 2005/2006; Kołakowski, 1989). Establishing history – for example, assessing a sequence of past events to be of a certain value or importance in order to understand and interpret present times – also includes myth-making as an element in the process of social memory, resulting in collectively organized and approved knowledge (Szacka, 2006; Wilshire, 1992).

Among anthropological myths – that is, those concerning the complications of human nature – we find several that try to explain the origin and meaning of sex/gender duality and reciprocity (Kopaliński, 1995; Plato, 1984; Tokarczuk, 2006). Here, male and female elements appear as complementary rather than as separable one from another. It also seems that gender-myths or myths containing gender images (feminine and masculine), ubiquitous in many cultures, reflect and cherish human beings' primordial propensities and original needs for expressing themselves through the most substantial roles ascribed to the individuals representing collective categories: women and men. Although this duality seems to be obvious, it is mostly in respect of earthly matters; among the gods it is usually abandoned.

For instance in Judaeo/Christian tradition, 'God the father' is self-sufficient in not having a feminine complement in creation; reversed in Japanese Shinto mythology where the goddess Amaterasu abstains from masculine help in conception. While on a divine dimension male–female dependence or reciprocity appears to be suspended or unnecessary, ordinary human breeding as effected through 'sex pairing', a biological necessity for variety in reproduction of offspring, becomes a principle for founding and organizing a society in its proper form, including the values of human culture (Kostera, 2003). It seems that the exclusion of the (evolutionary biology?) aspect, indicated above, can inform us to some extent about the most probable relation of origin/creation: rather from human to divine reality, then vice versa.

First among the gender-content-myths are those displaying the family model of spouses and couples – a man and woman staying together in order to maintain marital roles, expressing stereotypical images of wife and husband. They usually embody their expected parental roles; the state of motherhood and fatherhood, the way of creating a family, the basic human social unit.

In Judaeo-Christian myths and legends of human origin (Genesis), the first people in their dual sex/gender difference – Adam and Eve in Paradise – are confronted with God's taboo. Their curiosity for 'forbidden fruit' when tempted by a snake appears especially effective in Eve, resulting in 'original sin' when Adam listened to Eve and then 'humanity's fall' from heaven down to earth. According to many interpretations this sequence of symbolic events and evaluations is used to express the main psycho–behavioural differences between the sexes as well as a hierarchy: the superiority of man *vs.* the subjection of woman. Here is the basis for the patriarchal system – ordained by God the father through his sinful daughters and sons.

In the secular dimension, we shall consider an example from Polish prehistory, which 'every Polish child' will easily recognize as the 'mythical' beginning of the Polish state.

This popular legend describes the founding of the very first Piast dynasty of the peasant tribe of Poles (*Polanie*). The story begins with an ordinary, and happy, family consisting of: *Piast Kołodziej* (Piast the Wheeler) with his wife/woman *Rzepicha/Rzepka* (turnip) and their son *Siemowit/Ziemko*. The everyday chores, responsibilities and amusements were shared but also divided 'naturally' between the sexes, continuing the legend of ancient Polish rural inhabitants. Among these customs is the crucial role played by an event relating the ancient Slav rite of the first clipping of the son's hair, celebrated as his 'masculine maturity'. When little Ziemko has undergone the ritual of cutting at seven the modest party is unexpectedly visited by two unknown persons (or angels?) who in thanks for the hospitality they received prophesied the future Piast kingdom. The common interpretation was clear that in this way the nation gained acceptance by the heavens and given a sign for it to be governed honestly and justly, in reverse to the previously mischievous rule by king Pompilius (*Popiel*), whom 'the mice have eaten for his crimes'.

Now the legend is treated rather less seriously than earlier (in the nineteenth and twentieth centuries) when the Polish state did not exist, though it is still a common theme for many Poles (Anonim (Gall), 1989; Mikołajczakowie, 2001; Mistrz Wincenty, 1992). Some parts of this pagan family image can be recognized as being grafted in later (after Poland's 'birth' in 966) and resemble the Christian religious myth of the holy family; composed of Joseph the Carpenter, the Virgin Mary and their divine son – Jesus Christ, on the way to Bethlehem and Egypt. This similarity, however, is strong in folk interpretations of the symbolic Christmas; in carols, crèche performances etc.; and this same tradition still attaches a peculiar role to the mother and son relationship, which, it seems, truly reveals the bonds between earth and heaven.

* * *

The myths of single motherhood, i.e. immaculate, like that of the Virgin Mary, or unwanted hence in solitude (but also uniting humankind in spite of the challenges and obstacles), appear in many ethnic and religious cultures as well as national traditions. This kind of maternal image is usually cherished by a well-established nation when it is in crisis: endangered by an enemy; dissolution; dispersion; or undergoing a state of war or threat of extinction. The quite well known Mother Pole myth can serve as an example, still treated today as a valid pattern of proper Catholic motherhood.

This model of heroic femininity, borrowed it seems from a Spartan image, was taken up and circulated among Poles by some political writers no earlier than during the partitions of the country in the eighteenth century (Bogucka, 1998). It proliferated through the nineteenth century in many poetic embodiments, and without any real change still survives, mainly in today's pro-natal policy rhetoric. However, it has also undergone critique and deconstruction through the recent iconic transfigurations in Polish feminine/feminist art as well as reasoning (Kowalczyk, 2003). When analyzed through the tools of semiotics, this image of a powerful and 'nationalized' motherhood is rather recognized as a phantasm – a figure between (real) myth and stereotype – since it hardly reflects any clear referent between *significant* and *signifier* or have any direct correspondence, possibly so not only in the Polish tradition (Ostrowska, 2004).

Therefore, other 'great mothers' are also known, not just among Slavic nations: like Mother-Britannia, Mother-Lithuania, *Matushka-Russia* (compared to the Volga river in the lyrics of a famous song). The question is this: do they more-or-less resemble the solitary position of the Virgin Mary (with child), expressed through her endlessly multiplied icons in Christian nations? Or is their content rather of a secular and folk character? And why are the female figures abandoned by males; or, where are the fathers of the nations in need? Are they either dead on the patriotic battle fields or just indifferent to the ordinary problems of their children (Darowska, 2004; Janion, 1996)?

In relatively new nations, founded in the first half of the twentieth century, like India or South Africa, images of 'common to all nation' mothers were purposefully re-created and distributed in order to unite different ethnic groups into one Indian or Afrikaner citizen state. In the first case, of India, the development of independence and folk culture reveals the presence of strong feminine images, embodied by Indira Gandhi and Phoolan Devi, both being considered as incarnations of 'Mother India', although taken from the opposite poles of the social strata and certainly without direct connection to Christianity (Browarczyk, 2005).

The latter modern myth of folk mother (*volksmoeder*), invented after the Anglo–Boer war (1913), was only for Whites; but later on was supposed to represent a medley of nationalities in South Africa, Eurasian (White and Yellow) as well as African (Black) races. However, after so many years of repressive apartheid really mixed populations still seem to be quite problematic (Coetzee, 2003; McClintock, 1995). This phenomenon is rather evident in the case of Latin American colonial history and mythology.

Its aboriginal Aztec feminine hero, la Malinche (Malinzin, dona Marina), was first sold by her native tribe (Nahuatl) as a slave to the Mayas, and then in 1519 offered to Hernan Cortes, the Spanish conqueror of Mexico, becoming his interpreter and lover as well as the mother of their racially mixed children (the *mestizos*) (Todorov, 1991). Later on in the era of Mexican independence (in the 1920s) she was cursed by the native Mexicans as the main cause of their post-colonial misery (Tyler, 2006). However, there are rare attempts to vindicate and deconstruct this sad story, and in some opinions dona Marina is considered a scapegoat of her heirs as a result of a double superstition: of patriarchy mixed with a colonial past (Lenchek, 1997a,b). This, in many respects artificially reconstructed myth, is especially interesting when considered through its particular cultural context, revealing Christian elements intervening here also: that is, opposition between genders or *machismo-* vs. *marianismo-* attitudes, supporting the prevailing masculine and feminine behavioural patterns in Latin America (Śniadecka-Kotarska, 2003).

Going further North, let us inquire about the reputation of the 'Indian princess' Pocahontas vel. Matoaki (ca. 1595–1617; Lenchek, 1997a,b). Is she, like Malinche, 'blamed' for the unhappiness of Native Americans in the US today? Rather not. But the confrontation between the famous Disney film's plot (*Pocahontas*, 1995) and the story of Native Americans (Green, 1992) sheds certain light on a way a legend/myth grows. The former recreates an infantile picture of a *noble savage* teenager, who, throwing her body over an Englishman, Captain John Smith, saved his life during attacks on Jamestown (the first English colony in America), but is condemned by the people of her own tribe, the Algonquian (Powhatan) Indians. The latter tries rather to justify this sacrifice of a 10 or 11-year-old girl as the traditional Native American custom towards strangers and 'a way of symbolic adoption'. Regarding also the similar story of the Shoshone woman named Sacagawea (ca. 1788–1812), the only female participant of the famous Lewis and Clark expedition exploring a route towards the Pacific, we can see these two heroines, recovered only recently, as participants of the North American colonizing process whose biographies oscillate between the stereotypes of 'filthy squaw' and 'noble princess'. Therefore, in the background we can recognize elements far more similar to la Malinche, or the Middle and South America situation, with this juxtaposition of 'the founding fathers' poly-figure epitomizing American 'carved in stone' patriarchal rule there (Kopaliński, 1995; Oleksy, 1998).

In this context arises another mythical creation of a literary type, hence of quite a different origin than the previous ones, but also postcolonial and postmodern, though considered today as negative enough in its literal meaning to be mentioned here. Its name is *Madama Butterfly* or geisha Cio-Cio-San, a Japanese female lead character from Giacomo Puccini's opera (1904), now recognized as a postcolonial symbol of the legendary 'Oriental woman'. First easily conquered and hasty married, then abandoned by Pinkerton, an American Navy lieutenant, who after three years, now as bigamist (remarried), reappears claiming rights to their natural child. Cio-Cio-San after giving back the boy to his father commits suicide. The plot, originally a David Belasco short story (1900) later adapted for the opera by Luigi Illica and Giuseppe Giocosa, had been preceded by some earlier stories in the late nineteenth century; *Mme Chrysantème* by Pierre Loti (1887) and *Mme Butterfly* by John Luther Long (1903); relating the literary fates of oriental women which appeared on a wave of so called 'Japonism' then in fashion. There is perhaps also a reminiscence of this drama in the post-Vietnam War climate of the 1960s in the musical *Miss Saigon*. Only recently has it been thoroughly deconstructed by David Cronenberg's film, *M. Butterfly* (1993), based on the French-Chinese espionage play by David H. Hwang (an earlier success on Broadway). This cinema adaptation is a distant image of Mme Butterfly, enhanced with many layers of complicated entanglements, including homosexual deception, transvestitism, performativity of gender and gay elements etc. However, in spite of its reinterpretation of 'real femininity', it apparently does not loose the original story elements symbolizing and denouncing postcolonial implications of race and gender dependence entangled with politics (Chow, in Quillen, 2001). It is quite astonishing how great is the potential of a phantasm of a betrayed geisha under the etiquettes of Mme Butterfly-type performances, or rather how great is the power of the submissive Oriental image of femininity when exploited by the media, business and advertisements today (Ahmed, 1996).

* * *

Finally, let us try to make some suggestions concerning a number of preliminary ideas for recognizing the power of the above gender-myths as a new branch of research in women's/gender studies today.

In seeking the traces of a mythical deep past, we have studied the prehistory of Matriarchy or the heritage of the Great Goddess/Great Mother, using both critical and affirmative approaches to Maria Gimbutas archeomythology (Błaszczyk, 2005; Wilshire, 1992). Research on other patterns responsible for reproductions of Patriarchy will be conducted to go beyond the famous 'circulation of women in "primitive cultures"' by Claude Levi-Strauss (Szczuka, 2001). However tempting a superficial application of this theory is in the case of the singular mothers of the *mestizos* in both American cases, truly interdisciplinary and multicultural studies should reveal other neglected conditions of gender, race and social strata, shaping ancient and modern femininity (and masculinity too).

Careful studies on fulfilling the main female 'destination', i.e. the maternal role, in particular one which includes overcoming a 'nationalized' private sphere, should provide a vast amount of material for claiming female citizenship and power in both new and old nation states.

In spite of its equivocal demonstration performing art and media shall evoke and distribute a number of hidden collective memory images being of certain value for further historical exploration on gender relationship traces in transcultural scope. We can also try to discover other possible variants and variables of sex/gender dependencies in connection with today's recognized states of fuzziness, for example homosexuality and gays.

10
Adulation, Abandonment and Amputation: Images of Women in Vedic Mythology

Sumohon Matilal

Living women: women in myth

This chapter offers a range of insights into images of women in Vedic mythology. Here the story-teller is writing from an unusual perspective. This is a story of lives observed and of ancient mythologies. It is woven from the stories heard in childhood. It is also the case that it is written not by a story teller or an ethnographer but by an accountant. Yet, there is some happy coincidence in this. It is in many ways *an account*. It is an account written in the lived experiences of women. It is not written with a background of theoretical connections, although there are some; it is a story told from life. This is the story of many Indian women. It is the story of my mother.

According to Halpern (1961, p. 137), the study of myths is a study of 'the origin of beliefs out of historic experience'. Eliade (1963) suggests that

> Myths narrate not only the origin of the world, of animals of plants and of man, but also all the primordial events in the consequence of which man became what he is today – mortal, sexed, organised in a society, obliged to work in order to live and working in accordance with certain rules. (cited in Dandridge *et al.*, 1980, p. 80)

In other words, myths offer 'the motive for ritual and moral action, as well as with indications as to how to perform them' (Malinowski, 1955, p. 108). This chapter examines how the narratives of three central female characters of Vedic literature have 'expressed, enhanced and codified' (ibid.) the perceptions of women in India. It speculates whether these three characters serve as archetypes of the feminine in India and examines the workplace consequences of such perceptions.

Adulation: the story of Durga

This section of the chapter focuses on the legend of Durga, particularly on her emergence as the 'Mahishasura Mardini' (slayer of the buffalo demon). It then goes on to identify how Durga is worshipped in India as 'Ma Durga' and as an emblem of power or *shakti*.

According to the Puranas,[1] thousands of years ago, the universe was close to destruction in the hands of the demon king, Mahishasura. Through intense prayers, Mahishasura had become so powerful that no man or God could kill him – he was invincible. Soon he assembled one of the deadliest armies known to man and launched a fierce attack on the Heavens. The Gods, completely caught by surprise lost miserably and barely managed to escape. The cosmic order[2] was thrown into complete disarray as Mahishasura unleashed a reign of terror.

A saviour was needed to preserve Creation, but who could defeat Mahishasura?

> Driven out of their heavenly abode the divine personages went to Brahma[3] and sought protection. Brahma emitted dazzling effulgence from his many limbs which assumed the form of a woman. She looked awesome and when the gods saw Her they took heart. Then each of them created replicas of their own special weapons with which they equipped her. (Bhattacharji, 1995, pp. 32–3)

Durga led the Gods against Mahishasura's armies and a fierce battle ensued. Nine days and nine nights later She and Mahishasura alone remained standing on the corpse strewn battlefield:

> Now, the thirsty Goddess drank her fill of wine and smiled with eyes reddened in intoxication. The buffalo demon was uprooting hills and mountains and hurling them at her. She pierced and smashed them with her arrows and said, 'You fool, roar and yell as long as I drink. When I destroy you the gods will roar and shout.' She then leaped upon the demon, pierced him with her spike and struck off his head. (Bhattacharji, 1995, pp. 32–3)

In this way, the universe was saved and the cosmic order restored.

The worship of Durga, as Ghosh (2000, p. 295) suggests, 'epitomises the search for protection and benevolence of the Goddess'. She is considered to be a personification of the Divine Mother – the Supreme Being who is the creator and protector of this universe, the source of all beings, divine and mortal. She is worshipped each year for four days across most of Eastern India as 'Ma Durga' that is, as the Mother who preserved Her creation from the clutches of evil. However, in other parts of India she is worshipped as an embodiment of *Shakti* or power, reflecting the dynamic warrior aspect of the Goddess – as the woman who saved and restored order, a role traditionally attributed to the masculine.

These two adulated sides of the feminine – the maternal and the aggressive – will be revisited in a later section of the chapter where I attempt to explore how these perspectives influence perceptions of women at the workplace in India.

Abandonment: the story of Sita

The story of Sita is taken from the oldest Indian epic, the *Ramayana*. Written in Sanskrit by the sage Valmiki in the fourth century BCE, the Ramayana could be described as a biography of a north Indian king called Rama, considered by many in India as an embodiment of the ideal man and the ideal king. This section focuses on the story of Rama's consort, Sita, to identify the second strand – the notion of abandonment.

Sita was found in a furrow in the ground by King Janaka when he was tilling the land with a golden plough in fulfilment of a sacred ritual. The king saw celestial beauty in the child and decided to adopt her as his daughter. Sita thus grew up as a princess and was married to Prince Rama, with whom she fell in love at first sight. However soon after her marriage, the day before Rama's coronation, Rama's scheming stepmother had him banished to the forests for 14 years. Sita happily chose to accompany her husband to the forest rather than living the luxurious life of a princess.

Forest life was romantic and pleasant and full of adventure for the couple. Disaster struck when Ravana, the demon king of Lanka (modern Sri Lanka) kidnapped Sita and took her away to Lanka. Ravana held Sita captive for one year, continuously asking her to marry him and become his queen. But Sita rebuffed every advance and refused even to sleep under his roof.

Eventually Rama arrived with an army of monkey warriors and attacked Ravana; the latter was killed and Sita rescued. However Rama refused to accept Sita; he questioned her chastity since she had lived in another man's company for a year. He said to her:

> What illustrious man of good family would take back a woman who had lived in another's house though he longs to? The reason I won you back was to restore my fame. I have no attachment to you. Leave

here as you wish! This is what I have decided. (*Ramayana*, 1975, 6.103, pp. 19–23)

Stung by Rama's cruel words, Sita undertook an ordeal by the fire to prove her fidelity. She called upon Agni, the God of fire, to testify to her purity. But Agni recognizing her purity refused to consume her. Rama said that he knew all along that she was *pure*; he only wanted his subjects to be satisfied. He embraced her and returned home where Rama was crowned king and Sita, queen.

Unfortunately their happiness did not last long. Soon Rama learned that doubts about Sita's fidelity were still circulating among his subjects. Unable to endure the rumours he ordered his brother Lakshmana, to take the pregnant Sita to the forest and abandon her (*Ramayana*, 1975, 7.41, pp. 42–58). As Sutherland (1989, p. 77) observes, 'Rama rejects her so completely that he himself cannot even carry out the deed.' However, Lakshmana took her to the sage Valmiki's hermitage and abandoned her there. Safe in the sage's keeping Sita gave birth to twins, Lava and Kusa, who were brought up by Valmiki and taught the *Ramayana*.

In the meantime Rama decided to undertake the Ashvamedha Sacrifice.[4] During the sacrifice, Lava and Kusa recited the *Ramayana* as composed by Valmiki. Rama was so moved by the recitation and by the story of Sita's sufferings therein that he decided to take her back, ignoring the slanderous talk of his subjects. He had Sita brought before him and asked her to prove her fidelity once again. Dejected and forlorn, Sita appeared in Rama's court and took an oath: 'Since I have never thought of any man but Rama, let the Goddess Madhavi [the Earth] split open before me' (*Ramayana*, 1975, 7.88, p. 10).

As soon as Sita uttered these words the Earth split open and she disappeared into the furrow. The story of Sita provides a model of chastity – a woman who is under suspicion of not being chaste is abandoned despite her fidelity. Sutherland (1989, p. 77) comments, 'Throughout the epic we see her as a faithful and loyal wife who suffers precisely because of these virtues.'

How does Indian society perceive Sita's rejection by Rama? The answer to this question and its implications for the working Indian woman will be explored in a later section.

Amputation: the story of Draupadi

The story of Draupadi is taken from the other Indian epic, the *Mahabharata*. Composed in the sixth century BCE in Sanskrit by the sage Vyasa, the *Mahabharata* could be described as a poem that tells the story of two sets of paternal cousins – the Pandavas and the Kauravas, who became bitter rivals and ended up fighting each other in a bloody war for possession of the ancestral kingdom.

Draupadi and her brother Dhrstadyumna had emerged together from a sacrificial fire lit by King Drupad who was praying for a son. Draupadi grew up into an exceedingly beautiful woman (The *Mahabharata*, 1973, 1.155.10). Eager to win her hand in marriage princes and kings from every corner of the world assembled at her swayamvara[5] but it was Arjuna, one of the Pandava brothers whom she chose as her suitor. When Arjuna returned home with his new wife, he exclaimed to his mother, 'Mother, look what I have brought.' His mother, without realizing what Arjuna was referring to, replied, 'Whatever you have brought, you must share it with your brothers.' The mother's order could not be questioned and consequently Draupadi ended up having all the five Pandava brothers as her husbands (*Mahabharata*, 1973: 1.176.29–30)

Soon after the marriage the Pandavas were invited by the Kauravas to a game of dice. As the game progressed, the Pandavas, represented by their eldest brother Yudhisthira, lost all their wealth and even their kingdom. Having lost all his material possessions, Yudhisthira started putting his younger brothers and finally himself at stake but lost again. The Pandavas were reduced to slaves of their cousins. In a frenzy to win back his kingdom Yudhisthira placed Draupadi at stake as his last possession and lost her too. What followed can only be termed as a very ugly episode in Vedic India.

The eldest Kaurava brother Duryodhana commanded one of his younger brothers to forcefully bring Draupadi into the court. The princess, who had just finished her bath and was drying her loose hair, was dragged into the court all the way from her palace by her hair. 'Dressed in only one garment which had its ends tied low and menstruating, she entered the assembly' (*Mahabharata*, 1973, 2.60:10). She went before her father-in-law and begged not to be brought before the assembly but he did nothing. Infuriated, she looked at her five husbands for protection but they did not come to her rescue either for they had all been reduced to slaves. To taunt her further, Duryodhana bared his left thigh and asked her to sit on it. When she refused, he ordered his younger brother, Duhsasana, to strip her:

> Then Duhsasana forcibly took hold of Draupadi's garment and began to take it off. But, just as Draupadi's garment was being pulled off, other garments, one following the other, of the same type appeared![6]

All those kings, observing that miracle on earth, let forth a loud, terrifying sound of 'hala hala'. (*Mahabharata*, 1973: 2.61:40–6)

Although Draupadi was also an innocent victim like Sita, unlike Sita she was not happy to live life resigned to her fate – she sought revenge on the Kauravas for her public humiliation and would rarely let go of an opportunity to complain to her husbands, particularly Yudhisthira, about her ill-treatment and her ill-luck at having such a lot of husbands (Sutherland, 1989, p. 67).

Scholars (see Hopkins, 1901; Sutherland, 1989) have suggested that the final war between the Pandavas and the Kauravas that resulted in the complete extermination of the latter can be attributed to a certain extent to Draupadi's continual harping on the insult she received in the assembly and her husbands' failure to avenge it. For example, she complained bitterly to Krishna about the dice game:

> I was forced to become a slave. I blame only these strong Pandavas, men to be held best in battle, who watched their lawful and illustrious wife being tormented. A curse on Bhimasena's strength, a curse on the archer Arjuna's; both of them stood by while vile men insulted me, Krishna. (*Mahabharata*, 1973, 3.222:4–7ab)

This thirst for vengeance was further illustrated later in the epic when Draupadi was subject to two sexual assaults. First, by the King of Sindhus, Jayadratha, who madly fell in love with her and abducted her. The Pandavas rescued her but Yudhisthira decided to spare Jayadratha's life. Draupadi on hearing that Jayadratha would not be punished was enraged and spoke to her two husbands Bhima and Arjuna in fury: 'If you want to do me a kindness, kill that lowest of humans, that outcast ... that evil, wretched defiler of his family' (*Mahabharata*, 1973, 3.255, 44–5).

The second assault occurred when the Pandavas were in exile hiding behind disguises in the court of King Virata. A furious Draupadi mocked the strength and prowess of her husbands, calling them eunuchs enduring passively the assault on their wife. She asked Yudhisthira: 'Where is the anger, the virility and courage of those who do not wish to defend a wife from a wicked man?' (*Mahabharata*, 1973, 4.15:21). Later that night she approached Bhima and told him her woes urging him to take action on her behalf. The incited Bhima swore to protect her and killed her assaulter the very next day.

In stark contrast to the compliant, placid and all perfect Indian wife, Sita, these instances portray Draupadi, as a woman who is obsessed with revenge. Her aggression resonates with the warrior aspect of Durga–Shakti, representing the active dynamic principles of feminine power. Draupadi attempts to restore herself (the dignity of the feminine) through the use of aggression against those who have humiliated and emotionally amputated her, that is the patriarchal and male dominated society. Sutherland (1989, p. 72) suggests that the aggressive behavior of Draupadi can be seen as a 'powerful defense mechanism, a means by which she can express feelings of rejection and depression'.

Perceptions of women

These stories all offer insights into the ways in which women are perceived in Indian Vedic mythology. However, the question remains whether or not these images have any contemporary relevance. Are women in India today subject to the same adulation, abandonment and, in the specific sense in which I have used the term here, stripped down to nothing, without hope of help or rescue? This section focuses on the sociological and workplace implications of these three mythological heroines for an Indian woman.

A survey of 1,000 young men and women in Uttar Pradesh, the largest state in India by P. Pratap (cited in Sutherland, 1989, p. 63) indicated that from a list of 24 Goddesses, literary heroines, and historically famous women, a strikingly large percentage chose Sita as the ideal role model. As will be apparent from the discussion in this section, the conduct and character of Sita – a submissive acquiescence to the whims of an often cruel husband – is regarded as normative in Indian society. Jejeebhoy (2002, p. 299) writes that in India, the family is mostly patriarchal, patrilocal and patrilineal; husbands are assumed to own women and to have the right to dominate them. According to Bloom *et al.* (2001, p. 75): '[a] mong Hindus the transition from daughter to bride is particularly intense because a woman arrives as a stranger to the groom's family ... [and] ... during the early period of her marriage she has the lowest societal status of any household member'. She has left her family and needs emotional support which is usually lacking. Roy (1975, p. 33) suggests that as a consequence young Indian women often feel rejected and depressed after marriage.

Sita at work: the case of Lieutenant Sushmita Chakravarty

Twenty-five year old Lt. Sushmita Chakravarty shot herself to death on 17 June 2006 (Singh and Gupta, 2006). She had joined the army only 10 months earlier. Originally from Bhopal she was posted in Udhampur a town in Northern India where she was living alone. According to her father, his daughter, a gold medallist in Chemistry, joined the army 'with dreams of serving the nation' (p. 7) but was asked to work in the supplies department where her responsibilities were to organize parties for her bosses, supervise the food, drinks and entertainment and stay back until the party was over, which usually was early morning. Her father said: 'She was depressed... despite her capabilities the Army had reduced her to arranging parties' (Singh and Gupta, 2006, p. 7).

Like Sita, it can be argued that Sushmita was feeling rejected and abandoned by her male superiors. Commenting on Sita's final disappearance into the furrow, Sutherland (1989, p. 78) argues:

> Idealised traditional Indian values refuse to allow a wife, or for that matter, any subservient person, to admit disaffection or disloyalty. However such a denial by no means negates the existence of such feelings. One socially accepted manner of expressing such disaffection, it has been seen, is found in masochistic actions, actions turned against the self as a form of revenge against the aggressor.

In other words, one can argue that by shooting herself Lt. Sushmita Chakravarty was trying to protest against her ill-treatment by her male superiors. Feeling rejected by the army she decided to abandon it altogether through her suicide – like Sita repudiated Rama:

> Thus Sita's repudiation of Rama comes to represent to the vast majority of the audience, not merely a wife refusing a husband but an expression of a socially acceptable and highly sublimated act of counter-aggression against a figure of authority. (Sutherland, 1989, p. 78)

The perception of the feminine in Indian Hindu society however undergoes significant change as she grows older from a young woman to a *mother*. The same woman who would often be rejected and abandoned now becomes a figure of authority, all the more if she is the mother of a male child. Bloom *et al.* (2001, p. 68) observe that position of women in Indian society pivots around their reproductive capabilities, especially to produce male kin, because sons continue the patriline and provide age old security. It can be argued that the supreme authority of the mother can be attributed to a certain extent to Durga's iconic status as the Divine Mother who protects and preserves her creator. It is worth remembering here how the Pandavas accepted Draupadi as their mutual wife when their mother asked Arjuna to share his prize with his brothers. None of the five brothers dared to remind their mother that Arjuna was not referring to a thing but his wife, as the prize. Interestingly Draupadi did not protest either.

Mothers at work

Politicians make widespread use of the cult of the mother to garner the popular vote. Rushdie (1979) (cited in Ali, 1985, p. 3) points out how during elections Indira Gandhi used 'the cult of the mother – [and the] Hindu mother-goddess symbols and allusions – and the fact that the dynamic element of the Hindu pantheon [i.e. Durga] is female' to her advantage. Indira projected herself to the electorate as Mother Indira who would protect her children against demons like poverty, rising prices, unemployment etc. Hancock (1995, p. 919) suggests how the Chief Minister of Tamil Nadu, a state in the southern part of the country, sought popular support by popularizing mother-goddess devotion. Right wing Hindu fanatics also use this concept to incite male Hindu citizens to protect their 'motherland' against 'foreigners' (Basu et al., 1990 cited in Hancock, 1995, p. 919).

The discussion so far has focused on the maternal and passive aspects of the feminine. The obvious question now is what about the aggressive side of the feminine? In other words does the mythological Draupadi have any relevance at all? Certainly there are illustrations which can be offered to suggest that the dynamic warrior aspect of Durga still has some validity. However before discussing these examples it is useful to remind the reader that it is the placid, complaisant Sita who is regarded as the Hindu ideal of womanhood: a chaste, self-sacrificing wife who dutifully follows her husband into exile. Forbes (1980, p. 1) points out:

> because women are generally regarded as passive, those who engage in violent activities are usually seen as acting unnaturally. Past literature has promoted this idea of aberrance, labelling these women as either goddesses (the positive version) or social rebels (the negative one).

The following examples endorse these two dichotomous views of the aggressive Indian woman at work.

Laxmi Bai and the Bombay textiles workers

Laxmi Bai was the Queen or Rani of the Jhansi province, in British India from 1842 to 1857. Hills and Silverman (1993, p. 742) suggest that she was a 'rare confluence of the modern and traditional'. She was a tom-boy who became a capable warrior, training her maidservants in horsemanship, jumping and swordsmanship. Widowed at 18, she led her troops in person against the British Army to save Jhansi from becoming a part of the colony.

Considered by many as the driving force behind the Revolt of 1857, she died in battle when she was only 22 years old.

The Rani of Jhansi continues to be idolized as possibly the greatest nationalist heroine the country has ever had and is also regarded as one of the first symbols of defiance to British rule. When the Indian National Army had its first female unit, it was named the Rani of Jhansi Regiment, thereby employing a 'powerful metaphor of [feminine] resistance' (Hills and Silverman, 1993, p. 743). Thus the Rani represents a positive attitude of the Indian patriarch towards aggressive women. The following example will illustrate the negative view – how women are labelled 'social rebels'.

A study on discrimination against women in the textile industry of Bombay by Ralph James in 1962 showed that managers preferred fewer women in the textile mills. The reason being, women workers were regarded as potential sources of violence and indiscipline. Managers and union personnel found women to be more assertive and defiant than men in day-to-day work situations. Women would frequently assume the lead role in organized demonstrations of protest and would be at the head of almost every strike procession. James (1962, p. 213) observed that the direct violence exhibited by the female worker was in no way similar to the irrational, unrestrained violence of her male colleague; it was more purposeful and calculating than the occasional male outburst. Thus, from the point of view of the mill managers, who were all men, elimination of women was seen as a step forward toward greater managerial control.

These archetypes serve to foster and endorse a pervasive view of women in Indian organizations. Höpfl (2007) has talked about the ways in which definition functions to control and capture experience and, in a similar way, these stories help to create a typology of women in Indian society. As seems to be common in many societies, women are mothers or whores, worthy of adulation or abandonment. As Höpfl (2007) suggests, '[t]he masculine attitude, dominated by rationality and the rejection of dependency, reduces the notion of the feminine to nurturing, domestic and servicing functions.' In other words, it can be argued that the myths underpin ritually mediated attempts to control women's *shakti* that is channelling it towards ends such as fertility, subordination to male authority and adherence to the behavioural code of Sita, with its emphasis on patience, chastity and self-sacrifice (Wadley, 1982). However, as Höpfl (2007) says, the power to define always rests with patriarchal logic – the female is always being categorized, pigeon-holed – she is prescribed... always reduced and amputated.

Notes

1. Collection of stories written in Sanskrit, between the fourth century BCE and 1000 CE (Ghosh, 2000), to popularize the Vedic religion among the masses.
2. The Cosmic Order or Rta is, in essence the ordering principles of nature which gives to everything from the vast galaxies, down to the nucleus of an atom, their nature and course.
3. The Hindu God of Creation.
4. A sacrifice performed by a king to establish his control over neighbouring kingdoms. In this sacrifice, a horse is set loose, with the armies of the King following it. Whenever the horse enters another kingdom, the ruler of that kingdom has to either fight the army or has to surrender to the authority of the King conducting the sacrifice.
5. A way of marriage in Vedic India where the bride would choose her groom from a group of suitors, sometimes through the completion of difficult tasks.
6. Sutherland (1989, p. 69) observes 'completely degraded in front of all the kings and nobles her grim situation was ameliorated only by supernatural intervention'.

11
Romanian Socialist Directors: Heroes or Tricksters?

Mihaela Kelemen and Dirk Bunzel

This chapter explores the ambivalent identity of Romanian directors operating in the socialist regime. It suggests that one way to understand their identity is by reference to Romanian fairytales. As symbolic renderings of crucial life experiences, fairytales embody the accumulated wisdom of collectivities and individuals (Campbell, 1949/1993), making the unbelievable believable and the impossible possible in people's minds (Bettelheim, 1976). The traits of the archetypal characters present in the most popular Romanian fairytales appear to be reflected in how the directors studied represent their abilities, aspirations and motivations to themselves, their bosses and workforces.

The centrality of language forms to understanding organizations

The arrival of the 'linguistic turn' within management and organization studies (Gabriel, 2000) has lead many organizational scholars to turn away from the 'scientific method' and focus on stories and narratives as an alternative way to engage with the world of organizations (Boje, 1991; Kunda, 1992). Such storytelling draws on the rich cultural baggage of a nation, being more sensitive to the subtleties and complexity of organizational relationships and identities than most classical management theory (Patient *et al.*, 2003).

More importantly, stories are central to how individuals construct and maintain a sense of self-identity. In this chapter, we embrace the view that identity is a narrative construction, the product of the self's reflexive process (MacIntyre, 1981). As such, we will bring together the individual stories of ten Romanian directors who operated under the constraints of the previous socialist regime. Their individual stories are however not entirely private to themselves as they are constructed through language and within a particular cultural, social and political context. These stories are indebted, *inter alia*, to folk culture; in particular, fairytales and as such reflect the cultural virtues, morals and values that have been predominant in Romania for centuries.

The directors talk about themselves not in some abstract terms but with respect to their immediate circumstances and those who populate such circumstances (workers, The Party, the ministers, etc). They come to be who they are (however ephemeral, multiple and changing their directorial identity may be), by being located or locating themselves in social narratives rarely of their own making (Sommers, 1994, p. 606). Their stories are also placed within certain time coordinates. The past, in particular, figures importantly in their self-representations: Romanian directors draw on past experience and previous socialization processes in their attempts to justify their role as economic leaders in a socialist regime. Moreover, given that the interviews were retrospective, taking place more than 15 years after the collapse of the communist regime in Romania, the narratives put forward relied more heavily on recollections of past experiences than would otherwise be the case. Despite the varied background of the directors' interviews, central themes coalesced around the economic and political context of their activities as leaders as well as the coping strategies developed to accommodate the contradictory demands placed on them by the socialist system.

The context of Romanian economic leadership

Torn by political imperatives imposed by the omnipresent authority of the Communist Party and the economic predicaments of a state-socialist economy, enterprise directors were placed between the rock and the hard stone of 'real existent state-socialism'. While often portrayed as ideological simpletons or obedient technocrats, their complex behaviour eschewed classification such as mere apparatchiks. Rather, their subordination to a double line of political and economic authority rendered them versatile arbitrators among different rationalities, obligations and coalitions.

In the light of this, often, impossible task, many of them turned cynic or corrupt and succumbed to the common manipulation of plan figures and illegal practices in an increasingly fictional and grayish state-socialist economy. Yet, there were also those who – against all odds – were still dedicated to the communist ideal of building a better future for all working people. These directors combined a strong work ethos, idealistic values and paternalism and showed innovativeness, creativity and genuine concern for their staff (Weinert, 1995). As our data show, some directors turned into 'kings of improvisation' to deal with common lack of resources (Biermann, 1995); other struck 'compensatory deals' with workers and their supervisors to meet, at least narrowly, imposed target figures (Voßkamp and Wittke, 1990).

The chapter explores the extent to which the individual narratives of the directors interviewed for the study draw on archetypal types and characteristics evoked by fairytales peculiar to the Romanian culture, as an unconsciousness strategy to resolve these paradoxical demands at least on a psychological level. MacIntyre (1981) argues that folk stories are central to how we understand the various roles available in our society. Referring to them as 'dramatic resources', MacIntyre suggests that such folk stories contain both universal and particular elements, being quintessential to how we make sense of the world and how to justify the roles we take up in day-to-day life at work and outside work.

The role of fairytales

For Campbell (1949/1993), fairytales have a central role in helping to awaken and maintain a sense of wonder of the whole mystery of the universe. Second, fairytales provide a map or picture of the universe and of our relationship to it. Third, they validate and maintain the moral systems and life-customs of a particular culture. Their last function is psychological, according to Campbell, aiding individuals in their passage through life's stages, from the dependency of childhood to the responsibilities of maturity, to old age and the transition through death. As such, fairytales are central to the process of identity construction, influencing directly or indirectly the way individuals talk about their deeds, values and aspirations.

The fairytales collected by Petre Ispirescu (2004) have certain characteristics in common: they all have happy endings and talk about heroes and their journeys. These heroes strive to overcome many difficulties and obstacles and always triumph. The message that there can be no success without effort or even an enduring struggle also comes across in many of the Romanian directors' stories.

Evil is another theme that is recurrent in these fairytales either in terms of a character who is terrible and does brutal deeds or the evil inside the hero, his own conflicts, temptations and obstacles faced in the journey. 'In the traditional fairytale, the hero is rewarded and the evil person meets his well deserved fate' (Bettelheim, 1976, p. 144). The idea that one learns from mistakes and can better themselves through experiential learning is also apparent in some of the directors' stories. Also, the idea that the good always triumphs and the bad is always eradicated is a message that many of the Romanian directors are keen to stress in their stories about themselves. Finally the 'wise old man' theme is also common in the fairytales collected by Ispirescu. The person who provides guidance and often has magical powers may not be very different from the image the Romanian director portrays about himself.

The chapter juxtaposes two distinct sources of evidence: semi-structured interviews carried out in 2005 with ten socialist directors, on one hand, and a collection of Romanian fairytales collected by Petre Ispirescu, on the other. In particular, the analysis concentrates on the fairytale of Greuceanu (The Heavy and The Great Man, see appendix I). This fairytale is one of the most popular, best-known Romanian fairytales, recounting the story of a hero who embarked on a journey to rescue the moon and the sun from the tentacles of three fierce dragons. Many other strong men tried to so do but failed. Thanks to his cleverness, forward planning, social and communicative skills as well as physical strength, he triumphed. In return, the King gave him half of the kingdom and his daughter in marriage.

Ispirescu fairytale's main characters and Greuceanu in particular, possess the following traits/virtues:

- cleverness;
- good communication skills;
- well networked;
- willingness to sacrifice for the good of the others;
- good improvisation skills;
- heightened need to accomplish the task at hand (the need for self-actualization);
- quick learner;
- courage;
- chameleonic qualities including the ability to lie when necessary; and
- physical strength, health and other similar bodily characteristics.

Not surprisingly, many of these characteristics feature highly in the self-narratives of the Romanian directors interviewed. Only 'courage' and 'willingness to sacrifice for the good of the others' are characteristics unsupported by the evidence. This may be explained by the fact that directors felt that rocking the boat would achieve very little either for their companies or for the employees.

Directorship self-portraits

Our analysis suggests that the directors interviewed were engaged in a complex web of relations, which required extensive communicative work and flexible social traits. Among such traits, cleverness featured highly: without necessarily referring to themselves in a direct way, the directors interviewed argued that those in economic leadership functions were intellectually above the board and excellent professionals.

A director from a Chemical company said:

> my own bosses were extremely capable. They were not some wasters. They were all trained at CEPECA, a centre of management education that taught Western management models and theories. The general director did training courses at the London School of Economics. So, you could see that these guys were smart and extremely talented at management.

Another director recounted his life story saying that he was not allowed to belong to the party because his brother emmigrated to France and therefore, he could not be trusted politically. Economically, however, because of his professionalism, he had been promoted all the way up to being a director in the ministry. He had also been trained at CEPECA: 'we were taught by Western experts. The Party was very clever: it knew that this was the only way forward, applying all the new techniques developed and tried in the West.' A director of a mining equipment firm reinforced the idea that the directors were highly competent at managing: 'I was a strong believer in scientific management. I applied its principles to all spheres of my activity and have achieved great results. But I always asked for the opinion of my collaborators. My style of leadership has been participative and inclusive.'

Relationships with the others is another theme that comes across in many of the directors' narratives. The directors saw themselves as good networkers: networking above with the state agencies and Party organizations and below with the workers and other collaborators appeared as high on their management agenda.

All the directors interviewed suggested that they had to negotiate with the central planning agency and auxiliary forums to ensure that the plan targets imposed on them were realistic and achievable. A director from a mine explained the process by which plan targets were set:

> In the centralized economy, The Party had certain State objectives, which were set every five years and represented the five year

centralized plan. The five year plan stipulated a rate of economic increase decided by the Party (to catch up with the industrialized West) and had physical indicators such as tones of coal, steel, foodstuff. From the five-year plan, annual plans were derived. The process was theoretically two ways ... The real process of setting plan figures was in reality more complex than this: the charisma and the personal relations of the enterprise directors with state functionaries as well as the political position of the economic leaders played an important role. All economic leaders were Party members and depending on the size and the economic importance of their firms they were part of various superior political structures.

Another mine director hinted at the importance of personal connections and negotiating with powerful State officials:

Once the plan figures were decided, the material resources for achieving plan targets were also in the plan. But for some reasons we always faced shortages of materials. The firm's position in the economic network depended on the importance of the objectives that we had to achieve and the level of achievement. But your personal connections were also important: certain levers had to be oiled: you could not pay money because there was not an underground economy in Romania at the time, but you offered protocol objects to various functionaries and invited them to spend holidays in the mountains.

Indeed: 'one had to know how to talk to the decision-makers in the ministries and above: I had to be careful not to upset certain individuals if I wanted to carry on leading the company in my own way' (Director of a chemical company), and: 'If one had relationships above and you said the right things to the right people, you could lead your company in an ideologically free way. The party only intervened when they did not like what you were saying' (Director of an energy company).

More importantly, economic leaders had to 'negotiate' below. Smith and Thompson (1992) talk about a social contract that existed between the enterprise and its workers: employment security and other rewards (subsidized goods and housing) were expected in exchange for a degree of participation in the work place and broader social terrain. They also talk about the fact that in practice enterprise directors were forced to rely on workers' good will to maintain production.

Our evidence suggests that most directors applied a Theory X style of leadership:

> I forced the people to participate effectively to the production process. My leadership style was correct, honest, demanding but I did respect the individuality of the workers. If I was beaten up from above, I had to beat up my workers: I used bad words to get them to work harder but it was for their own good. I was always able to pay their salaries and they knew that. (Director of a mine)

Another director does not shy away from calling his style of leadership dictatorial:

> My style was dictatorial, unfortunately. I had to give directives. The level of education among my workers was very low and they did not understand it any other way. But I was also very close to them: I knew their families, their kids, I helped them in many ways so if I said to them we have to work day and night, they'd all come to work.

The intimate knowledge of one's workers is however key to the relationships forged by the directors:

> I knew my team very well. The production depended on them, so I had to know their strengths and weaknesses. Some needed little direction, others needed more, I had to repeat things a few times to them. I did all I could to help them. (Ministry director)

The directors interviewed described themselves, not as good motivators, but as quick learners and excellent improvisers. The irregular arrival of supply led to the continual reallocation of the temporal sequences of the production process, re-organization of work and resetting of the machines. Thus, the need for being imaginative and resourceful at all leadership levels becomes apparent. In the words of a Romanian director from an engineering firm:

> The way we coped with ambiguities in the supply of raw materials was to reorganize the production flow and finish all those parts that did not need the missing materials. When the materials arrived, the work was distributed to other workshops that could help. This was the happy scenario: the most common one was to ask the workers to work harder and longer.

Another director from a construction company talked about the way in which they mobilized workers to economize in resource use in order to cope with existing shortages:

> The workers themselves were expected to find solutions for rationalizing and minimizing the consumption of raw materials, electricity etc. below the national standards. The starting point was the design engineers who in collaboration with skilled workers looked for ways to make more from the same.

Modernization via new technology was also high on the directors' agenda. Economic leaders engaged in constant negotiations with the State apparatus to obtain funds for new technologies, the argumentation being that new technologies were instrumental for meeting plan targets and ensured better working conditions for the workers. Selling the idea of new technology to the workers did not appear to worry the directors. In the words of a director from a large engineering enterprise:

> If at the beginning the workers were slightly reticent in accepting the implementation of new technologies they very soon realized that working conditions improved and salaries increased. Soon, workers started to associate the new technology with increases in salaries and were welcoming both.

Flexibility is another key characteristic of the directors interviewed. As one of the directors of an energy company said: 'if you wanted to keep your seat as director you had to be adaptable, flexible and put up with a lot of things that you may have not liked; you had to go around the political system and not engage in it.' Being flexible involved a certain amount of chameleonic behaviour as well as lying to the right audiences:

> Lying was part and parcel of being a director: but you had to lie in a plausible way. The most plausible lie was in itself a difficult task. I once met with a top official (the deputy Prime Minister of the country) and I told him it was impossible to produce what we had been asked to. He took a liking to me and advised me to lie and not to keep saying that the plan was unrealistic: this was the advice from a top official. (Director of an energy company)

Interestingly, none of the directors interviewed regarded themselves as privileged by the socialist system. The system privileged the workers not their economic leaders:

> socialism did not hit the workers, because it was the Workers Party. The intellectuals (engineers, economists and other professionals) were in theory their friends and their support but we were paid below capabilities. My salary was the salary of a unskilled miner. (Mining director)

Directors describe themselves as people who had to cope with contradictory demands, which made it impossible for them to please all stakeholders. On the one hand, they had to meet economic targets, on the other they had to contribute to the glorification of the system and do so with less and less resources.

> any economic development was taking place not because of existing economic needs but because of some political directive that was completely removed from day-to-day realities: the politic decided the economic. Everything was imposed top down: we had to do more with less, and in the end the ability to produce decreased because of lack of investment, maintenance policies and so on. (Director of a construction company)

Their position as directors was also precarious and subordinated to the political system:

> The director was named by the superior economic organism (the same organism could also fire me) but with the Party's OK. Directors were usually demitted when the plan targets were not met, when they upset their bosses in meetings, or when there were work accidents and fatalities. Of course, the Party could also suggest the demission of a director particularly when their enterprises did not contribute to the society in the way expected by the Party. There were extra curricular activities such as making fences for the city, or irrigations for agricultural cooperatives for which we had to find resources internally to demonstrate that we were good citizens. (Director of a construction company)

However, the preferred strategy for the Party was not to demit directors but to keep them under close observation and cajole them constantly:

> we were given ultimatums, always being told off and treated badly by the superior forums. They realized that this is a better strategy than having to replace directors periodically. 'Just give them a good and constant bashing to keep them on their toes.' The Party also kept a close eye on us: there were two microphones in our offices so everything we said was being recorded. Because of this environment, we, the directors, had a tacit understanding and relationship with each other: we had a common language that was only known by us, we helped and respected each other. (Director in the ministry)

Given these tactics of control and subordination practised by the Government and the Party on the directors, they had to be inventive, resourceful, learn quickly and have excellent communication skills to convey different messages to different audiences. In more direct terms, the directors interviewed viewed their jobs as heroic and monumental tasks and believed they had always acted like the old wise man in the interest of the many and for the good of the people. Retrospectively, the directors did not blame socialism *per se* for the evils of the economic system they were supposed to manage but the party officials who did not understand the economic premises of efficiency, productivity and strategic planning.

Conclusions

Most of these directors are now retired and running businesses of their own. Yet, there was a feeling of regret that their leadership skills were not sufficiently valued and rewarded by the socialist system, and that they were completely ignored by the transitional system that followed (with the exception of one director who stayed in his job until 2000). Given the contradictory demands placed on them, the directors interviewed felt that they had fulfilled their leadership duties. Their own behaviour and traits mirrored the cultural values upheld by the society, as reflected in the prevailing folk culture and fairytales. However, their credibility was undermined by the very essence of the socialist system, which asked them to do one thing officially, but expected them to do something else in real terms. Heroism and trickstery were equally needed to navigate through such muddy terrains and getting the right balance between these was what most of the directors interviewed aimed to achieve.

Appendix I: Greuceanu – the Heavy and the Great Man

Once upon a time, there was an emperor called the Red Emperor. He was very upset because some dragons had stolen the sun and the moon. He spread the message to his people that if anyone brought back the sun and the moon, he would give them half his wealth as well as his daughter in marriage. If they didn't succeed, he would cut off their heads. Many strong men tried to bring the sun and the moon back but failed: their heads were cut off.

There was a strong and wise man called Greuceanu. When he heard about the promise made by the emperor he picked up courage, based on his strengths and belief in God, and went to the emperor to let him know he'd take up the challenge. On the way, he met two people whose heads were about to be cut off because they ran away from a battle. These people were very upset but Greuceanu gave them some encouragement because he was very good with words. The people felt much better. Greuceanu thought: 'if I could persuade the Emperor to forgive these people, then I'll take on the challenge to find the moon and the sun. If not, I'll go back home.'

He told the emperor that there was no point in killing the people, for it was better to have two more men worshipping the emperor. Moreover, his people would appreciate a merciful emperor. The emperor listened to Greuceanu and the men were freed. The two men thanked Greuceanu and told him they would pray for his health and success. Greuceanu told the emperor that he would like to take on the challenge of finding the sun and the moon but he would need some mercy and help from him. In reply, the Emperor said: 'My word is my word, I can't alter my promise'. Seeing that the emperor was decisive and seeing the truth in his word, Greuceanu accepted the challenge on its own terms. He said: 'I'll do my very best to achieve this task, whatever it takes.'

Before leaving, Greuceanu thought long and hard about what he would need to take with him on his long and arduous trip. He and his brother set off after a short while. They went a long way until they arrived at Greuceanu's brother in arms, The Earth Steel Maker (ESM). He was not just a steel maker, he also knew how to make magic. For three days and three nights Greuceanu and ESM talked and talked and planned what needed to be done to achieve success. After Greuceanu and his brother left, ESM made Greuceanu's face out of steel and kept it warm in the furnace.

Greuceanu and his brother went a long way, then they stopped to have a picnic. There they embraced each other and cried big tears for they decided to go separate ways. Greunceanu went to the right and his brother to the left.

After a long journey Greuceanu arrived at the dragons' house: he rolled over three times and turned himself into a pigeon. He learnt this trick from ESM, his brother in arms. But one of the daughter dragons realized that the pigeon was a human and said to her mother and the other two sisters: 'this pigeon has Greunceanu's eyes! Oh dear, our end has come!' It seemed that the dragons had heard about Greuceanu and his strengths and were getting worried. But Greuceanu rolled again three times and turned into a mosquito, went through the keyhole and heard what the dragons said to each other. Greuceanu found out that the male dragons were out on a shooting expedition in the Green Forrest and the first was planning to come home in the evening, the second one at midnight and the last one in the morning.

Greuceanu went to the edge of the forest and waited for the first male dragon, by a bridge. As the dragon approached the bridge, his horse started to make a funny noise. The dragon knew there was danger. Greuceanu showed himself and said: 'do you want to fight me?' The dragon said 'yes'. They fought and fought, but after a short while Greuceanu threw him on to the ground and cut off his head. He threw the body under the bridge. Then he rested, awaiting the next dragon. The same happened with the second dragon. Now Greuceanu was waiting for the last dragon, the father dragon who was the strongest and cleverest of the dragons. First they fought with their swords, then with their bare hands. The fight lasted for a long time and they were both exhausted. A big black bird was flying above them: the dragon promised the body of Greuceanu to the bird in exchange for some water. Greunceanu promised three dragon bodies in exchange for water. The birds brought water to Greuceanu and he plunged the dragon onto the ground. Then he asked the dragon where the sun and the moon were hidden. The dragon did not want to tell him initially but after some negotiation he told Greuceanu that the sun and the moon were hidden in a cave deep in the forest and the key was tied around his little finger. Greuceanu killed the dragon, cut off his little finger and set off to find the cave. He took the sun and the moon out of the cave and put them on the sky. Everybody was very happy to see the sun and the moon in the sky.

Greuceanu returned to the place where his brother had said good-bye to him. He found him there, they hugged, bought two horses and set off to the Red Emperor's kingdom. On the way, they saw a pear tree with golden pears. Greuceanu's brother wanted to eat a pear but Greuceanu would not let him. He knew what the dragon women were planning so he took his sword and cut the tree: black blood sprung out and a voice said: 'you killed me, you killed me.' It was the voice of one of the female dragons.

They started on walking and arrived at a beautiful garden with a lovely fountain. Greuceanu's brother wanted to drink the water but Greuceanu took his sword and hit the bottom of the fountain; black blood sprung out. It was the second female dragon. As they set off, they could feel something hot blowing from behind: it was the dragon mother who lost her daughters, husband and sons-in-law. They went faster and faster until they reached ESM: there, they locked themselves in a room. The dragon asked Greuceanu to show her at least his face. ESM made a hole in the wall and put the steel made face which was still very hot. The dragon ate it up and died.

Greuceanu thanked his brother in arms for the help and set off to the kingdom of the Red Emperor with his brother. As they got closer, he asked his brother to go ahead of him and announce his arrival.

Greuceanu was resting in the carriage when a devil came his way. The devil removed a pin from the carriage and then told Greuceanu that he had lost his pin. Greuceanu went looking for it but forgot his sword in the carriage. The devil stole it, then rolled over three times and turned into a large stone by the edge of the road.

In the meantime, at the palace, one lord of the manor who had connections with the devil, told the Emperor that it was him who found the sun and the moon. The devil promised him Greuceanu's sword and in return he wanted the lord's soul and his first baby. The emperor believed the lord and arranged for the marriage to take place. In the meantime Greuceanu arrived at the palace but he realized he had lost his sword: without it, he was like any other man. He remembered the devil and the big stone by the edge of the road. He returned there and rolled over three times, becoming a large mace. He hit the stone so hard that the devil asked for forgiveness but Greuceanu hit and hit until the stone became sand and then he found his sword at the bottom of it.

He went back to the emperor and asked him to invite the lord to prove his strength and fight an honest battle with him. When the lord realized that Greuceanu had found his sword, he asked for forgiveness. The emperor banished him from his kingdom.

Then there was a big wedding and they all lived happy ever after.

12
The Hard-working Hero/ine among Phantoms, Donors and Dark Forces: On Mythical Features in Polish Organizational Imagination

Katarzyna Wolanik Boström

Introduction

Myths and tales may be considered as a culture's way to conceptualize important values and paradoxes of reality. They try to find a symbolic solution to profound – and actually unsolvable – problems and dilemmas (Barthes, 1957/1973; Lévi-Strauss, 1981). In this chapter, I discuss mythical features occurring in 30 extensive life-story interviews that I carried out with well-educated Polish specialists at the end of the 1990s (see Wolanik Boström, 2005). Almost ten years of the Polish 'transition' from socialism to democracy and market economy had passed; a turbulent period for working-life values, which were subjected to challenges and renegotiations in the interviews.

Even though the reality of working life is seen as rather mundane and inherently politicized in the Polish professionals' stories, it is presented in strangely mythical ways. Actual people, organizations, institutions or time periods are used as narrative resources, given different *functions* and become mythical figures such as Donors, Phantoms, Dark Forces or Paradise Lost. I shall analyze the stories as 'heroes tales', drawing freely on Propp's, de Vries', Campbell's and Holbek's models (see Arvidsson, 2005; Holbek, 1987). The narrator is a hard-working Hero/ine, driven by a passion for his/her chosen occupation, enduring politicized trials and common foul play and striving to do a good job against all odds. The Hero/ine's ultimate objective – as I interpret the underlying logic in the stories – is a *rightfully earned* career, implying peer recognition, societal prestige and economic rewards, none of which is an unproblematic issue.

Helpers and donors

In the interviews, the ideal scenario for getting a job or a promotion is doing it by strictly professional means, and such achievements are mentioned with much pride and satisfaction. Strikingly enough, much more elaborated stories are told about situations which do not meet this ideal. The hard-working Hero/ine is certainly an individualist, happiest when s/he can rely on his/her own agency and competence, but s/he works in a world where objective qualifications are sometimes just not enough. In the case of attractive positions, there may be other power relations involved, making such qualifications null and void. The interviewees spend a lot of narrative energy explaining how sometimes it was/is virtually *impossible* to get a job within narrow professional limits – and this applies both to beginners and to those with an excellent reputation. Getting aid from helpers (relatives, friends, 'contacts') and Donors (public institutions and organizations) is sometimes the only means of occupational survival.

The Donors have substantial resources and can make the impossible come true, such as providing a good job, or even a flat attached to the job. However, they may also demand unreasonably hard work (which is a minor problem for the Hero/ine) or even expect you to sell your soul (which is a problem). Donors can be whimsical – sometimes there will be manna from heaven, sometimes favours are withdrawn. Very often, a Helper's interventions on the Hero/ine's behalf may be vital to get a Donor in the right mood. Let me give some examples.

Teresa, a 55-year-old specialist in child medicine, told me how she got her first job in Krakow. As vacancies were rare and the competition stiff, this unlikely achievement was entirely thanks to her mother, who was acquainted with 'just everyone in Krakow'. She accompanied the young Teresa to the head of the clinic (a potential Donor) and, in a leisurely and charming way dropped some important references. The man was slightly irritated and amused, but sufficiently impressed by her social connections to give Teresa a very good position. In the story, it borders on the magical. The well-connected Helper, acting out of kinship loyalty, makes a miracle happen.

Teresa was very concerned to motivate her choice of action, as I suppose it is not quite in line with her professional ideals. She points out that relying on social contacts was really the *only* way to get a job in the city if you did not have support from the Party. She took her work very seriously, with a whole-hearted commitment; constantly working overtime to stand in for sick colleagues; always willing to learn new methods, doing research – and loving every minute of it! The story proves beyond any doubt that Teresa was *well worth* the position.

Many years and jobs later, an elderly woman doctor provided Teresa with a job on her ward, created especially for her. Teresa admired the lady's competency and cultivated manners and felt well taken care of, even though the help was not altogether altruistic: the lady asked Teresa rather often to stand-in for her night duties. 'She did it in such a *charming* way that I just could not blame her.' This indicates the logic of a gift, with social obligation and prolonged reciprocity, when no explicit transaction of services is ever mentioned.

Informal connections were of profound importance also for Adam as a young aspiring writer and critic in the eighties. He got a part-time job in a renowned literary journal thanks to his father, a Marxist writer: 'there was *no other way* to get into these institutions!' Adam says. The chief editor had just published an 'underground' book, and was afraid that Adam's father would make a fuss about it, so he gave Adam a job. However, he mercilessly cut down Adam's articles and reviews: 'I had to write *very* thoroughly, *very* good, well-documented texts – which were just cut down and thrown away.' The Hero's competence and commitment to the job is stated beyond any doubt, but he is unjustly punished by the reluctant Donor.

The Party is *the* Donor in Adam's stories, but still a rather unreliable one, sometimes giving him unrealistic options. At the end of the 1980s, Adam was offered a position as chief editor of a journal. He was thrilled: 'Finally a chance to make a career!' Unfortunately the co-workers thought he was a security officer and did not accept him, so he chose not to take the position. Then 'the Party gave up on him' and his possibilities to publish stopped altogether. Another potential Donor, which Adam absolutely refused to make use of, was the Opposition with its considerable 'underground' publishing. Adam is viciously ironic about those fellow writers who became 'convertites' when it was most suitable, to gain the possibility of publishing! In the story, Adam stands morally impeccable, while the Marxist writers sell their political souls for the Opposition's resources.

In all the interviews, it is unthinkable to let any Donor affect the Heroe/ines' *own* political opinions; only 'The Others' are prone to this. Hieronim, a 60-year-old senior lecturer, says with emphasis: 'I can be a pauper, but I'll have my honor!' – meaning that he would rather manage on a low wage then put his integrity into question. Once, he obviously did take a good offer from the Party, namely a college job and a flat, but he was asked to do the work for his professional competency and with no political commitment. In the interviews with people who are reasonably successful, such a defensive, justifying attitude is quite common; they seem eager to prove that they have *not* strayed too far from their professional ethics. In a sort of a self-imposed scrutiny of their consciences, work trajectories are often told as a serial of trials and tribulations, through which the Hero/ine shows his/her values and moral standards.

Trials, challenges, harassments

The core cultural dilemma which the myth of the hard-working Hero/ine conceptualizes is the *difficulty* of doing good work and making a career on strictly 'professional' grounds; a mission impossible in a world profoundly marked by a proliferation of political or social entanglements. As researchers point out (e.g., Marody, 1991), during socialism the ideal of professional excellence was contested by an ideal of 'political engagement' in all professions. The very concept of 'career' became problematic when the Party interfered with the selection of candidates to important positions and distributed benefits and privileges on the basis of a person's political capital (Bourdieu, 1999). However, since different social circles used ingenious strategies of counter-power, such a 'success' was not always considered legitimate and could mean losing a great deal of professional status (Marody, 1991; cf. Wolanik Boström, 2005).

In the interviews, the Hero/ine's work trajectory is (ideally, it seems) characterized by trials, contests, harassments, injustice, too little economical rewards and societal appreciation. S/he tries to stand up against Villains (rivals, evil colleagues) and Dark Forces (demonized centres of power). The battle is often uneven, but even if s/he loses in career progress, at least s/he gains in moral superiority.

Hieronim says that when he was a doctoral student, and very much committed to his topic, the head of the department (a Villain) persecuted doctoral students. Hieronim left the academy for many years, but did finally complete his thesis in his spare time: 'it was only thanks to *my own* efforts!' For some years, he worked in a small newly started museum; on his own initiative he travelled around Poland to find interesting exhibits and 'carried them on his own back' to the museum. Nonetheless, a local Party secretary (a False Hero) took all the credit for the exhibition. Hieronim made a fuss – and was instantly fired. Here, the antagonized Party becomes a Dark Force.

After some years, a newly built college in another town that was looking for senior lecturers, offered both a job and a flat (this time, the local

Party was a benevolent Donor), and Hieronim agreed. His work and commitment were much appreciated and he became a member of the college's management board. However, in 1981 martial law was proclaimed, and as Hieronim was active in the local Solidarity trade union, the Party (turned into Dark Force again) and the military authorities called him to a very unpleasant interrogation. He was not however arrested, 'which is a pity, it might be creditable', he says with a smile; these confrontations are apparently a source of a somewhat bitter pride. A record of being harassed, fired or arrested seems to be a desirable supplement to an academic CV – I would guess that it implicates a personal integrity against bullying authorities, and thus political and symbolic capital (cf. Bourdieu, 1999).

Adam has also lived through many confrontations, but his Villains and Dark Forces were oppositional ones. Adam's father was a Marxist intellectual pursuing many liberal ideas, which interested the opposition. Nevertheless, the father absolutely refused to get involved in the opposition and gained many bitter enemies, a fact with considerable implications for Adam's own career. When Adam was a doctoral student, his department let him know in every possible way that he did not belong, refusing to give him a position (which went to a young catholic poet) and persistently criticizing his texts. He gave up, until his father recommended him for a research project at another university. While there, Adam wrote a thesis which received excellent reviews. However he was still not welcome back to his former department. What is even worse, his books and articles are consistently omitted in many bibliographies. 'This is a shabby way, beyond a researcher's dignity', he says. In the story, he loses the battle but is morally superior, doing excellent work and simply expecting collegial fair play.

A very special case is Teresa's work at the Militia Hospital in Krakow during the 1980s, an episode resembling a mythical journey to another world. The topic is sensitive. Teresa received violent reactions from friends and relatives to her choice of workplace, and she says defiantly that she had young children, the Militia Hospital was near her home, and there was a special food-shop with a splendid supply of food in a time of notorious shortages. Still, it turned out to be a mistake. The Militia was 'a state in a state' and most of the staff in the hospital belonged to a political category of 'militia doctors', with double salary and lots of privileges. Teresa's superiors tended to regard the 'civil doctors' with suspicion and her closest boss, 'a terrible security officer' with poor medical competence, was arrogant and sarcastic about her church visits. She had an intolerable suspicion that some of her patients could have persecuted people from the opposition. Eventually, after a year, she found another job. In the story, the Militia is a distinctive Dark Force, luring the hardworking Heroine with a promise of enticement and benefits – but as its world proves to be distorted, unjust and evil, the Heroine runs away to save her mental health and integrity.

Gabriela talks with nostalgia of 'normal' times during socialism. She worked as a secondary school head teacher. The teachers were a merry, closely-knit group. The Party people who checked on the school's activities were sensible and friendly, quite happy with just the obligatory socialistic ceremonies and providing financial support for the school's equipment. For many years, she was also engaged in a socialist women's organization.

This description of an almost ontological security is effectively contrasted by Gabriela's occupational trials during the 1990s. Her feminist activity was then interpreted as left-oriented, and to her great surprise she was made redundant at work by an unfair manoeuvre. In spite of an impressive teaching record, she could not find a job anywhere in Krakow. When she finally did, it was in a primary school in a suburb, teaching the school's 'problem class'. Gabriela decided to make the best of it. She taught in an unorthodox, personal and committed manner, and as it turned out this was just the right thing for the 'problematic' youth. 'Almost all of them turned out to be really fine', she says with pride.

Gabriela then applied for a high school head teacher's job. It soon became apparent that this position was the subject of intensive lobbying on another candidate's behalf – a man with an oppositional record. A lady in the committee told Gabriela in confidence: 'you certainly presented the best programme, but you don't stand a chance'. After some time, the winner turned out to be extremely autocratic and was fired; then finally it was Gabriela's turn. She enjoys the work, though it is certainly not easy to manage a school these days; the administrative absurdities are beyond belief, and as there is 'an overall authority crisis in Poland', the teachers are suspicious and easily antagonized. Gabriela is keenly scrutinized. She makes sure her decisions are always transparent and fair and everybody feels secure – and this is really appreciated by the staff. In the story, the Heroine does splendid work in all societal circumstances, and gets the upper hand in spite of severe trials.

Work-related problems can also be blamed on the Dark Force of 'wild capitalism' in Poland. Ania is a 30-year-old schooled actress who really loved her theatre job and was fairly successful, but she had to give up her profession as her financial status became unbearable. She says that state cultural politics have become outrageous and the public is letting the theatres down. People would rather watch all the new TV-channels. Now she works as a radio reporter and her programmes are very popular, but as jobs are scarce, the employer knows that she will accept a ridiculously low wage and insufficient social security papers. 'It is the early-capitalist exploitation which I cannot help', Ania says.

In all of the trials narrated, the problems are due to structural (political, economic, etc.) injustices or someone's foul play, and *not* to any shortcomings in the Heroes/ines' competence or eagerness to work. The Heroes/ines are attacked using unprofessional means. Even if they lose an uneven battle, they still get satisfaction from doing a good job against all odds, and a conviction of moral superiority. The message is that they did their best in a complicated world, providing proof of competence and moral standards.

Favourite phantoms

Let me narrate a typical story of hard and honest work. When Teresa got married and had a small child, she took a job in a town where a hospital offered her a tiny flat to rent. She was so happy because of the flat! The work burden was *huge*, every day she worked first at the Delivery Ward, then at a Care Centre and finally made home visits in 'godforsaken villages' far from the town. As well as that, she took her second postgraduate course. As the job involved much skill and responsibility, it was highly satisfying: 'I felt a lot of professional pride, I could solve *every* problem', she says with a happy smile.

This kind of self-presentation is frequent in the interviews. To the Hero/ine, the occupation s/he has chosen is very meaningful, often bordering on passion or vocation. S/he is not *primarily* interested in money or titles (although they are most welcome) but in a sense of meaningfulness and professional pride. In this regard, the Hero/ine makes a sharp distinction between him/herself and some phantoms: the *careerist*, the *businesswoman* and *Homo Sovieticus*.

A most favourite phantom is the careerist – a clever, utilitarian, goal-oriented climber and a distinctly male figure. He uses illegitimate means to get to the top, for example social connections or political support, not as a complement to but *instead of* hard work and competence. The careerist sells his soul – or rather: pays lip service to the Party, Opposition, Church or any other centre of power, but may easily 'convert' if he gets a better option. Teresa talks indignantly about her former school-sweetheart: 'such a talented careerist, with smartly chosen career'; in his youth an engaged choirboy, later a Marxist and a university rector: 'They made a department just for him!' Adam muses about some Marxist writers who 're-oriented' when socialism was dissolving; as the Opposition and clergy gained in political influence they suddenly became very oppositional and 'the local priest's right-hand'.

The interviewees also relate some collegial counter-strategies against careerists. A powerful weapon is social boycott, making a person painfully aware that he is not tolerated by colleagues. Another is word of mouth; the careerists can be branded in the professional circles' opinion. Teresa says: 'The world of physicians is small and *we know who is who*.' A laurel wreath or a professor's title is not enough: 'we know exactly how he obtained it, how much he deserved it!' The careerists' cynical methods and alliances with those in power make some interviewees suspicious of the very concept of career. An attitude which they simultaneously take pride in and regret, as it diminishes their own capacity to compete for well-deserved positions.

In stories about capitalism, the careerist is sometimes aggressively self-marketing. Piotr, 40, is a rather unwilling manager in a private firm. He would most of all like to write historical books, but as 'nobody wants to pay for them', he has taken a friend's offer to become 'a manager, ha ha' in his private firm. Despite the irony, he takes the job demands seriously, not wishing to disappoint his friend. Still, he feels like an alien in a world where 'hordes of young, new, skilful people' grasp the entrepreneurs and people make much fuss about themselves. 'I know this sort of life-style pays off. But I *can't*, I don't *want* to do it!' My interpretation is that his aspirations lie in the cultural field rather than the economic one; he does not respect either its principles for success nor the goal-oriented careerists thriving in the capitalistic reality.

A female variant of the careerist, characteristic of the post-socialistic period, is the phantom of businesswoman. Monika, a remedial teacher and a school head teacher, says she is definitely *not* a 'uniformed' businesswoman! Gabriela, a high-school head teacher, does *not* approve of women trying to show they have 'more male genes' by acting in aggressive and tough ways. Both women stress that they are 'feminine' in their management style – meaning competent and well-articulated, but also elegant, agreeable and pleasant, even a little flirtatious.

Another mental model is Homo Sovieticus, who either read too much Lenin or has simply been damaged by the socialist system: helpless, narrow-minded and leaning heavily on authority. Teresa says that her former boss stood to strict attention even when talking on the *phone* with someone from the Party. Jarek, a 30-year-old manager in a joint-venture company, says that the elderly state-employed workers used to be guided and taken care of by the omnipotent State, and now feel lost and incapable of any entrepreneurial initiative. Monika, the school head teacher, criticizes those employees who just whine, complain and make demands, instead of putting in effort.

In these examples, a contrastive self-presentation is implied: the Hero/ine's own work mentality is honest, open-minded, flexible and energetic. Even if s/he happens to get some informal career-help, it is never an excuse *not* to do a really good job or *not* to take on a traditional gender role.

Images of paradise

In the interviews, wages and social position are delicate matters, especially for state-employed persons. The message is that the Hero/ine's societal and economic status is certainly not satisfying; not as it *should be* by other standards, for example the inter-war period, the socialistic period, 'the West' or private job alternatives in Poland.

Some people depict Paradise Lost. When Hieronim was a young research assistant, his elderly colleagues told him that in the inter-war period, a research assistant could afford to travel around the world to collect data for a thesis. During the socialist period he could hardly make ends meet, as education was economically punished rather then rewarded. On the contrary, Ania says that actors are sadly pauperized now, they were so much better off during socialism! The public loved them as representatives of the forces of freedom and subversion. The Party cherished them, giving them money, apartments and benefits, just to show the world that Poland is 'a free and creative nation'.

There are some imaginary paradises in the stories. For some interviewees, private, well-paid workplaces fill this function, but the most mythologized of places is 'the West'. Hieronim thought he was doing fine during the 1980s. A family of five living in a 4-room flat in a prefabricated multi-storey house ... but then a visitor from the USA first refused to believe that Hieronim had a doctoral degree, and then told him how much he could earn in the West. 'He took my breath away!' Hieronim says, shaking his head. When Polish researchers went to Western conferences, they could give brilliant lectures but had barely money for dinner. Monika tells me that when she travelled in Western Europe, she got *very* upset by the comparison with Poland. 'The remedial teachers there have really good incomes and are *so* appreciated by society!' Nevertheless, when a professor from Canada visited Monika's school in Poland, she was truly overwhelmed by the things they did with so little money.

Depicting images of Paradise is not so much an exercise in conjuring up unreachable utopias, as showing what the status and economic level should be – as it was and is in some other (imaginary) times and places. The interviewees often dwell on the difficulties in obtaining a life-style appropriate to their deserved and rightful social status. The message is that getting the same income and appreciation as their lucky predecessors or colleagues is only fair for exactly the same, or better, achievements.

Mission impossible accomplished

The myth of the hard-working Hero/ine conceptualizes some of the dilemmas left by the organizational baggage of socialism and the labour pains of democracy and capitalism in Poland. The professionals express the paradox of being both a societal elite and a political and economical punch-bag; the state-employed professionals, especially, consider the relation between their work and wages as being strongly unfair. Proud of their professional achievements, they argue that they are worthy of more appreciation by society. Stereotyped representations of persons, organizations and time-periods are used as narrative resources to illuminate the Hero/ine's point. The *functions* of those stereotypes vary: the Party may be a benevolent Donor or an evil, treacherous Dark Force, seducing people into unwelcome obligations.

In the stories, The Hero/ine's successes are always well-earned and mostly due to his/her agency. In quite impossible circumstances, a helping hand is gratefully accepted, but the Hero/ine is eager to prove that it was well-deserved aid. The Hero/ine's adversities and misfortunes are explained by outer circumstances and illegitimate means; as they are thoroughly unjust they do not diminish the Hero/ine's qualities and agency, rather, they can be a source of moral strength. Making a career on a professional basis among the proliferation of obstacles seems often a mission impossible, but the Hero/ine shows how it can still be accomplished. Even if it does not lead to wealth and power, then it at least results in professional and moral *satisfaction*. The solution is honest, conscientious work, standing trial, and balancing with retained integrity among political and social entanglements. Even though this solution does not sound spectacular, it still takes a Hero/ine to live through it.

13
Mighty McManus: Mystery, Myth and Modernity

Tony Watson

It's good to see you again

The scene is an academic office – B32 – on the ultra modern campus of an English university. The room looks out onto the narrow end of an artificial lake. Ducks swim on the water and a heron with an intent professorial look is standing statue-like at the water's edge.

A computer is whirring away, unheeded, on the long curved desk close to the windows and two men are sitting at a circular table at the other end of the room. One is the occupant of the office. He is called Tony. The other is his visitor. His name is James.

It's good to see you again, Tony.

Good to see you, James. I do hope that I can help with this project of yours. It sounded quite exciting on the phone.

Yes, it is but I'd like to use you as a sounding board for some of my ideas.

That would be a pleasure.

I want to write this book about the world of journalism that has preoccupied me since my youth. I want it to be truthful as well as an exciting read. But the truths I want to present – or perhaps I should say 'the truths I want to look for' – aren't truths in the sense of simple facts. I know it sounds a bit pretentious but I want to get at some of the deeper truths about the world I have lived in than I would with a documentary approach.

And why not?

I'm not a sociologist like you but I think that my own reading of military history and bits of anthropology over the years have been about trying to go beneath the surface of the everyday events that I write about in my 'day job'. I think we share some key interests here. I see you, in that fiction science piece (Watson, 2000) and the one about the Scottish ballad (Watson, 2004), as using what you might call 'literary' techniques to fulfil what I see as a serious social science intent. Is that right?

I wish I could have thought of those words myself. But you're not telling me that you are intending to make a late career-shift into sociology.

No, I'm not. If I can get this book right, that will satisfy me. I want to write about the journalistic tribe – and the broader social world in which the tribe exists – in a way that goes way beyond what can be done in a memoir style of book or in a straightforward novel. I am not concerned with theorizing as such. But I do want my thinking to be well informed by good theory, whether it is from sociology, anthropology or whatever. I've read quite a lot as you know but I need to pull it together before I start writing.

Enter McManus

What do you think the focus of the book will be then?

I've got this mythic bloke that I want to make the main character in my … in my … in what I might risk calling, for now anyway, my ethnographic novel. They called this man 'the mighty McManus'. There are all these tales about him. I have been intrigued for years about the McManus myth.

And I assume he was a journalist. Am I right? You are going to write about the quintessential journalist; a hero of the newspaper world, a legend in his own 'Times'; the epitome of the seeker after truth. It sounds good, James.

I think you are taking the piss, Tony.

Sorry. Do go on.

For a start, he was mainly a photographer. I mean, it appears that he was originally a photographer who then moved on to produce his own written copy to go with his pictures. And you're also wrong about his being a hero – in the sense of somebody that everyone admired or used as a model of how to be a newspaperman. He was sort of that, but he was also, well, to some very much a villain. That is if he ever actually existed – other than as a mythic figure. There are all these stories that I have picked up over my career with the newspaper. So you could say that they are just 'stories'. But I feel it's more than that, which is why I talk of him as 'a mythic figure'. But what is 'myth' – beyond the everyday label that people put on things that aren't true.

So the main thing we need to talk about is myth. That's a good idea. I am going to write a book chapter on this – so our interests really do come together. McManus might be a subject for me as well as for you!

Myths and the shield against terror

Well yes, fine. But I am not sure whether we can talk of myths as such in modern societies. That's what I want your thoughts on because I have a suspicion that perhaps myths are altogether something of the past; that we are beyond a mythic age. What I take from your work – and I want you to explain where your ideas here have come from – is that there are deep and frightening issues which human beings always have to face up to and that human cultures, whether they use myths or something else, help people deal with. Look, I marked this bit in your ethnography book. I've got it with me. You say that there are deep issues for all of us, like death, the nature of love, the meaning of fidelity and so on and that we need help with these things in order to stay sane.

Indeed, and to be part of a functioning society.

Yes. And you say that this does not mean that we agonize all the time about these issues – presumably because this would send us mad and divert us from getting on with any kind of worthwhile social life. Instead, you say we engage with these issues in a way which allows our culture to do our worrying for us. We do this – yes here's the bit on page 21 – 'through looking at, reading about, engaging in stories in novels, newspapers, films, jokes and gossip – stories about love, death, hate, infidelity, illness, bliss.' Now, here is the bit I've underlined in red on page 22: 'The "mythic" element of all these cultural products function like fairy tales do for children (reference here to Propp, Betelheim blah blah . . .). Our anxieties are raised as the ogre storms from his castle, the murderer creeps up behind the victim, the adulterous seducer slips in, and out, of the bedroom of the erstwhile faithful spouse. But order and calm is restored to our lives as the fairy tale ends with "and they all lived happily ever after", the murder film comes to close or we shut our newspaper and go to empty the dishwasher.'

OK. Anyway, tell me more about this McManus.

No, let's clear up some of these theoretical things first. They are important to me. I would like to understand where you developed your line of thinking from?

I think it was originally Peter Berger's sociology of religion (1973) and his idea of religion as a sacred canopy, part of the socially constructed 'nomos' that acts as a 'shield against terror'. And all of this relates to his work with Thomas Luckmann on the social construction of reality (1966/1991). A key influence on that work – someone I've been trying to read up on recently – was Arnold Gehlen.

A spooky diversion: the Nazi spymaster and the philosophical anthropologist

Oh yes, believe it or not, I know about him. He was the famous Nazi spymaster, one of Hitler's key intelligence officers. And when I was working in the States at one time, there was all this stuff about Gehlen and the CIA. There was this black orchestra of spies and ...

Just a minute, James ...

No, I must tell you: McManus allegedly got caught up in all this stuff in America. We thought that some of his unexplained wealth might be to do with the Gehlen gang in the states.

James, stop. This is not the Gehlen I was talking about. You are talking about Reinhard Gehlen and I am talking about Arnold Gehlen, a sociologist and philosophical anthropologist who influenced Berger and Luckmann.

Oh dear, so no Nazis for now.

Well, here is the great coincidence. Arnold Gehlen was also a Nazi.

Seriously? You don't mean that literally? You don't mean he actually was an active Nazi?

Oh yes he was.

Spooky!

You could say that. But it's pure and simple coincidence. Anyway, Berger and Luckmann in The Social Construction of Reality *clearly indicate their dependence on his thinking.*

What was his main argument then?

In his book Man: His Nature and Place in this World *[1940 trans. 1980] he developed a philosophical anthropology based on Nietzsche's idea that humans* are 'not yet finished animals': they are dependent on society and culture for a long period of maturation; they have 'world-openness' because of a lack or deficit of instincts; thus modern life is precarious and humans require a secure political and social environment to provide discipline. 'Human dependence on social institutions and culture creates ontological frailty and existential precariousness'.

And if I understand Berger and Luckmann properly ...

You've read the book?

Quite closely, actually. I was very taken with their idea of 'symbolic universes' – the totality of meanings that gives us societies, histories and human biographies.

And gives legitimacy to the social order with which it is associated. But did they deal with myths in the book? They presumably play a part in symbolic universes.

I don't know. And I can't see a copy on your shelves.

OK I'll go and borrow my friend Gerardo's copy. [Tony briefly disappears and comes back into the room already having looked up myth in the index]. Here we are, on page 110: 'Mythology represents the most archaic form of universe-maintenance, as indeed it represents the most archaic form of legitimation generally. Very likely mythology is a necessary phase in the development of human thought as such. In any case, the oldest universe-maintaining conceptualizations available to us are mythological in form.'

Now this is interesting. They are making myths something of the past. And do they define myth?

Myths and sacred forces

Well they define mythology: 'For our purposes, it is sufficient to define mythology as a conception of reality that posits the ongoing penetration of the world of everyday experience by sacred forces. Such a conception naturally entails a high degree of continuity between social and cosmic order ...'. Aha, and listen to this: 'all reality appears as made of one cloth'. Now that does suggest the myths are part of the symbolic universe of the sort of society where there was a tight monolithic community all more-or-less believing in the same things.

It is clear, then, that they also see myths as involving the supernatural – well the sacred anyway.

Yes, this is something that Monika Kostera recognizes [see page 1]. She sees myths originating in what she calls the sacred realm of experience. And I think she connects this to what she calls the 'spiritual sphere' of social life. All this is suggesting that your McManus is perhaps more a figure of organizational folklore than a mythical figure. Organizations and businesses are, as Monika points out, usually seen as distinctly profane. And we can look to another of my friends here. Go along to the G's on the middle book shelf and pass me those Yannis Gabriel books, would you. Thanks. He is anxious to discourage us from looking at organizational stories in the way a number of management and organization theory writers do – yes, here it is: when they 'use the idea of myth to denote any symbolically charged organisational narrative'. (2000, p. 24).

OK, pass the book to me please, Tony. Uhm, and listen to this: he says he is disinclined to see organizational stories as being part of a 'mythology' because '[T]he stories lack the sweeping grandeur, narrative complexity, or overwhelming emotional charge of ancient Greek, native American, and other myths. Their characters can be interesting, unusual, or even brilliant, but they lack the towering presence of true heroes.'

And here look, James, in his other book: '[S]tories do not have the larger-than-life heroic presence of mythical heroes, nor the sacral qualities of myths' (2004b, p. 6).

OK, I see the point of all this. But I have a feeling that there still a strong element of 'the mythic' about McManus even if there isn't the full-blown archaic style of myth at work – something that, if we follow Gehlen, Berger, Luckmann and co, we would only expect to see in a pre-modern society.

McManus: hero and villain

Let's see, then, James. I really think it's time you talked more about good old McManus.

Or you might think bad old McManus when you hear about him.

Let's see. Off you go.

I first heard of McManus in the first few days of my joining the paper. I was more-or-less just a tea-boy. I had been lucky to get a job on a national paper straight after leaving school, without having to work on a local or a provincial paper first. But the price I had to pay for this was a whole series of humiliations – ritual and otherwise. They made me stay at the paper all the way through the night in my second week on the grounds that someone needed to be near the phone to 'take copy from McManus'. Of course, he never called and it was only the next day that I asked why one of the usual copytakers could not have handled his expected call. All I got in response to my question was a lot of eye-rolling and I was told that I would have been 'made as a reporter' had I actually had a telephone conversation with the 'great McManus'. I decided that it was all just a simple 'wind up', especially after I was told that he was actually a photographer. But then, one of the other reporters explained to me that this 'picture man' was a 'loner' who never went out into the field with a reporter. Consequently, when there was copy to go with his pictures, he would write it himself and send it in. Show me some of his pieces, then, I said. So they gave me several pieces, all of which had different by-lines – different names – on them. He appears always to have hidden behind names that weren't his own, on pictures as well as with text. Indeed, I was shown some photographs and these were all either anonymous or attached to various names which were nothing like McManus.

And what were the photographs like?

They were all of a high quality. There was always a subtlety to them – as if there was something more there in the scene than was actually visible. You found yourself staring at the pictures to see if they could tell you more than was actually presented on the page. At the time, I took it that this man really must exist, because the pictures that people pointed to as 'McManuses' seemed to have this peculiar quality in common. However, since then, it has occurred to me that it might be that pictures with this extra quality that were not known to have come from any particular photographer might simply have been attributed to the so-called 'McManus'.

But surely some of the people you were working with, sub-editors, photographers as well as journalists, must have been willing to provide some detail about the man.

Oh yes they provided lots of detail. And I have collected lots of material on him and his adventures over the years. The thing is, though, that it was always 'a good pal of mine' or 'my old friend x' or 'a former editor' who was the source of the information. Nobody has ever given me anything that we could call first-hand. And yes, before you ask me, I have regularly asked people if they had ever personally worked with or known McManus. Now, a common pattern was for people to say something along the lines, 'No, but I know someone who knew him well.' But there was also a much more coy type of response; more along the lines, 'I might have done,' wink wink. It was almost as if some of those blokes felt that they would be diminished in the eyes of other men if they were to admit that they had not been touched by the hand of this god.

Aha, 'this god' eh. This is getting interesting. But we'll come back to this. I want to hear some more. But I note that you talk about 'blokes' and 'men'. Does this mean that women never spoke of him?

Oh they did. With one very important exception, I think I always heard women speak in a disparaging way of McManus. If they saw a bloke getting a bit 'above himself', then a women might say, 'so you think you're the great McManus, do you?.' And I remember well when one of the news editors rather cruelly dumped his wife for a younger woman. Several of the women in the office spoke sneeringly of the bloke as 'that bloody McManus'.

No men spoke of him this way?

No, a lot of them were envious enough of the fellow anyway. But I think it was more than this. It would have been sort of, well, blasphemous for them to attach a profanity to the name of McManus. For many of the women, however, I think that McManus represented the villainous in the sort of men they saw and disapproved of in the newspaper industry; men who were unfaithful to their wives, men who preferred to go abroad to exotic or dangerous places to escape from the mundane lives of their wives and families.

The beautiful Maria-Vittoria

But you mentioned an important exception.

Yes, this relates to rather a significant episode in my personal life. It was an experience, an adventure if you like, that will feature rather centrally in my book, if I actually get round to writing it. It was an amazing love affair that I had with this woman, Maria-Vittoria, in Milan when I was in my late twenties. Mavì, as she liked me to call her, was quite a bit older than me and more experienced in almost everything; opera, food, architecture, fashion and sex. She had been a catwalk model and was now a fashion editor on a Milan-based magazine. She was stunning. I could not believe my luck. It was just wonderful, wonderful for about three months.

It only lasted three months?

No, it went on for quite a while after that, until I was moved to the Rome office in fact. But it changed all of a sudden one Sunday morning. I remember it so well. We were sitting on the wall of a fountain after strolling through the Parco Sempione and the grounds of the Castello Sforzesco. Mavì had seemed distracted when we were sitting on one of those stone benches in the Castello and I was trying to get her to finish the story she had started to tell me in bed that morning about Guiseppe Verdi's death in Milan. She seemed somewhat distracted. When she appeared to be reluctant to have any kind of conversation, I simply let things go quiet. I just gazed at her beauty, her long legs, her golden hair, her perfect eyes, nose and cheeks. And I thought of how she had made love to me earlier that morning. And I thought back to something she said in Italian one night, in a flight of passion, something I thought was 'Vuoi sposarmi?'

Oh mio Dio.

Did Mavì really think of settling with me for life at some point? Maybe, maybe not. Anyway, on the day I was talking about, we eventually walked out of the park and sat by the fountain. And then she spoke those fatal words.

Fatal words! This is getting dramatic. What were they? Come on.

'You are not McManus.'

Gosh.

Yes, 'gosh'. What do you say? I was stunned. I had never mentioned McManus to her. I had no reason to.

So she knew the legend, the myth or whatever we are going to decide it was.

Oh no, it wasn't as simple as this. Mavì told me that McManus had been her lover.

So now you had actually met someone who had first-hand knowledge of McManus – if 'first-hand' is not too tame a word here!

Well that is it. I do not know to this day whether she really was involved with the man or not. I knew that among her various affairs had been a couple of entanglements with people from my paper – a long time ago when she was a young model. So perhaps one of these was McManus. Or perhaps she had simply heard stories from them about him.

But what did she say about him?

Oh it was always mysterious, ambiguous sort of stuff . . . a bit embarrassing to speak of here in the cold light of day.

Like what?

Well, things like 'you are not the love of my life, you are not McManus.' That was one of the early things she said on that Sunday. Another time, would you believe, she said, in her slightly drawled deep-voiced southern Italian accent: 'you are a man but he was a god.'

Gods again!

Yes, and I felt over those next few months that the gods were trampling all over me. Maria-Vittoria, my once-passionate lover, became more and more remote from me. And now and again, in these nasty cold rages that she could get into, she would throw in references to McManus. Even though I was horribly in love with her I could see that I was, in the end, just one of the string of men she had been involved with. I was just another one of what she once referred to as her 'piccoli esperimenti amorosi'. When she spoke of McManus, always with a lot of eye flashing and half-drunk jumbled-up Italian and English, it was difficult to tell whether she was rambling on about a real lover in her past or whether she was invoking some perfect hero-lover that she could dream about in the face of her growing realization that there was never going to be a real 'love of her life'.

You're not still in love with her are you?

God no. I saw her only once after my move to Rome. I realized that the whole affair, for all its intimate dinners, nights at the opera and passionate couplings had been a semi-fantasy for me much as it had been for her.

McManus and masculinity: capturing, shooting and taking

But you hate McManus, don't you? I can now see him as a diabolic sort of figure rather than a hero or a god.

Well if you had seen these stunning erotic photographs that my lover presented to me one evening as the work of McManus, you'd wonder just what he was. He had captured her perfectly. He had captured her sophisticated side and her wild-animal side, often in the same photograph. He had shot her several times at what looked liked the height of sexual abandon.

Did you say 'shot'?

Yes, why? Oh, I see. That's the normal language that photographers use. And models too, talk of 'shoots'. But you are noting the rather unfortunate metaphor here, aren't you?

Yes and there's another rather interesting metaphor there: 'capturing'. It's all very aggressively masculine, isn't it, this photographer stuff? I think I can picture this McManus figure now: Don Giovanni just before he gets dragged to hell at the end of the opera – with a phallic long-lens camera poking out of his cloak.

And a flash gun at his side. More aggressive machismo: why, I wonder, should a source of light be called a gun?

Oh dear, so where are we now, James? Our McManus is both a god and a devil in the guise of a superman sharp-shooting photographer and divine lover.

Modernity and the demise of gods, heroes and devils?

I think that our conversation earlier rather confirmed my feeling that 'myths' in what we might call the full sense are something of the past, something of an earlier period when societies were more unified, sharing the same beliefs and values – with these beliefs and values being exemplified by supernatural or semi-supernatural gods, heroes, devils and the like.

Well, I am not sure about that historically or sociologically; all this stuff about a solidaristic unified past.

OK, but I was very taken with a lovely little book by Karen Armstrong (2005/2006) who is not, by the way, a sociologist. I've got it here in my bag. Again, Armstrong talks of the need for humans, who are different from other animals, having to make meanings to cope with their awareness of their own mortality and to avoid the danger of sinking into despair. She shows how myths played a key part in such meaning-making in the various earlier periods of history that she examines. But here's the crunch for us. When she comes to the modern world, 'The great western transformation, 1550–1899', she sees the death of mythology coming about. Modernization and the growth of science discredit mythology.

So we don't need myth any more?

Modernity and a continuing role for the mythical

Yes, we do need the mythical, says Armstrong. She insists we are still 'myth-making creatures' (on page 142 in her book). The twentieth century gave us some 'very destructive modern myths, which have ended in massacre and genocide'. And she seems to think that we can turn to novels to help fulfil the role that myths once played. This, of course, appeals to me as a would-be novelist. Here's some more of my underlining on the last page of her book, look: 'A novel, like a myth, teaches us to see the world differently; it shows how to look into our own hearts and to see our world from a perspective that goes beyond our own self-interest.' And what really got me excited, reading this, was that one of the novels she talks of here is Conrad's *Heart of Darkness*.

So why should that have got you so excited? It's certainly a great book. And Apocalypse Now, *based on it, is a great film.*

Can't you see: McManus could be my Kurtz! So come on, what do you think?

The novel is a great idea. And I think I agree with you that we don't have what you called full-blown myths of the type that were allegedly socially significant in 'the past'. McManus does not comply with all the features that Joseph Campbell identifies in the archetypal heroes and gods of the Joycean 'monomyth'. And I doubt if all your stories about McManus fit closely that pattern of what Campbell calls, if I remember rightly, 'the standard path of the mythological adventure of the hero' (1949/1993, p. 30). However, I think that we can still see strong elements of 'the mythic' here. There is a lot of mystery in the stories; there is a hint of another world of the journalist/photographer beyond the mundane world of the ordinary newspaper people who pass the tales around. His is a world of adventure, sexual freedom, control over his own circumstances (unfettered by editors, deadlines and all that). It is a world of masculinity: loving and 'shooting' beautiful women. Taking pictures (note how, again in this aggressively masculine photographic discourse, we 'take' photographs; rather than 'make' photographs) is to capture the world, pull it through the lens into that little 'room' that we hold in our hands – the camera. And I think that central to the functional rationale of the McManus myth (or semi-myth) is the handling of men's fear of women and men's desire to control women. I clearly go along with Barthes (1957/1973) here on myths supporting material interests or, as we might put it sociologically, functioning ideologically.

Are you serious, Tony?

I certainly am. Like most gods, kings, queens and mythic heroes from Ulysses and Arthur to Morse and Taggart) he only has one name – McManus. He disappears off into the wilderness like all the classic mythic heroes. But when he does it in this modern setting he is not just escaping from the work-based mundaneness and routine of the newspaper office. He is also escaping from responsibilities of marriage, family, children and so on. His stories help your newspapermen wish away their marital, parental and domestic responsibilities. He is a nice fantasy for them.

And this is why women dislike him?

Yes, with Maria-Vittoria being the exception who proves the rule. You suggest that she was a woman who was never going to marry, whatever you think she might have whispered to you one night in bed. She knew the McManus myth and was using it to push you away. But, let me stress, I am not saying that he didn't actually exist, or even that he was not Mavì's lover. It seems to me that myth or 'the mythic' always incorporates a suggestion that some of the events that they cover just might have happened.

So, to bring this to a close, what are we to conclude about myths and modernity? You seem keen to insist that McManus is indeed a mythic figure, not just a character in a bundle of organizational folk tales. You do see an element of grandeur and complexity that people like Gabriel require of a myth.

Yes, an element of it. And Yannis talks of myths having an 'overwhelmingly emotional charge'. Well your telling of your Italian love story, and McManus's intrusion into it, certainly had an emotional charge to it! I think that what I would conclude is that there is not the archaic full-blown myth here in the McManus narratives. But there is a strong strain of 'the mythic'. While I go along with the basic ideas of Gehlen, Berger and Luckmann and Bell about cultures – and indeed the mythic element of cultures – having to deal with fundamental existential issues, I do worry about the philosophical conservatism which is implicit in their work (as it is in much classic sociology, as Nisbet [1970] convincingly showed in his book). These neo-conservative thinkers seem to look back for inspiration to an earlier, simpler, more spiritual age of solid and unquestioned institutions (and look where this took Gehlen: into bed with the Nazi myth-makers). I just don't think that there was an 'age of myth'. The basic mythic form has been around for a long time – Armstrong goes back to the Neolithic age I notice – but I bet people through the ages traded looser and more fragmented versions of the basic form in different circumstances, just as your newspaper people have traded in tales of the mythic figure of McManus in the age of formally rational work organizations and modern gender relations.

'The mythic figure of McManus', I like that. Do you think your friend Monika might put him in her book?

That would be good, wouldn't it?

It certainly would.

14
Myth and Charisma as Symbolic Capital: The Case of Architecture

Alexander Styhre and Mats Sundgren

Introduction

This chapter presents a study of Sweden's most prestigious firm of architects, Wingårdh Architect Firm, and suggests that resources such as myth and charisma are not additional or external to regular organizational practices but woven into the very fabric of everyday practices. Myth and charisma are socially enacted beliefs, circulated in narratives and symbols, and helping to structure a particular field. In the field of architecture, the importance of such resources must not be neglected or ignored. In this view, myth and charisma constitute what Durkheim (1895/1938) called *faites sociale*, social facts. In the general wake of interest in mythology and other forms of 'non-rational' (i.e. emotional or symbolic) resources in organization, for example charisma, myth is often portrayed as something that is, of necessity, deceiving and poorly related to actual conditions (Gabriel, 2004a; Gemmill and Oakley, 1992; Ogbor, 2000). Here, myth is used in its anthropological sense, as something capable of making what is ambiguous or fuzzy intelligible and widely shared between groups of humans (Douglas, 1963/1999). Contrary to such a view, myth may also be used as an organizational resource, both internally and externally to the organization, to promote certain ideas or to reinforce the image of the organization or its employed professions. For instance, management consultancy firms are eager to underscore its scientific principles and its actual effects on organizational performance; theatre companies emphasize artistic creativity and autonomy *vis-à-vis* financiers; and university professors are at pains to safeguard its detachment from political power and specific interests. In this view, mythology is not only, in the words of Geertz (1973), a 'system of meaning' making sense but also a resource actively mobilized in order to affect a specific field (Barthes, 1982). Following the analytical framework of Pierre Bourdieu (2005), myth is a part, here, of the symbolic capital that individuals or groups of individuals may use to accomplish objectives and gain the prerogative to define and inscribe social reality. In this perspective, myths do not fall from above but are actively formulated, reformulated, circulated, and reiterated. Following Boje (2001), myths are ante-narratives, stories being retold in various communities, and never becoming fully finished or wholly enclosed.

The empirical material explored in the paper derives from a study of an internationally renowned firm of architects whose founder and chief architect is one of Sweden's few 'starchitects' (to use Jones' phrase from 2006). While architecture is generally portrayed in the literature as a profession struggling to maintain its jurisdiction over the architecture and design of buildings (Blau, 1984; Blau and McKinley, 1979; Cuff, 1991; Gutman, 1988), the field is also characterized by its belief in strong individuals' foresight and vision, something which breeds a certain *faiblesse* regarding mythologies of 'lone geniuses'. In addition, the insistence on seeing architecture as what strikes a balance between the engineering sciences and art, the symbolic and ornamental and the material, between what is public and private, further reinforces the image of architecture as what bridges scientific rationalities and artistic expression. Even though there is a corpus of texts examining the social function of architecture (see, for instance, Le Corbusier, 1946; Koolhaas, 1978; Obrist and Koolhaas, 2001; Venturi *et al.*, 1977) and a general interest in the aesthetics of organization (Guillén, 1997; Linstead and Höpfl, 2000; Strati, 1999), and in society at large (Julier, 2000), architectural work is rarely the subject of analysis in management studies. To date, little research has been conducted on architectural work in management studies and the few studies that do exist (Blau and McKinley, 1979; Ivory, 2004; Pinnington and Morris, 2002; Winch and Schneider, 1993) primarily examine the formal organization of architectural work and not the practice *per se* or its symbolic resources. In this chapter the function of mythology and charisma in architecture is examined *qua* the symbolic capital exploited in the day-to-day practice of architects.

The nature of architecture

The management literature examining architecture is rather limited and tends to regard architects as a professional group that has gradually lost its status and influence upon construction projects. 'Architects, as a professional group', argue Pinnington and Morris (2002, p. 190), 'have sought to preserve a narrowed professional jurisdiction in the face of a weakened authority over clients and contractors'. Similar to all professions bridging aesthetic and commercial concerns, architects have to pay allegiance to a variety of conflicting interests. On the one hand, they adhere to ideologies praising aesthetic values, functionality, and predominantly architectural solutions; while on the other hand, they have to pay close attention to the client's expectations and demands, and the financial resources dedicated to the project (Pinnington and Morris, 2002). This two-sided concern, in many cases representing conflicting interests, leads to many trade-offs with regard to decisions and negotiations. However, in the formal rhetoric, innovativeness and the ability to conceive new solutions to architectural problems is praised within the industry and the most prestigious architectural firms are those winning major competitions and being capable of presenting intriguing architecture. The strong emphasis on awards and competition makes the field of architecture susceptible to myths about talent and creativity as innate and extraordinary qualities demonstrated by certain architects. This is referred to as the 'lone genius myth' by Cuff (1991), who rejects this view of architecture. Cuff (1991, p. 245) writes, on the basis of his evaluation of architecture: 'Perhaps the most basic discovery I have made during this research is that the mythical architect as lone genius-artist is a false image, insofar as it represents a simplification of actual circumstances'. Instead, Cuff (1991, p. 245) advocates a 'social practice view' of architecture wherein the architect is capable of aligning and harmonizing a broad range of interests and of collaborating with various stakeholders.

Even though the lone genius myth is gradually losing its appeal to architects and to the general public, its reputation remains the gold standard for architectural firms. Reputation is the accumulated credibility gained from a number of successes in the field, including the winning of prestigious competitions, coverage of the work of the architect or architectural firm in leading journals and magazines, and, to a minor extent, the review of the architecture in daily newspapers and the public's recognition of the work. Similar to researchers who make their reputation by being published in leading scientific journals, architects gain credibility through their work. Architecture is thus 'path-dependent' in terms of previous successes enabling future activities. Ivory (2004, p. 506) explains:

> Clearly, for the architect, reputations are tied to previous works. Every building is, as one architect noted, 'a sort of database, a living advertisement'. In other words, these buildings as they appear in portfolios

and in presentations, become key to winning future business. Innovation becomes central to the process because a building which looks good, even if it is only because of an innovative roof or cladding system, will always speak better of the architect than a more mundane creation.

Expressed differently, individual architects may actively promote an image of themselves or their firms (or even other firms which they regard as innovative) as being extraordinarily creative and capable of envisaging new buildings and new design solutions. Rather than being passive actors who are evaluated by others, architects can, like scientists, take on the role of active agents promoting an image of themselves as being at the forefront of architectural theory and practice. In this view, myth and charisma are symbolic capital mobilized and employed in the field of architecture. Myth is thus not a meaning-making system which is out of control of relevant groups, but something that is actively shaped and translated in narratives and storytelling.

Myth and charisma as symbolic capital

The notion of myth is key to anthropological research and thinking. Claude Lévi-Strauss (1979, p. 17) speaks of myth as that which gives meaning to what cannot be fully controlled or understood:

> Myth is unsuccessful in giving man more material power over the environment. However, it gives man, very importantly, the illusion that he can understand the universe and that he does understand the universe. It is, of course, an illusion.

Myth gives what is poorly understood or elusive a function, a sense, or a certain linearity; myth imposes systems of meaning onto what is unfamiliar and puzzling. In this view, myth does not merely deceive but instead actively promotes shared worldviews and a joint outlook on social reality – myth is thus a collective agreement regarding how to perceive and examine social reality. Such affirmative views of myth have been advocated by, for instance, Vico (1999, p. 145) who argued that the task of great poetry is 'to invent sublime myths which are suited to the popular understanding'. More recently, the representatives of the *Collège de sociologie*, including thinkers such as Roger Caillois, Georges Bataille and Michel Leiris, thought of myth as a substitute for traditional and obsolete forms of transgression and thus playing a decisive role in modern life (Richman, 2003, p. 34). In anthropology, Joseph Campbell (Boa, 1994) has pointed out the productive functions of myths as capable of making sense and sharing meaning. One specific form of myth embedded in social psychology is the concept of charisma. The concept of charisma is part of Max Weber's sociological vocabulary and denotes a specific form of domination (German, *Herrschaft*) based not on legal or traditional authority but on extraordinary individual traits and skills: 'Charismatic domination rests on the affectual and personal devotion of the follower to the lord and his gifts of grace' (Weber, 1999, p. 104). For Weber, the concept of charisma is what paves the way for enchantment in a de-traditionalized and disenchanted modern world; charisma is what opposes scientific knowledge and bureaucratic procedures and what operates on the level of emotionality and desire rather than intellect. It is affectual rather than rational. Charisma is what enables disruptive change in an increasingly continuous and rationalized society. In organization theory, it is primarily in the leadership literature that the notion of charisma has been operationalized and studied (see Yammarino *et al.*, 2005, and Conger and Kanungo 1987, for an overview of charismatic leadership). Just like the notion of myth, charisma is a concept that helps to make sense of certain events and conditions at a specific point in time. In addition, charisma is what is produced in terms of being a collective inscription of extraordinary qualities into certain individuals. By using Pierre Bourdieu's (2005) notion of symbolic capital, it will be argued that myth and charisma serve as resources that various groups may actively promote in their struggle to maintain authority, jurisdiction and control over resources within specific fields. Speaking in terms of architecture, reputation and myths or narratives regarding extraordinary talents are part of the symbolic capital mobilized by individual architectural firms. Architects may thus expand their jurisdiction and domain of expertise in the field of construction work if they achieve a position whereby they are regarded as charismatic and surrounded by an aura of creativity and innovativeness. Architecture is thus not detached or isolated from beliefs and assumptions that rest on little more than mythological thinking and attributional phenomena.

Architecture and symbolic capital

Wingårdh Architect Firm is an architectural consultancy founded by its chief architect and CEO, Gert Wingårdh, in 1977 in Gothenburg, Sweden. This firm has grown organically and today about 100 people are employed at its offices in Gothenburg and Stockholm. Wingårdh Architect Firm became internationally renowned following the exhibition of a building at the 1996 Venice Biennale, and following achievements when designing the Swedish Embassy in Berlin, where Wingårdh, according to one critic, expressed original creativity, architectural ability, and a sense of humour which is quite rare among Swedish architects (Wærn, 2001). Today, the consultancy is one of the most respected in Northern Europe and Gert Wingårdh has been awarded the Kasper Sahlin Architecture Prize, which is the most prestigious national architecture award in Sweden (Postiglione, 2004), four times (1988, 1993, 2001, 2006), exceeding all other Swedish architects. As a consequence, Gert Wingårdh, if not a celebrity, is well-known by those members of the Swedish public who are interested in architecture. Recently, the company won several prizes in international invited competitions including the chancellery of the Swedish Embassy in Washington, Ericsson's headquarters in London, the Swedish National Science Centre (Universeum) in Gothenburg in 2001, and *R&D Magazine*'s 2001 Laboratory of the year for the AstraZeneca R&D Waltham site in Boston, USA.

Among his co-workers, Wingårdh is the great visionary who leads day-to-day activities at the firm without being involved in details. Wingårdh has claimed that he could 'allow himself to act a bit like an elephant in the office' even though that may 'repel some talents' because, in his view, it is the shared interest among his co-workers in producing good and interesting architecture that matters at the end of the day. At any given point in time, there could be as many as 40–50 projects running concurrently, so Wingårdh is not involved in all the details. Instead, he participates during the more creative phases when concepts are developed and new thinking is articulated. During the higher-profile projects, such as the embassy buildings, Wingårdh plays a more active role. Failing to produce high quality solutions during such projects would be detrimental to the firm so the chief architect invests more time and energy in the project.

Wingårdh is praised by his co-workers for his ability to communicate his architectural visions with various stakeholders that include clients, politicians and construction industry representatives. One of the architects at the firm emphasized the ability to share ideas about architecture as one of the most important leadership skills in the domain of architecture:

> Besides creative abilities, leadership skills also entail being able to communicate the idea further; to explain to others how you were thinking

and why you have to engage your co-workers in thinking in similar terms. A good leader is capable of making his or her co-workers believe that the idea is their own, one might say, and then you can work towards the same goals. That is very important; it is pivotal for the creative processes of the firm. (Lead architect)

At the same time, internal communication, or what could be referred to using the more mundane term 'talk', plays a key role in bridging between and bonding individual co-workers, visions and architectural practice. Internally, talk serves to constitute a joint vision within the project, to motivate co-workers, and to create a sense of *esprit de corps*; externally, communication plays a similar role, albeit with other stakeholders that do not, of necessity, share the architectural credo – that is, the interest in a certain aesthetic in the built environment. One of the data visualization experts argued: 'I think Gert's personality plays a substantial role. His way of communicating and convincing people, as well as making them go for something that will make a difference, matters I would say.' One of the design engineers argued along the same lines: 'Gert is great at promoting his ideas. He is very eloquent. I think that is number one. Additionally, he does not recognize any limitations. If he wants it a particular way, then he works hard to accomplish this and he makes his co-workers join him in that work.'

Within the field of architecture, the reputation of the architectural firm is of key importance to its ability to compete at the cutting-edge of the industry and to win the most prestigious project competitions. One of the principal means of exposure in the field is architectural journals covering ongoing and recent work. Wingårdh has pointed out the importance of being represented in 'visual spaces' of architecture, that is to say, winning competitions in major cities like Berlin. Chief architect Wingårdh argued:

The entire community of architects is continuously in contact with architectural journals and there is an institutionalized market . . . There is little doubt that if you conduct a project in a 'visible space', you will receive more attention, OK. Our most widely published project is the Swedish Embassy in Berlin because Berlin, as a city of architecture, is closely monitored. All of the architectural journals cover it. It is in print much more than, for instance, the Museum of Modern Art in Stockholm, not because it is better – but because of its location.

The architectural journals not only review ongoing and recent work, thus establishing mechanisms for the distribution of prestige and reputation in the field, they are also a source of inspiration for individual architects. Wingårdh actively promotes an attitude in his architectural firm whereby one is influenced by one's peers, that is, other architectural firms. One of the 3D-visualizers providing animated computer-designed images of the building said:

> A lot of inspiration comes from others. He [Gert Wingårdh] reads incredible numbers of magazines. He knows what kinds of feelings he wants a building to convey. If he cannot express in words what he wants to say, he goes to his room to pick up a magazine and then we see an image of how he wants it to look. You know, the type of stone to use on the façade and so on. His creativity is undoubtedly an inspiration. I can imagine that most people who are creative in design professions are inspired by many different sources.

In general, the co-workers at the architectural firm regarded the CEO and founder as the leader of internal creative work as well as the external representative of the firm. In both domains – intramural and extramural – the ability to embody certain aesthetic values and norms, as well as extraordinary skills and capacities, served as symbolic capital; among the co-workers, Wingårdh's track record and his ability to 'think outside the box' was a source of inspiration for older as well as newer co-workers; for outsiders, the rhetorical skills and didactic tactics of Wingårdh convinced stakeholders of the value of taking risks and paving the way for new architectural spaces. In this view, architecture is not only a matter of bridging the symbolic (e.g., sketches, blueprints) and the material (the actual construction of the building on the basis of the work of the architect), but also a matter of rhetoric, storytelling, and what Goffman (1959) calls 'the presentation of self'. This latter category of resources, so central to the success of architecture, is captured by the concept of symbolic capital, including the ability to narrate myth and to be attributed charismatic features.

Discussion and conclusion

From Lévi-Strauss (1979) we learn that myth is not solely deceiving or misplaced but that it actively promotes a shared outlook on social reality, helping to make sense of what is obscure and puzzling. While myth has taken on a slightly negative meaning that denotes premodern and traditional explanations that are inherently in opposition to a more scientific and 'rational' worldview, one may also think of myth as that which is already always in place in various guises. (Think for instance about what Milburn (2004/2005) calls the Feynman myth in nanotechnology discourse, as discourse otherwise being, using Holmberg et al.'s (2002) apt phrase, 'stuck in the future', preoccupied with narrating potential but as yet no actual contributions from nanotechnology.) In architecture, myths of extraordinary talent or aesthetic vision are part of a symbolic capital that is mobilized within the relevant fields. A part of such myths is the idea of charisma, denoting individuals' characteristics and skills. Since so-called 'creative work' (e.g., design, architecture, advertising, research) pays substantial attention to peer review procedures, formal awards and the ranking of individuals and communities, or firms/universities, there is little chance of individuals controlling such activities. Instead, both reputation and charisma derive from outside of the focal individual, that is to say, they are attributional phenomena. Nevertheless, once an individual has taken such an entrenched position within a field, he or she may actively promote such an image. Robert Merton (1973, p. 442) spoke of the Matthew effect in scientific work meaning that '[e]minent scientists get proportionately great credit for their contributions to science while relatively unknown scientists tend to get disproportionately little credit for comparable contributions.' As stated in the Gospel according to Matthew (25:29), 'For unto everyone that hath shall be given, and he shall have abundance: but for him that hath shall be taken away even that which he hath.' Favourable positions within a field tend to perpetuate themselves.

However, charisma is a transient and temporal phenomenon and thus there are always things at stake when being promoted as charismatic. Charisma and reputation are, of necessity, produced by others and there are examples where attempts at inscribing individuals with charismatic qualities have failed (Bryman, 1992) as, for example, the case of the German Emperor Wilhelm I who could not, despite the authorities' propaganda, compete with Chancellor Bismarck to attain the position of founding father of a united Germany (Hobsbawm and Ranger, 1983, p. 264).

In the case of the Wingårdh Architecture Firm, the co-workers claimed that Wingårdh wielded an influence through his ability to communicate his ideas internally within the firm and through persuading external stakeholders to embark on innovative projects. The national and international success of Wingårdh Architecture, then, is not solely the outcome of architectural skills and competencies but is equally dependent on the ability to exploit reputation and images of creativity and charisma entrenched in the field. Much creative work tends to succumb to what Freud (1963) once called – speaking of nationalism – the 'narcissism of minor differences'; that is to say, small differences between individuals tend to be regarded as major deviations and thus representative of extraordinary qualities (Nixon, 2005, p. 9). There is thus a thin and rather permeable line between the ordinary and the extraordinary in most creative occupations. Nevertheless, such lines of demarcation play a key role when prestige, credibility and access to material resources are being distributed and shared. Consequently, myths about creativity, skills and charisma must be regarded as social facts which actually constitute and structure social life. If an architect is regarded as being of an extraordinary calibre, then he or she will be given the resources to accomplish his or her visions. No wonder, then, that the struggle within certain fields is ongoing and persistent.

15
Paradise Lost: Impartiality of an Arbitrator

Joanna Jemielniak

> So judged he Man, both Judge and Saviour sent;
> And the instant stroke of death, denounced that day,
> Removed far off; then, pitying how they stood
> Before him naked to the air, that now
> Must suffer change, disdained not to begin
> Thenceforth the form of servant to assume;
> (John Milton, *Paradise Lost*, Book X)

Introduction

The chapter discusses the demand of impartiality from an arbitrator in the context of his or her role as compared to the role of a judge. Although both the arbitrator and the judge pursue the goal of impartiality, their ways to achieve it differ significantly.

The role of a judge, primary in the Western legal tradition, is rooted in the logocentric, state-oriented concept of law, based upon transcendental authority. In this chapter, mythical figures of judges are analyzed to capture recurring, symbolic patterns, which construe links between the spheres of *sacrum*, state (represented by royal power) and adjudication. Those patterns are reflected in the social construction of the role of a judge. The impartiality of a judge is perceived as a consequence of his or her symbolically elevated (otherworldly) condition.

International commercial arbitration as an alternative to litigation abandons this ideal. The chapter discusses the reasons for the current rapid development of this method of dispute resolution. Contrary to state-authorized litigation, arbitration is considered 'human' and 'profane'. Accordingly, the power of an arbitrator is ascribed locally, not universally. He or she is also continually challenged with the requirements of work in a culturally, linguistically and legally diversified environment. Impartiality is, therefore, a laboriously achieved state of balance among those factors.

Absolute justice

Judgmental deities

The skill of finding the truth and repaying people according to their actual deeds has often seemed a virtually superhuman feature. It has been expressed through popular Western iconography, where the figures of goddesses, Greek Themis and Roman Iustitia, were blended into a general allegory of this virtue. The scales and blindfold, originally worn by Iustitia and symbolizing unbiased attitude, quickly became much more recognizable than a cornucopia as proper attributes of the personalization of justice. 'Stop judging by appearances and make an honest judgment' warned Jesus (*The New American Bible*, 2006, Jn. 2:23). While human capacity to remain neutral in judging was often perceived as fallible, the divine power cannot be influenced, misguided or overcome. It can, however, be manifested in different ways. Respectively, in various mythologies and religions, the figures of divine guardians of law seem to represent several patterns.

A supreme male deity, head of the pantheon, is a source of general order and a patron of forces organizing the world. Such male deities commonly provide law and justice – hence the role of the Greek Zeus (Grant, 1995), the Roman Jupiter (Iovis) (Wiseman, 2004), the Egyptian Osiris (Ions, 1983), and the Sumerian Shamash (Finkel and Geller, 1997) as protectors of social regularity. Shamash, the god of the sun, reveals sins and wrongdoings by bringing them to light. One of the earliest monuments of written laws, the Code of Hammurabi, was erected to praise the solar god. Law-making and execution are also performed through powerful manifestations of monotheistic deities, such as Jalal, who is Allah in his aspect of *al-hakim* 'the judge', *al-qadi* 'the ultimate judge', and *al-'azim* 'the tremendous' (Lindemans, 2000), and Jehovah, founder of the Commandments and severe punisher of the renegades (Brague, 2007).

In Greek and Roman mythology, the idea of justice distinguished as a separate virtue was personified by female figures: Athena, Themis and Iustitia, the last two of whom being, albeit rather eclectically, incorporated into the popular Western legal imagination. They are balanced by their antithetic deity, Nemesis, a merciless executrix, representing justice as fate and vengeance and often interpreted as a remaining aspect of the Great Goddess (Cybele, Demeter, Aphrodite), whose supremacy supposedly preceded Zeus' Olympic rules in the history of ancient Greek religious beliefs.

Whereas the sole idea of justice may be represented by female allegories, mythological acts of judgment are performed generally by male deities, often connected with underworld, who command the souls of the dead. Powerful gods, such as the Egyptian Osiris, the Hindu Chitragupta (Dallapiccola, 2003), the Greek Hades or the Roman Pluto, represent ultimate justice, deciding upon repayment for the deeds of a whole human life. A female figure, such as the Akkadian goddess, Mamitu, seems extremely rare in the ranks of underworldly judges (Lurker, 2004). Traditionally depicted as terrifying and pitiless, deities can even appear regularly in the popular tales told to frighten young children, as did the Japanese Buddhist god Emma-o (Lindemans, 1998).

While judgment is a divine act, impartiality appears to be a necessary consequence of the immensely superior nature of the gods, who could not possibly have found any interest in the wishes of mortals. An exception occurred only when a human surpassed the limits of his or her own condition, through, for example, the use of supernatural talents. Still, the interest of a deity in a human can be only conditional and eventually turns against the hero, as in the myth of Orpheus.

The ultimate equality among people occurred when they faced death and the afterlife, when they would be judged alike without regard to their earthly status. Such judgment was perceived as both dreadful and edifying. It is also one of the basic concepts of Christian ethics. Popular medieval *danse macabre* paintings, in which death is depicted leading a line of dancing figures, typically including such persons as a king, a pope, a monk, a young lad, and a beautiful woman (Clark, 1950), illustrate this belief, along with the vast iconography of the inevitable Last Judgment.

The figure of Jesus in this context combines, analogically to Osiris, the solar and the underworldly aspects through the mystery of God's death and resurrection. The evangelical redeemer, who died for the sins of humanity, returns in the Book of Revelation as Jesus of Justice, a figure so terrifying that St. John fell as though dead at his sight:

> The hair of his head was as white as white wool or as snow, and his eyes were like a fiery flame. His feet were like polished brass refined in a furnace, and his voice was like the sound of rushing water. In his right hand, he held seven stars. A sharp two-edged sword came out of his mouth, and his face shone like the sun at its brightest. When I caught sight of him, I fell down at his feet as though dead. He touched

me with his right hand and said, 'Do not be afraid. I am the first and the last, the one who lives. Once I was dead, but now I am alive forever and ever. I hold the keys to death and the netherworld.' (*The New American Bible*, 2006, 1:14–18)

Divine judges

A close connection among divinity, state power, and adjudication is strongly present in both Roman and Christian origins of the Western legal culture. The monarchial position of the lords of the underworld is evident, even more so in the case of principal deities. Regal attributes, such as an ebony throne or sceptre, held by Hades and Pluto, as well as the super-royal position of Jesus, King of the kings in the Biblical visions of the Last Judgment (*The New American Bible*, 2006, see Matt 25:31–34) demonstrate supreme power in their domain. Such power was often executed through judgments. In ancient Rome, Jupiter was not only the keeper of the cosmic order and the justice of the universe, but also the patron of laws and social order and protector of the Roman state. Without any doubt, adjudication is one of the key aspects of supreme power.

How could human actors successfully undertake a titanic task of separating right from wrong? It required superhuman abilities, manifested through a supreme position in the society. Adjudication perceived as a regal privilege is widely exemplified in mythological and biblical sources. Human judges famous for their decisions, such as King Solomon, derived their powers from divine appointment and support. The tribunal appointed by Hades to decide the fates of the souls acted solely upon the will and authorization of the lord of the underworld. It consisted not of ordinary mortals, but of dead kings, known for their reason and justice: Minos, Rhadamanthys and Aeacus, all of whom descended directly from Zeus. 'Justice and judgment are the habitation of thy throne,' wrote the Psalmist (*The New American Bible*, 2006, Ps. 89:14). Correspondingly, a Christian tradition of anointing a monarch in the act of coronation symbolizes the divine origins of a king's powers, including an authority to render judgment.

In modern times, secular versions of the myth of a divine judge are still widespread. The logocentric character of Western legal culture, stemming from both Roman and Christian sources, is also present in the prominent, positivistic monist concept of law. The link between the state and the enactment and execution of laws, including the power of adjudication, is assumed here to have been necessary. Divine legitimization of this order was yet sublimated into a more abstract form.

Its core is a central position of the original (Logos), associated with deity and assumed after Plato by Christian philosophers. For centuries it has been a characteristic motif of Western thought (Banasiak, 1993).

In jurisprudence, this assumption was transformed into a concept of an ideal model of adjudication based upon direct application of legal rules. Legal interpretation and reasoning is reduced to the supposedly straight repetition of the words of law. The Montesquieuan travesty of the biblical quotation, stating that judges should serve as no more than the mouth of the law (Montesquieu, 1748/1989, p. 163), has had a tremendous career in the doctrine of adjudication. This approach is shared by authors advocating theories of legal interpretation described as linear or static (see Eskridge et al., 2000), including positivistic and textualist concepts, and partially by those who focus upon the intent of the lawmaker. The goal of legal reasoning in this context is a discovery of external, superior rules.

This logocentric perspective is present in jurisprudence of both Western traditions: continental (civil law) as well as that of common law. From this point of view a judge is perceived as an instrument for the enactment of a supreme and transcendent order, a vehicle for legal Logos (Jemielniak, 2002). Still, he or she is elevated above ordinary mortals, staying beyond their reach both physically and in a symbolic sense. Judges are appointed by the state and arrive at their decisions in its name. Their special status is emphasized, for example, by ceremonious clothing and by official formulas by which they are addressed during judicial proceedings. Their impartiality is a result of the general rule of independence of the judiciary declared, often constitutionally, by the state.

The link between the state's authority and administering justice is still widely recognized as self-evident. Correspondingly, litigation remains a presumed, 'natural' way of dispute resolution. However, this established picture is currently undergoing a serious change.

Leaving paradise

Arbitration: departure from a state

As is still not commonly known, arbitration has become the primary method of adjudication (Varady et al., 2002). For centuries, it remained overshadowed by litigation, to enjoy rapid expansion in the past several decades. Particularly in the field of international commercial disputes, arbitration has undergone an impressive revival, becoming the predominant method of conflict resolution (López Rodríguez, 2003). Different reasons for this phenomenon have been indicated. Demands for expeditious, competent, predictable and relatively economical proceedings have increased, together with a growth of global trade and, inevitably, the number of controversies connected therewith. The parties to such disputes frequently come not only from different legal systems, but also from various cultural backgrounds.

According to numerous authors (see Drahozal and Naimark, 2005; Lew *et al.*, 2003), the fact that international commercial arbitration is not connected with any particular state seems to facilitate conflicting parties to seek a nondiscriminatory decision. The possibility of applying new *lex mercatoria* (New Merchant Law) – autonomous law of international trade (Berger, 1999; De Ly, 1992), to the merits of the dispute augments the a-national character of this method of dispute resolution.

Indeed, the staggering growth of international commercial arbitration is frequently considered jointly with the impressive development of the New Merchant Law. They appear to be two sides of the same coin: a growing transnational trade exchange, which requires a transparent and flexible legal framework. Such a framework has to be secure in two respects: substantive (norms regulating the relations between the parties) and procedural (rules of dispute resolution). While arbitration aims at securing the latter, the new *lex mercatoria* is an attempt to provide a uniform set of substantive regulations for the needs of businesspeople operating in the international environment (Berger, 2001).

Historically, the origins of Merchant Law lay in universal commercial customs. According to numerous authors, they can be traced to ancient history among the usages of trade by ancient Egyptians and Phoenicians (Miller, 1996) and in those adopted by Roman *ius gentium* (Goldman, 1983). The term *lex mercatoria*, however, emerged in the Middle Ages to describe a common set of regulations observed by merchants coming from different parts of Europe (Berger, 2001). The phenomenon started at the beginning of the eleventh century and is attributed to the growing expansion of commerce. Tradespeople travelling often from very distant lands could expect a uniform and predictable treatment. *Lex mercatoria*, developed by international *societas mercatorum* (community of merchants) and not by local authorities, was also executed in the significant market cities by special tribunals, which were independent from feudal power.

The contemporary version of Merchant Law originated from processes analogous to those that brought its medieval counterpart into being. Rapid growth of international trade and the increase of globalization processes in past decades resulted in the spontaneous and pragmatic search by businesspeople for model legal tools. Such methods as standard clauses (e.g., Incoterms), self-regulatory contracts, recourse to trade usages (now also privately codified), and opting for international commercial arbitration are traditionally noted as typical of the new *lex mercatoria*. The decisive role of private initiative in solidifying the corpus of the New Merchant Law has led the positivist thinkers to deny its status as law, as it is not legitimized by state authority (see, e.g., Carbonneau, 1990). Although this debate has occasionally recurred during the past three decades, attempts to hamper emancipation of *lex mercatoria* seem to resemble a rather unsuccessful spell-casting. The movement has started and is progressing without regard to the particular name it is given.

The need for professional and expeditious dispute resolution seems to be one of the natural consequences of the described processes. National courts, presumably foreign to at least one party to the dispute, offer decisions reached by the judges who did not necessarily undergo a specialist training in the field of international trade regulations. In the domestic courts, to determine the substantive law to be applied to the merits of the controversy, collision (private international law) rules are to be used. As they are a part of *lex fori* (law of the state of the court) legal order, the finding of applicable substantive law, as well as the final result of the dispute, can frequently be difficult to predict by the parties. Contrarily, a-national and universal character of the rules of procedure offered by arbitral institutions enables the parties to avoid the rigours of domestic adjudication, often inadequate to the demands of fast commercial exchange in the international environment (Berger, 1999).

The current renaissance of arbitration as a method of resolving international trade disputes can therefore be interpreted as a product of postmodern pragmatism (Rorty, 1982; Dickstein, 1998). International commercial arbitration has emerged to a great degree due to the grass root movement of businesspeople and as an alternative to state-regulated and formalized litigation. It serves the needs of transnational, global trade, while being based upon local and individual legitimizing grounds and deriving from the will of the parties.

In search of impartiality

Neutrality and providing equal footing among the parties throughout all of the proceedings are recognized among the most basic and rudimentary duties of an arbitrator (Gaillard and Savage, 1999). An arbitrator's status in this regard has to be reviewed in the context of the relationship between him/her and the parties, significantly different from that between the parties and a judge. In arbitration, the parties themselves determine the way of choosing an arbitrator for their case if not directly selecting the arbitrator themselves. The authority of the arbitrator derives from the will of the parties and not from an external, supreme source, as in the case of a judge.

Procedural instruments introduced to prevent biased conduct by an arbitrator resemble those known from domestic regulations in civil procedures. Once the arbitral proceedings have started, an arbitrator can be challenged by a party only if an objective doubt as to his/her impartiality or independence arises. Still, as emphasized in literature (Gaillard and Savage, 1999), if the doubt is grounded, it is a duty of an arbitrator to decline the subsequent request by the parties to resolve their case. If the proceedings have already started, an arbitrator is obliged to disclose all relevant circumstances to both parties and, in the case of an arbitration involving an institution, also to the institution and, if any of the parties objects, he or she should resign. Since a correctly issued arbitral award is as binding as a court's decision, the parties not satisfied with the ruling cannot escape liability.

An important difference between the status of a judge and of an arbitrator is that the actual occupation of the latter depends far more constantly and directly upon his or her recent professional credit, experience and knowledge. Parties to a dispute can easily avoid persons with insufficient competence or with a long history of decisions being subsequently changed as a result of appellate proceedings. An established reputation of an arbitral institution might serve as an additional assurance of the quality of the services being offered. Still, the decision upon the personal choice of an arbitrator and/or upon the method of selection is determined by the parties.

An arbitrator issues a final, binding award based upon his or her application of the law to the facts found, which distinguishes his or her role from that of a directly involved mediator (Varady *et al.*, 2002), for whom consensus is a goal to be achieved and whose proposals in this regard are not conclusive upon the parties. Still, the sources of an arbitrator's powers are purely human, not transcendent, as in litigation, since in each arbitration, it is the will of the parties that makes for a commencement of the proceedings. Impartiality is not an effect of an elevated, 'divine' position, supposedly resulting in no interest in the affairs of the mortals. For an arbitrator, neutrality is an ethical duty, but also a necessary component of his or her professional condition. It would be highly unreasonable not to meet the requirement of impartiality if one intends to be invited to another arbitration again.

Although arbitrators do not enjoy a symbolically superhuman status, their task of keeping equal footing toward all parties might often seem to require excessive powers. Balancing the procedural interests of the parties in international commercial disputes is a charge that frequently exceeds the challenges that a domestic judge typically confronts. The process of reaching a final decision to be expressed in an award has to be conducted with due respect to the diversity and integrity of the parties' legal environments. Decisions regarding the location of the arbitration, the language that will be spoken, and the admissibility of particular types of evidence – predetermined in litigation – are just a few examples of choices to be made by the arbitral tribunal with regard to providing the participants with the opportunity to present their respective claims (Frommel, 1999).

Since an arbitrator must be knowledgeable regarding the international trade customs as expressed in *lex mercatoria* regulations, and as he or she assumes the power to act as *amiable compositeur* or to decide *ex aequo et bono* if the parties have so chosen, the task of keeping equal distance is even more complex and delicate. The rules of the New Merchant Law lack state authorization. Consequently, their character of commonly accepted norms has to be evidenced, not taken for granted. Decision-making on the grounds of justice and equity, affecting parties coming from varying legal cultures, is particularly sensitive and demanding.

Not enjoying the symbolic status of the mouth of Logos, arbitrators seem to be entirely human in their undertakings. As pioneer protagonists of the concept of 'law without a state' (Teubner, 1997), they co-create a phenomenon described as emerging multicentrism of contemporary Western legal systems (Łętowska, 2005). These processes, resulting from globalization, advancement of technology, and such economic and political endeavours as European integration, do not necessarily provide an openly revolutionary change. Rather, they involve an increasing outflow of regulatory efforts that traditionally belonged to the sphere legitimized by the state.

International commercial arbitration has taken the form of a highly professionalized and efficient alternative to state administered litigation. The current renaissance of this form of dispute resolution cannot be perceived as an act of rebellion against the state's *imperium* in its legal aspect. Rather, it has been a creative and successful use of unrestrained areas of freedom left to the will of the parties. The massive scale of this activity and the establishment of common, transnational standards have been truly novel and have made the phenomenon non-reducible to separate individual endeavours.

Conclusion

The story of an arbitrator is not a Grand Narrative (Lyotard, 1979/1984). It is not titanically Promethean, as it does not involve appropriation of sacredly divine property at a tragic cost that only a superhero can pay. It is rather a micronarrative of human, private and pragmatic entrepreneurship, which can, without assuming heroic dimensions, develop profane solutions suddenly more popular than the solemn ones. Judging gods were neither killed nor expelled. They still reside on their thrones. The only difference is that people have gained a choice. They no longer have to seek relief exclusively in the form of their judgment.

An arbitrator cannot hide behind the external, supreme authority, but must demonstrate his comparative worth through recognition and the balance of diverse legal and cultural components and the facets of the case. He or she has to embrace the 'differend' (Lyotard, 1983). Although Eden, where all had their determined places, is lost, the amazing gardens of earthly delights are waiting to be discovered.

16
The Film Producer: A Scapegoat or/and a Midwife in the Film Making Process?
Marja Soila-Wadman

Introduction

Making a new film is demanding and risky for both the film director and the film producer, who hold the two leading positions in a film project. It is commonly believed that the director is responsible for the artistic/creative part of the film, whereas the producer works with administration and finances (Bordwell and Thompson, 1997). The relationship between the director and the producer is not always unproblematic, which I noticed when doing a study on leadership and organizing dynamics in a film project (Soila-Wadman, 2003).

My interest in the theme of the producer as a scapegoat in filmmaking arose when I interviewed *Film director Volcanoes X*. Inspired by ethnography and narrative practices (Czarniawska, 1997a; Van Maanen, 1988), I had previously observed *Film team X* on location during the shooting phase of *Film X*. The interview was conducted during the editing phase of the film, after the shooting phase was finished. In other words, the final film text had not yet taken form. During the entire interview I was repeatedly told how disappointed the director was with the producer's cooperation during the project. S/he accused the producer of not being professional in her/his administrative duties, and argued emphatically that s/he should never have chosen to work with this producer. For instance, s/he maintained that the producer hadn't made plans in advance for the complex situations that are likely to occur during the turbulence of film making. What made her/him particularly angry was the notion that the producer didn't care about the artistic aspects of film making:

> This producer doesn't care about the artistic spirit in the film. The person doesn't care about what it's like for the actors, not to mention

the part of the team who is there to do the artistic work. S/he just wants to get the production finished, like any other job. (*Film director Volcanoes X*, in Soila-Wadman, 2003, p. 53)[1]

The shooting phase of any film project is demanding; this project was no exception. For a director it means making hundreds of decisions throughout the process – some trivial, others of great importance – about the artistic result, the organization of the film team, and even the project's finances. Despite all of the planning before a project starts, it is impossible to predict everything. Actors in the film industry use words such as *battlefield* and *circus* to describe the turbulence that shooting can entail. It occurred to me during the interview that the director gave the producer a scapegoat role. It was the producer 'who only cared about the finances', and who was to blame when shooting and editing hadn't flowed as smoothly as the director had expected. However, when I subsequently interviewed several actors in various positions in film production, tension in the producer – director relationship was quite frequently mentioned. Claims about the producer being interested in only the finances of the project, not the artistic outcome, were repeated so often that it sounded like a ritual. 'Some film producers are like brake pads for the creative work in a film project. Others are invisible, which maybe is better' (*Film director MA, ibid.*, p. 78).

Accordingly, the aim of this chapter is to explore how the scapegoat myth can create understanding of the role of the producer in a film project and, consequently, how leadership/management in filmmaking is influenced by the important relation between the film director and the film producer. Yet the scapegoat myth explains only a part of this understanding. Therefore, I propose to explore the role of the producer as a midwife.

The scapegoat myth and its enactment through ritual

Throughout human history we have looked for something or someone to blame for all the misfortunes that befall us; through assigning blame, we are released from guilt. The scapegoat is a well-known concept that is described in different disciplines to characterize the object, people, groups, animals, etc. in this role.

In the anthropological tradition, Frazer (1913/1951) has identified several ceremonies and rites ever since ancient Greece, where it was believed that all types of economic, political, psychological and physical hardship could be avoided directly by either expelling 'the evil' from the collective, or indirectly by labelling someone/something as the scapegoat. These carriers of evil could then be destroyed or driven out of the community, taking the suffering, the evil, or the sins of the collective with them. By letting the scapegoat bear our sins we do not need to feel guilty and can deserve our feelings of justice, Perera (1986) states.

In classic Greek tradition the scapegoat myth was based on the idea of sacrifice: the god of the kingdom of the dead could be appeased by sacrifice, and the community was thereby purified of sin. Perera (*ibid.*) writes that the scapegoat is a *pharmakon*, a means by which one can become a part of the purifying force. In the ritual the scapegoat was consecrated to divinity; it was jointly identified with the god or goddess who was to be appeased. Through sacrifice, the divine powers could be persuaded to help communities that confessed their dependence on these forces. In the *Bible*, Leviticus 1–3 (1996), where several ways to conciliate God are presented, the scapegoat concept also has its roots in the ritual of sacrifice: on the great reconciliation day two goats were chosen. One of them was selected to bear the Jewish people's sins and evil deeds, which were transferred by laying hands on the head of the goat. This goat was then driven into the desert to appease Azazel, an evil demonic creature. The second goat was sacrificed as a burnt offering to God, who represented goodness.

Girard (1977/2005) discusses the double meaning of the classical Greek word *pharmakon*. It is both a poison and an antidote: 'any substance capable of perpetrating a very good or very bad action, according to the circumstances and the dosage' (Girard, 1977/2005, p. 100). On the one hand, Girard points out that the effect of the scapegoat myth and the ritual of sacrifice serves to create a frame within which the violence in a community can be structured and channelled by fixed laws; thereby, absorbing the internal tensions within the community and holding it together. On the other hand, Perera (1986) states that through the ritual of sacrifice, the evil and the dead can be combined with life and that which is good, thereby forming a coherent whole, magnificent and with a healing effect. The role of ritual in general has been to make life richer and draw attention to higher levels of existence (Douglas, 1966/2006).

Can we benefit from understanding these old myths and primitive rituals today? Hatch *et al.* (2005) argue for understanding the role of myths as an aid to understanding our world in general and our organizational world in particular. With references to Jung, they discuss the importance of myths as 'the dreams of collective unconscious'. Myths provide us with the symbolic and imaginary material, which we need when telling the stories through which we make the world comprehensible.

Douglas (1966/2006) writes that 'the ritual focuses attention by framing; it enlivens memory and links the present with the relevant past' (*ibid.*, p. 79). She states that we can look at our modern secular rites and how their symbolic enactment affects us in order to understand the mechanisms of older rituals.

Bowles (1989) maintains that modern work organizations have largely come to represent the institutions that influence our meaning making and thus how we structure our lives. He lists some secular rites and ceremonies, such as breakfast meetings, and after-hours company gatherings, as means to create desirable attitudes, values, and behaviour in a company. But he is doubtful that the organizations have succeeded in their attempts to create meaning, and argues that it is important to challenge the forms of mythology in contemporary organizations. Parallel thoughts are presented by Perera (1986), who maintains that we, surely, believe in the effectiveness of the rituals. But she wonders if we have lost contact with the source behind the individual, the realm where all human life has its origin. She criticizes our one-sided focus on worldly and material aspects, and doubts that the spiritual dimension is known to us at all. The original purpose of rituals was to connect us to the unknown. Today people believe in an almighty human being, who with help of some rites can inoculate himself against evil.

By talking about the scapegoat myth, Perera fears that it has become profane. She explains further that in Jungian terminology, appointing a scapegoat is a type of denial of the shadow that partly belongs to humans, partly to God, and is, actually, a part of life itself. Instead of seeing darkness and evil as a potential force within each one of us, we project it irresponsibly onto the other, the scapegoat, and lack the earlier conscious acts to expiate our sins.

But how is a scapegoat selected in a community? Girard (1977/2005) discusses the strict rules that guided the scapegoat ritual in earlier societies. Exploring the scapegoat mechanism in bullying in contemporary work organizations, Thylefors (1987) writes that it is not just anyone who can be made the scapegoat of a group. To be chosen, a person either has a specific role in the group, or differs in some personal, characteristic way. It is a question of interplay between the individual and the group. Inspired by an article of Brown (2002), I find Serres's (1982) concept of quasi-object useful in understanding how the scapegoat mechanism is activated in a specific group.

However, when talking about groups, one's view of human beings must be addressed. Drawing on social constructionist tradition and the relational perspective in organizing (Dachler *et al.*, 1995) I view our subjectivities as being constructed in interactive, relational processes in our world. Serres (1995) maintains that human relations emerge through stabilizing relations via things that we turn into objects (for example, a plate stabilizes eating procedures). A quasi-object is not quite a material object, but it is not a symbolic, relational phenomenon either:

> This quasi-object that is a marker of the subject is an astonishing constructer of intersubjectivity. We know, through it, how and when we are subjects and when and how we are no longer subjects. 'We' what does that mean? We are precisely the fluctuating moving back and forth of the 'I'. The 'I' in the game is a token exchanged. And this passing, this network of passes, these vicariances of subjects weave the collection. (Serres, 1982/2007, p. 227)

In the scapegoat ritual, 'owning' the quasi-object will be a kind of token, a symbolic marker. According to Serres (*ibid.*), it points out the one who the collective chooses as the victim to be sacrificed for the group. I propose that the financial aspect of filmmaking is this quasi-object. Consequently, the producer, whose role in the film team entails responsibility for the film project's finances, is chosen as scapegoat.

Ideas of art work and its organizing

After *Field study X*, my interpretations could have leaned toward identifying (negative) behavioural patterns in the work conditions of that specific film project. However, through the perspective employed in this chapter I wish to view the use of the scapegoat myth as part of the construction of the producer and director roles in a film project.

The task of a film project is to produce an aesthetic product. Therefore, some comments on the artistic/creative task and the role of the artist in filmmaking are discussed first.[2] That the art creating process is a demanding one is not an uncommon idea. The artist goes through a strenuous ordeal that finally results in some kind concrete work of art. Film projects are no exception. Deleuze and Guattari (1994) describe the art creating process as if the artist were returning from the land of the dead. In an article on arts management, Lapierre (2001) maintains that the most important thing for artists is to be true to their ideas. Then art is a means of self-fulfilment. A work of art originates from an idea that the artist wants to realize, not from market demands. Consequently, the myth of the artist as a lone, heroic genius greatly influences our beliefs (Bjurström, 1983).

However, a film is a result of several people's work. Nevertheless, it is mainly the directors who are presented in a kind of romantic hero role, just as people in leading artistic positions in the art field often are (Soila-Wadman and Köping, 2005). But can the director be viewed as 'The Author' of a specific film text, which has long been debated and discussed in film science? Bordwell and Thompson (1997) observe that the way detailed work is organized varies depending on the specific project. However, it is the director's role that comes closest to providing an overall grasp of the shooting and editing phase, where the artistic creation culminates. The director gathers the contributions of the co-actors. The director's everyday work in the turbulence of filmmaking entails navigating between the artistic ambitions, the practical organization and the financial demands of the project.

What is the role of the producer in this process? There is not much mentioned about the producers except the references to finances. How many people in an ordinary cinema audience know who produced the film, or what a producer does? After having studied some textbooks used in leading film programmes in the US, Lanz (2007) argues that textbooks present a picture in which the producer is quite neglected. Moreover, she stresses that the construction of the two leading roles in a film team, the director and the producer, are traditionally constructed dichotomously, which maintains ongoing competition between them.

The producer in the role of a scapegoat

Director Volcanoes X had lofty ambitions concerning the artistic creation of the film, and it was important for her/his sense of integrity to manage the project well. During the filmmaking process when a film is evolving, it is still in-between, and despite the script, it lacks a clear destination. Perhaps blaming the producer/finances helps the director to canalize frustrations and release stress during the problematic situations of the shooting phase and the insecurity of the editing phase. In addition to money, there is much energy and emotion invested in film projects. Viewing the producer as a scapegoat can be the *pharmakon* that holds the whole film team together in circumstances which often demand hard work and a good deal of overtime.

That the producer is chosen as scapegoat is not remarkable. The producer does not need to be on location during the filming process and does not directly participate in the creative process. Therefore, s/he is an outsider in the film team who is involved in the practical artistic creation. One of the producers I interviewed stated that the filmmaking process is very hierarchical: 'Certainly, the system has changed, but earlier it was hardly allowed for the producer to come to the shooting location' (*Producer BJ*, in Soila-Wadman, 2003, p. 75).

That the film's finances become the quasi-object, which the producer is responsible for in the team, is also understandable. Everyone in the team has a relation to the finances of the project, which in turn shapes mutual relations. Of course the practical organizing structures vary from project to project, but it is not uncommon for several team members to be freelancers. Thus they are responsible for the part of the budget concerning their own work. Aspects which have to do with finances are a continual part of the small talk and negotiations of a project as I observed during my field study: 'Is it possible to stay on location for one more day for additional takes; does the budget allow that?' 'How much does it cost to hire an extra camera?' 'Are we going to have to work overtime today?'

However, I ask if the scapegoat mechanism, by polarizing the artistic and financial realms, really is a productive one in leadership/management of film project dynamics today. As Lanz (2007) points out, the dichotomy between the director/art and the producer/finances is still maintained and reproduced in film school textbooks. Guillet de Monthoux *et al.* (2007) argue that if the art field is to survive and develop, there is a need to overcome the dichotomy in which art and the management sphere (which includes finances) are seen as two opposing fields. They propose that all of the fields that are involved when an artistic project is organized should be accepted: fields of management, administration and aesthetics. Thus it is important to develop flows between them in aesthetic leadership. Surely, the division of work practices is necessary. But in my interviews, a 'creative producer' who understands the creative process was wished for. And conversely, that the director should be aware of managerial practices, including finances, was also wished for.

A need for a new myth: the producer as a midwife

I propose viewing film making in society from an entrepreneurial perspective in its specific context in the aesthetic field (Soila-Wadman, 2007). This entails seeing the entire film making process – from the spark of an idea to the finished film – and additionally, when the film meets its audience and begins to have 'a life of its own'. Then the artistic vision and the finances, realized in the tasks and roles of the director and the producer, should not and must not be viewed as contrasts to each other.

The entire process of film making is risky, expensive and difficult to organize. The artistic creation of a film is demanding for everyone and involves the whole work team. The film producer's role in this process could be to act as a midwife and to assist in 'the passage through the realm of death'.

The midwife in Greek mythology is represented by the goddess Eleithya, who Burkert (1985) categorizes as one of the lesser gods of the Pantheon. The name Eleithya resembles the name Eleuthyia, which means *coming*. Eleithya comes when the cries and the pain of childbirth summon her. When Eleithya comes, so does the child. Perhaps *Film director Volcanoes X*'s accusations against the producer could be interpreted as this cry after Eleithya. Unfortunately, s/he didn't seem to hear and come, which perhaps activated the scapegoat mechanism.

Later in human history, midwives have periodically been compared to witches, and often with negative distinguishing features (Harley, 1990), but this area needs further exploration. However, in Pratchett's fascinating twenty-first-century book, *A Hat Full of Sky*, witches are depicted as the ones who make things happen and 'get past the "I can't" ' (2004, p. 297). They help people who live on the edge to find their way. But this requires making the hard choices that have to be made, similar to a comment from one of the directors I interviewed, who said:

> In addition to all professionalism in managing a project, I imagine that Producer BJ's way of co-operating with his directors is like a director's way to relate to the actors. He carries the directors through the practical turbulence and nuisances typical in a film project, guards them, so that they dare to take the creative leap in the unknown. (*Director MA*, in Soila-Wadman, 2003, p. 78)

Conclusion

I asked how the scapegoat myth can explain the role of the film producer, the director–producer relationship and the leadership–management question in a film project. Certainly, the role of the producer as a scapegoat can be to release the director and film team from the tensions of the artistic/creative process in filmmaking, to 'carry the sins', when the practical management and administrative problems are made the burden of the producer. There is a concept of 'the hands-on producer'.

That the finances of the project become a quasi-object, a token that labels the producer as a scapegoat, is understandable. Everyone in the project has some relation to financial matters, which can create a lot of controversy. Although the connection between the artistic result of the project and the economic matters as a part of managerial practices during the project is not a straightforward process, these aspects are nevertheless intertwined, as one of my informants stated: 'Can we afford a whole starry heaven, or only a half?' In film making aesthetic leadership, perhaps it is possible to handle the state of affairs via thorough cooperation and communication processes between the director and the producer.

Accordingly, it is important to note the double meaning of the scapegoat as the *pharmakon*, as a poison and an antidote. Instead of talking about the scapegoat in the narrow sense, when one projects her/his responsibility for the undesirable state of affairs onto someone else, a broader view which goes beyond the individual and 'puts one in contact with the gods' can be taken. Then we would perhaps view the producer in the role of the midwife, and consequently, start exploring myths for understanding the midwife role. However, I am not suggesting that changes will occur harmoniously in either the creative process or in old management/leadership traditions. As the myths remind us, the process of giving birth can be hard work for everybody involved.

Notes

1. Interviews have been translated from Swedish to English by the author.
2. Whether film is seen as art, popular culture, entertainment, etc., has long been discussed in film history (Söderbergh Widding, 1996), along the discussion about what art is (Becker, 1992). In our postindustrial world, several borders have been questioned. In this text I speak about art creating processes in film making, with inspiration from persons in film production, which means that there are so many different aspects in a film, for instance, photo, sound, story, etc., that it is difficult to say where it is art, and where it is not.

17
The Witchcraft of Professionalism: The Attractiveness of Ideal Types of Professions

Karin Jonnergård

'Granny Aching... that is, my grandmother said someone has to speak up for them as has no voices,' Tiffany volunteered after a moment. 'Was she a witch?'
'I'm not sure,' said Tiffany. 'I think so, but she didn't know she was. She mostly lived by herself in an old shepherding hut up on the downs.'...
'Good, good,' said Miss Level soothingly. 'Was she clever at medicine?' Tiffany hesitated. 'Um... only with sheep' she said, calming down. 'But she was very good. Especially if it involved turpentine, actually. But always she... was... just... there, Even when she wasn't *actually* there...'
'Oh yes', said Miss Level. 'Your Granny Aching... lived up on the downland, with the sheep, but people would look up sometimes, look up at the hills, knowing she was there somewhere, and say to themselves "What would Granny Aching do?" or "What would Granny Aching say if she found out" or "Is this the sort of thing Granny Aching would be angry about?" said Miss Level. Yes?'
Tiffany narrowed her eyes. It was true... But –
'How did you *know* that?' she said.
'Oh I guessed. She sounds like a witch to me, whatever she thought she was. A good one, too.'
Tiffany inflated with inherited pride.
'Did she help people?' Miss Level added.
The pride deflated a bite. The instant answer 'yes' jumped onto her tongue, and yet... Granny Aching hardly ever came down off the hills... But there wasn't a person on the Chalk, from the Baron down, who didn't owe something to Granny. And what they owed to her,

she made them pay to others. She always knew who was short of a favour or two.

'She made them help one another,' she said. 'She made them help themselves.'

In the silence that followed, Tiffany heard the birds singing by the road... Miss Levels sighed. 'Not many of us are *that* good.' from *A Hat Full of Sky* by Terry Pratchett, published by Doubleday; reprinted by permission of The Random House Group Ltd.

In Terry Pratchett's imaginary Discworld, witches belong to a prominent profession that exhibits most of the features usually connected with the folkloristic ideal-typical professional. She possesses knowledge impossible for a non-witch to possess; Tiffany tells us that she 'speaks up' for her clients who 'have no voice'; her incentives for engaging in her profession extend beyond profit making; and her work is dependent upon the trust and confidence of her clients. No one challenges her societal position.

This image of professions and professionals turned 'scientific' at the turn of the twentieth century, and was defined as one basis for the division of work during modernity (cf. Parsons, 1939). Today, many professionals have changed their shape and become 'knowledgeable organizational members' of knowledge-intensive organizations (Alvesson, 2001; Kärreman and Alvesson, 2004), and many new vocations are knocking on the door of professionalism, trying to gain admittance. In Swedish universities, a number of new vocational education programmes have been established and have changed their label from 'vocational education' to 'professional education', a move accompanied by various strategies from interest groups with a stake in transforming vocations into professions.

This chapter has two aims: (1) to investigate the development of the ideal-type profession(-alism) over time; and (2) to indicate how these ideal types can be combined in order to meet new demands that various interest groups are making on the liberal Swedish government, taking the 'academization' of new vocational groups as an example. I must warn the reader, however, that this is a most speculative paper – more of an essay than a proper scientific treatise presented in the name of the scientific profession.

Professions as the lackeys of modernism

The witches of the Discworld agree with our intuitive understanding of a professional, but they would not be allowed entrance into the professions of modern time. Parsons (1939), building on Durkheim's tradition, was one of the first to conceptualize the notion of 'profession'. Parsons views professionals as the source of technological and societal improvements and places strong emphasis on the importance of professions in the development of modern society. In Parsons's view, the two most salient features of a professional are 'rationality' and 'scientific knowledge'. In addition he (because the professional is a 'he' in Parsons's rendering) does not become emotionally involved with his clients; rather he maintains a relationship of functional specificity, is service-oriented, and works for the common good (cf. Brante, 1988, p. 121). Such caring vocations as witchcraft no longer fit the image of the professional.

Departing from the more cynical Weberian perception of professions, Brante (1988, pp. 129–34) outlines seven myths maintained by professionals in order to retain the status of the profession and the closure towards other groups. The first three deal with reasons for professionals to maintain their autonomy: the myths of *technocracy, increasing qualifications* and *certain knowledge*. Applying new technical knowledge is, according to these myths, the main factor in modernization, implying that technology is increasingly complicated and can be understood only by highly competent professionals. Thus professional activities can be performed and controlled only by professionals.

The next three myths deal with reasons for trusting professionals and their decision-making: the myths of *altruism, rationality* and *neutrality*. These first six myths are summarized in the seventh myth: the myth of *the hero*. As Brante writes (1988, pp. 133–4, emphasis in the original):

> Another central component of many professional ideologies stresses that professional activities concern things that are fundamentally *unknown* to the client, and that an element of *uncertainty* is always involved. Therefore the professional can act as the hero saving the client from danger by eliminating or reconstituting a threatening situation.

So the mystic still exists, but based on a division of scientific and context-dependent knowledge embodied in professionals who care for the common good rather than individuals.

Undressing the professionals: knowledge as a bits and pieces

As time passes, some of the attractiveness of modernity has faded away, although there is no agreement on whether we are entering late modernity (Giddens, 1990) or postmodernity (Bauman, 2002). There seems, however, to be agreement over the notion that scepticism over 'meta-stories' has been propagated and that the idea of *the* Science serving as the engine for developing a better world is outdated. A challenge to knowledge and science implies a questioning of the traditional definition of a profession. Abbott's (1991) article provides examples of changes in the professions and their claims on expert knowledge. Since the days of Parsons and Weber, self-employed professionals have typically acquired membership in large organizations such as hospitals or global accounting firms. Their expertise has taken various forms and is employed in three primary modes: in the professions, in organizations and in commodities. Expertise embodied in commodities has often been invented and controlled by the professions themselves. A new tendency is for more advanced expertise to be commoditized in, for example, expert systems of various types (Abbott, 1991, p. 22). Organizations contain their expertise through the encoding of knowledge and their division of labour. According to Abbott (1991, p. 25), it is organizational expertise that has recently experienced the most growth, leaving 'the esoteric and intellectual aspects of expert knowledge' for the professions (1991, p. 27). Viewing expertise in this manner, the professions may be defined through the ways they possess power over expertise in its various forms and through the way they succeed in retaining social status and closure.

More than 15 years after Abbott's (1991) observation, the growth of expert organizations continues. The Big 4 accounting firms are not only multiprofessional, but have virtually attained a global oligopoly in the market for large corporate auditing. The same is true for the large law firms and computer companies. In the scientific discourse of business administration, professions are hardly ever the objects of research. Instead the focus is on 'knowledge-intensive organizations' (Alvesson, 2001; Alvesson and Kärreman, 2004) or 'professional service organizations' (see, special issues in *Human Relations*, 2001, and *Journal of Behavioral Studies*, 2007). From an ostensive perspective, this move into the organization is conceptualized in the development of organizational ideal types such as the traditional professional partnership, P^2 (Greenwood *et al.*, 1990); the managerial-dominated professional organization, Managerial Professional Business (MPB) (Cooper *et al.*, 1996); and the Global Professional Network (GPN) (Brock, 2006). These ideal types are all experiencing decreasing influence over activities from the professional side and increasing globalization in the realm of business.

Although in areas such as sociology, the profession and the professionals still seem to be accurate categories, within the academic area of business administration, the professionals seem to be well-integrated organizational members and the features of professions are de-emphasized. Expertise is a property of and realized through the organization, whatever form it takes. Within the private sector, the profession became a category subordinate to the organization and the concept of professionalism gained new connotations. Development within the public sector is not as obvious, but probably similar. The reforms connected to New Public Management (NPM) (Hood, 1991) have been interpreted as one way of constructing organizations (Brunsson and Sahlin-Andersson, 2000). Before the NPM, hospitals could be seen as arenas where different groups – the professionals, such as physicians; the semi-professionals, such as nurses; people in vocations, such as administrators – met under relative equality while performing their respective tasks independent of each other. The new public reforms implied a more organization-like way of organizing; however, including a common identity for all employees, a common hierarchy and an organizational rationality. As Brunsson and Sahlin-Andersson (2000, p. 726) claim:

> Co-operation and co-ordination within hospital clinics, municipal offices or state authorities have been reinforced, while spontaneous co-operation among individual professionals representing different units is no longer encouraged... The idea is that the internal teams should be guided by organizational policies rather than by central rules of professional norms. This also means that any achievements are attributed to the unit as a whole. Achievements at many universities, for instance, are increasingly attributed not only to the individual researchers, but to the unit, the university or research institute.

The ideal type of profession in late modernity entails a transformation of professional knowledge from a personal capacity developed over the lifespan to a property possible for an organization to organize and utilize in manifold ways. The hero we remember from modernity is exchanged for the heroic organization to which we connect both knowledge and status.[1] It is our expectation that organizations care for the will of their principals (according to agency theory, cf. Fama, 1980); for their primary stakeholders (according to stakeholder theory, cf. Jones, 1995); or for their own survival (cf. Barnard, 1938); but more rarely for the common good, as the professionals of the modernity did.

Late modernity and the use of professionalism

Stripped of their knowledge and left with questionable status, what would become of the noble professionals? First and foremost: professional conduct. The professional within an organization is, like any other employee, subject to discipline. The most practical resolution would be to build upon what is already there: in this case, the discourse of professionalism (Aldrige and Evetts, 2003; Grey, 1997). Professional conduct implies the application of a behaviour that retains trust in the professionals' superior expertise and the appropriateness of professional autonomy. To achieve such trust, the profession is forced to exert discipline. Or, viewed in another way, one could say that in order to gain legitimacy, the profession must demonstrate professional competence that is dependent not only upon knowledge, but upon personal conduct and control over the practice.

The disciplinary logic of professionalism has been shown to be a most effective software for organizational control in project management (Hodgson, 2005), large accounting firms (Anderson-Gogh et al., 2000; 2005; Grey, 1998) and knowledge-intensive firms (Fournier, 1999), for example. Here the professionalism serves to: ' "responsibilise" autonomy by delineating the "competence" of the "professional employee", by instilling "professional like" norms and work ethics which govern not simply productive behaviour but more fundamentally employees' subjectivities...' (Fournier, 1999, p. 293). Disciplinary logic applies to professional groups both outside (see Aldrige and Evetts, 2003) and inside the organization. In addition it may apply to new occupational groups. Fournier (1999, p. 293) continues:

> We can here establish a parallel between the disciplinary logic of professionalism as a way of regulating the autonomous conduct of professions, and the extension of professional discourse to new occupational domains to regulate the increased margin of indeterminacy created by the introduction of flexibility and emotionalisation of work.

A new ideal type takes its form from professional conduct, norms and work ethics, and the emotionalization of work – not ruled not by the autonomous professional, however, but by the (self-)disciplinary vocations.

Letting the witches back in

It is time to return to the second aim of this chapter: to suggest how the ideal types of profession(-alism) can be combined in order to satisfy the demands of various interest groups on the 'academization' of new vocational groups in Sweden. The vocational groups that make these claims are primarily in the social welfare sector. They are, among others, nurses, social workers, and school teachers – groups that were previously defined as semi-professionals. In Sweden these are typically lower-middle-class vocations, with large work loads and relatively low pay. In previous times, people in these vocations were educated in special colleges but today their programmes have been moved into the university and have been reconstructed as scientific courses of study.

To understand this development, we need to comprehend the complexity of the phenomenon of profession. Following the Swedish sociologist, Asplund (1979),[2] profession as a social phenomenon may be thought of as one 'figure of thought' that acts as an intermediary between the material basis and the discursive level of our society. 'Figures of thought' are institutionalized, in the sense that we cannot think about the world without them. Asplund (1979) used the concept of childhood as an example; it is difficult for us to imagine a world without childhood. Yet Ariès (1973) has shown that the very idea of childhood is a relatively recent social construction. Figures of thought, therefore, have the ordinary features of an institution; i.e., social constructions that are taken for granted over time (cf. Berger and Luckmann, 1966/1991), yet they can elude our understanding of institutions as taken for granted, because they can take several shapes over time or many shapes at one time. Figures of thought are complex, and may include a number of aspects that are sometimes incongruous. At different times, various aspects of a specific figure of thought may be emphasized in societal discourse, but as long as the figure of thought continues to be a part of the societal institutions, other aspects may pop up or be developed, and the discourse may change.

In this short narration about the ideal types of profession, we can catch a glimpse of the figure of thought in professions. Over time we have defined four ideal types: the folkloristic, the modern, the late modernity and the disciplinary. Table 17.1 summarizes some of their features.

As can be seen in Table 17.1, the four ideal types differ in their nuances and composition. This implies that, even though some of the ideal types may be perceived as outdated, there is a palette of features that may be used in constructing a professional that suits the specific situation.

Table 17.1 Ideal types built upon the 'profession(-alism)' figure of thought

	Folkloristic/ the witches	Modernity/ the scientific hero	Late modernity/ organizational man	Disciplinary/ the caretaker
Societal position	Independent, high social status	Independent, high social status	Organizational, varied social status	Varied
Concept of knowledge	Discretionary Experience-based Mythical	Discretionary Based on science and experience	Possible to dissect and utilize in different form Based on science	Experience Possible to influence
Carrier of knowledge	The professional	The professional	Commodity Organization People	Organization People
Base for autonomy	Tradition Superior knowledge	Superior knowledge	Esoteric and intellectual aspects of expert knowledge	Work tasks impossible to measure or give detailed instructions for
Working for...	The client	Common good	Organization	Organization
In the mode	Personal involvement	Detached	Organizational loyalty	Personal involvement
Ethics	Traditional	Professional norms	Organizational rules	Professional conduct
Legitimacy	Traditional Based on conduct	Knowledge Based on conduct	Organizational- and knowledge-based	Based on conduct

Some of the features may be experienced as more 'attractive' than others: the claim for high social status, superior knowledge and different forms of autonomy, for example. By attaching these features (or the hope of these features) to certain vocational groups, professionalization becomes a desired path for the vocation. In addition, a choice may be made about whom to work for, mode of working, and so on.

The transformation of vocational groups into 'professionals' in the Swedish university system is, to a large degree, a political process that has been supported – not only by the professions, but by the state, various national boards, expert organizations and the universities. In this respect, professionalization may be viewed as a programme of government (Rose and Miller, 1992) rather than a search for power and monopoly from the vocational groups (e.g., Freidson, 1986; Larson, 1977). This implies that professionalization – at least partly – is a way of accessing a societal problem to assure governmentality. It further indicates the presence of several parties with interests in the process. I have not undertaken a complete analysis of the process here, but provide examples by discussing three of the aspects in Table 17.1 to indicate the attractiveness of the figure of thought of professions, and how the different ideal types may be blended to construct a desired 'professional'.

The attractiveness of status

One main advantage of being a professional is the status that the role has traditionally given to those who can carry the title. This might have been true for some of the vocational groups that now go through 'professionalizing university education', but may not be for all of them. Many of these vocations are female-dominated and involve low-paid work; and the public sector, in which many of these vocations are concentrated, is seen as conferring lower status than the public sector does. Thus to professionalize a vocation may lower the status of the concept of profession rather than raise the status of the vocation. On the other hand, the label of 'professional' education may raise the status of the educational institutions that provide education for these vocations. This re-labelling of vocational education moves it into the university sector, where the coded practice has long been to undertake research in all academic areas. This would suggest that moving vocational education into the university would be as great a gain for the university as it would be for the vocation, giving higher status to the former colleges and a wider field for scientific research.

The attractiveness of scientific knowledge

Being a professional most often implies that the work is built upon scientific knowledge. Part of the professionalization process is, therefore, to translate scientific knowledge into practice. In vocations such as nursing and social work, this has implied an attempt to build the work on evidence-based routines or quality assurance systems. Besides putting 'science into action', routines are established for ways to act in various situations, and the behaviour of professionals has become standardized and predictable (cf. Kurunmäki and Miller, 2006). It also implies that at least some aspects of performance become measurable, and thereby governable. In this way, putting 'science into action' may not only support the professionalization of vocational groups, but may also make it easier for the political establishment and bureaucracy to control them.

The attractiveness of mode of involvement

To be professional implies a specific relationship with clients. In Table 17.1, this notion is labeled 'mode of involvement', and the nuances range from involvement with the client to more detached approaches. My speculation – and this is the most speculative part of this chapter – is that the professionalization of the new vocations is part of the emotionalization of work that Fournier (1999) talks about in the quote about responsibilizing autonomy. Most of the vocations in question (especially social workers) handle difficult situations and vulnerable people. By including 'personal involvement' as part of the definition of the professional role, the same effect may be reached as for Pratchett's witches: speaking up for clients who have no voice and being perceived as successful when helping people to help themselves. This way of attaching accountability for the client to the professional is one strong ingredient of the disciplinary logic of professions. It may actually oppose the detached mode that may be a negative consequence of the routinization of behaviour that lies implicit in imposing evidence-based work processes. Thus the professional became controlled from the bureaucracy, but accountable to the clients.

If my speculations hold true, two valid observations have been made. First, in constructing the label of professional for new vocational groups, bits and pieces from various ideal types are brought together. The scientific approach from modernity is combined with the mode of involvement from the folkloristic ideal type. Had we continued the previous analysis, we would probably have added the ethics of the late modernity and the legitimacy processes of the disciplinary logic to the construction, for example. The figure of thought remains, but allows for various interpretations over time. The second observation is that labelling the new vocations as professional may be interpreted as an expression of the liberal state, including the manifold interests and ambitions of government and the professions. In the speculations put forth in this chapter, I have identified the universities, the state and the bureaucracy as three parties that share the interests of vocational groups. This implies a process of professionalization (or a labelling as professionals) initiated less by the vocational groups than by other interested parties. This process differs from the processes of professionalization described by researchers during modernity (cf. Freidson, 1986; Larson, 1977), when the professions' own striving for status and labour market monopoly were the main driving forces. The label, profession, thereby goes from being a desired state for the professional to a way for people other than professionals to resolve societal problems and organize the workforce.

So what has happened to the witches? Have we dismissed these proud and independent carriers of knowledge in exchange for poor, governable creatures, sentenced to never-ending self-disciplinary routines? We don't know. Practice will show. In putting their educational skills and codes of conduct into practice, the new 'professions' – just like the old ones – still have the freedom to utilize all aspects of the figure of thought of 'profession'. If they want to, they may let the witches return, irrespective of the proper ideal type or the thoughts of a scientist in business administration.

Notes

1. And people we meet at parents' meetings at school or at the children's football club proudly introduce themselves as 'a member of Sony Ericson development team' or 'the head of the surgery department at the University hospital' – not as an engineer or a surgeon.
2. Johan Asplund, the first professor of social psychology in Sweden, has had substantial influence over the development of social sciences in Sweden. He decided early in his career to write only in Swedish and not to have his work translated into other languages, because he believed that Swedish was the only language in which he truly could express himself. I believe that the social sciences have suffered a great loss because of this decision, but given the beauty of his writing and complexity of his theories, he might have been right.

Bibliography

Aaltio, I. and Hiillos, M. (2003) The Uniting Mother and the Body of the Organization. In Höpfl, H. and Kostera, M. (eds), *Interpreting the Maternal Organization*. London: Routledge, pp. 27–46.

Aaltio, I. and Takala, T. (2003) *Charismatic Leadership and Ethics from Gender Perspective*. Reykjavik: Proceedings in the 17th Nordic Conference on Business Studies, 14–16 August, Iceland.

Abbott, A. (1991) The Future of Professions: Occupation and Expertise in the Age of Organization. *Research in Sociology of Organization*, 8, pp. 17–42.

Ahl, H. (2002) *The Making of the Female Entrepreneur: A Discourse Analysis of Research Texts on Women's Entrepreneurship*. Jönköping: Jönköping International Business School.

Ahmed, S. (1996) Construction of Women and/in the Orient. In Consslett, T., Easton, A. and Summerfield, P. (eds), *Women, Power and Resistance: An Introduction to Women's Studies*. Buckingham and Philadelphia: Open Univ. Press, pp. 136–49.

Aldrige, M. and Evetts, J. (2003) Rethinking the Concept of Professionalism: The Case of Journalism. *British Journal of Sociology*, 54/4, pp. 547–64.

Ali, T. (1985) *The Nehrus and the Gandhis: an Indian dynasty*. London: Pan Books.

Alvesson, M. (2001) Knowledge Work: Ambiguity, Image and Identity. *Human Relations*, 54/7, pp. 863–87.

Ambjörnsson, R. (1999) *Mansmyter: James Bond, Don Juan, Tarzan och andra grabbar*. (*Male Myths: James Bond, Don Juan, Tarzan and Other Guys*). Stockholm: Ordfront.

American dream (n.d.). *The American Heritage® Dictionary of the English Language, Fourth Edition*. Retrieved on 17 February 2007 from: http://www.answers.com/topic/american-dream

Anderson-Gough, F., Grey, C. and Robson, K. (2000) In the Name of the Client: The Service Ethic in Two Professional Service Firms. *Human Relations*, 53/9, pp. 1151–74.

Anderson-Gough, F., Grey, C. and Robson, K. (2005) 'Helping them to forget' – Organizational Embedding of Gender Relations in Multi-national Audit Firms. *Accounting, Organizations and Society*, 30, pp. 469–90.

anniewalker (2006) William Roache Never Wanted the Role of Ken Barlow in the First Place. Retrieved on 8 April 2007 from http://www.soapchat.net

Anonim, (Gall) (1989) *Kronika polska* (*Polish Chronicle*). Wrocław: Ossolineum, Wrocław.

Antonacopoulou, E.P. (2004a) On the Virtues of *Practising* Scholarship: A Tribute to Chris Argyris a 'Timeless Learner'. Special issue 'From Chris Argyris and Beyond in Organizational Learning Research', *Management Learning*, 35/4, pp. 381–95.

Antonacopoulou, E.P. (2004b) The Dynamics of Reflexive Practice: The Relationship between Learning and Changing. In Reynolds M. and Vince R. (eds), *Organizing Reflection*, London: Ashgate, pp. 47–64.

Antonacopoulou, E.P. (2006) Working Life Learning: Learning-in-practise. In Antonacopoulou, E.P., Jarvis, P., Andersen, V., Elkjaer, B. and Hoeyrup, S. (eds), *Learning, Working and Living: Mapping the Terrain of Working Life Learning*. Basingstoke: Palgrave, pp. 234–54.

Antonacopoulou, E.P. and Bento R. (2003) Methods of 'Learning Leadership': Taught and Experiential. In Storey, J. (ed.), *Current Issues in Leadership and Management Development*. Oxford: Blackwell, pp. 81–102.

Ariès, P. (1973) *Centuries of Childhood*. Harmondsworth, Middlesex: Penguin.

Armstrong, K. (2005/2006) *A Short History of Myth*. Edinburgh: Canongate.

Arvidsson, A. (2005) *Vladimir Propp's Fairy Tale Morphology and Game Studies*. Retrevied on 15 October 2006 from http://www.umu.se/kultmed/forskning/Propp1.pdf

Asplund, J. (1979) *Teorier om framtiden*. Stockholm: Kontenta, LiberFörlag.

Banasiak, B. (1993) Na tropach dekonstrukcji. In Banasiak, B. (ed.), *Pismo filozofii (Selected essays by Jacques Derrida)*. Kraków: inter esse.

Barnard, C.I. (1938) *The function of the executive*. Cambridge, MA: Harvard University Press.

Barthes, R. (1957/1973) *Mythologies*. London: Paladin.

Barthes, R. (1978) *Image-Music-Text*. New York: Hill & Wang.

Barthes, R. (1982) Myth Today. In Barthes, R., *Selected writings*. New York: Hill & Wang.

Bauman, Z. (2002) *Det indvidualiserade samhället (The Individualized Society)*. (trans. Torhell, S.E.) Göteborg: Daidalos.

Bauman, Z. (2005) *Liquid Life*. Cambridge: Polity Press.

Beckett, D. (2004) Acting with Things: Distributed Agency and Practical Judgement. Paper presented at the *33rd Annual Conference of the Philosophy of Education Society of Australasia*, Fitzroy, Melbourne: Australian Catholic University.

Becker, H. (1982) *Art Worlds*. Los Angeles: University of California Press.

Belasco, D. (1900) *Madame Butterfly* (theatrical play).

Bellah, R.N., Madsen, R., Sullivan, W.M., Swidler, A. and Tipton, S.M. (1985/1996) *Habits of the Heart: Individualism and Commitment in American Life*. Berkley–Los Angeles: University of California Press.

Berger, K.P. (1999) *The Creeping Codification of the Lex mercatoria*. The Hague–London–Boston: Kluwer Law International.

Berger, K.P. (2001) The New Law Merchant and the Global Market Place: A 21st Century View of Transnational Commercial Law. In Berger, K.P. (ed.), *The Practice of Transnational Law*. The Hague–London–Boston: Kluwer Law International.

Berger, P.L. (1973) *The Social Reality of Religion*. London: Penguin Books.

Berger, P.L. and Luckmann, T. (1966/1991) *The Social Construction of Reality*. London: Penguin Books.

Bettelheim, B. (1976) *The Uses of Enchantment: The Meaning and Importance of Fairytales*. Knopf.

Bhattacharji, S. (1995) *Mother Goddesses of Calcutta*. Calcutta: K.P. Bagchi.

Biblia: Pismo Święte Starego i Nowego Testamentu (The Bible). (1975) Warszawa: Brytyjskie i Zagraniczne Towarzystwo Biblijne.

Biermann, W. (1995) Man musste ein König der Improvisation sein. In Pirker, T., Lepsius, M.R. and Weinert, R. (eds), *Der Plan als Befehl und Fiktion – Wirtschaftsführung in der DDR*. Opladen: Westdeutscher Verlag.

Bjurström, P. (1985) (ed.) *Myter*. (*Myths*) Utställningskatalog nr 470. Stockholm: Nationalmuseum.
Błaszczyk, D. (2005) Koncepcje starej Europy i wielkiej bogini w archeomitologii Mariji Gimbutas. (The Old Europe and Great Goddes in the Archeomythology of Marija Gimbutas). In Pakszys, E. (ed.), *Międzykulturowe i interdyscyplinarne badania feministyczne. Daleki – Bliski Wschód: Współczesność i prehistoria. (Crosscultural and Interdisciplinary Feminist Research: Far to Near East: Contemporary and Prehistory)*. Poznań: UAM, pp. 259–84.
Blau, J.R. (1984) *Architects and Firms: A Sociological Perspective on Architectural Practice*. Cambridge: The MIT Press.
Blau, J.R. and McKinley, W. (1979) Ideas, Complexity and Innovation. *Administrative Science Quarterly*, 24, pp. 200–19.
Bloom, S.S., Wypij, D. and Gupta M.D. (2001) Dimensions of Women's Autonomy and the Influence on Maternal Health Care Utilisation in a North Indian City. *Demography*, 38/1, pp. 67–8.
Boa, F. (1994) *The Way of Myth: Talking with Joseph Campbell*. Boston–London: Shambhala.
Bogucka M. (1998) *Białogłowa w dawnej Polsce: Kobieta w społeczeństwie polskim XVI–XVIII wieku na tle porównawczym*. (*Lady in Old Poland: Woman in Polish Society of 16–18th Century against Comparative Background*.) Warszawa: Trio.
Boje, D. (1991) The Storytelling Organization: A Study of Story Performance in an Office Supply Firm. *Administrative Science Quarterly*, 36/1, pp. 106–26.
Boje, D.M. (2001) *Narrative Methods for Organization Research and Communication Research*. London–Thousand Oaks–New Delhi: Sage.
Bordwell, D. and Thompson, K. (1997) *Film Art, an Introduction*, New York: The McGraw-Hill Co.
Born, G.B. (2001) *International Commercial Arbitration: Commentary and Materials*. The Hague–Boston: Kluwer Law International.
Bourdieu, P. (2005) *The Economic Structures of Society*. Cambridge: Polity Press.
Bourdieu, P. (1999) *Praktiskt förnuft. Bidrag till en handlingsteori*. Daidalos, Göteborg.
Bowles, M.L. (1989) Myth, Meaning and Work Organization. *Organization Studies*, 10/3, pp. 405–21.
Bowles, M.L. (1993) The Gods and Goddesses: Personifying Social Life in the Age of Organization. *Organization Studies*, 14/3, pp. 395–418.
Bowles, M.L. (1997) The Myth of Management: Direction and Failure in Contemporary Organizations. *Human Relations*, 50/7, pp. 770–803.
Brague, R. (2007) *The Law of God: The Philosophical History of an Idea*. (trans. Cochrane, L.G.) Chicago: University of Chicago Press.
Brante, T. (1988) Sociological Approaches to the Professions. *Acta Sociologica*, 31/2, pp. 119–42.
Brock, D.M. (2006) The Changing Professional Organization: A Review of Competing Archetypes. *International Journal of Management Review*, 8/3, pp. 157–74.
Browarczyk, M. (2005) Wybrane aspekty sytuacji kobiet w Indiach współczesnych. (Selected aspects of the situation of women in contemporary India). In Pakszys, E. (ed.), *Międzykulturowe i interdyscyplinarne badania feministyczne. Daleki – Bliski Wschód: Współczesność i prehistoria. (Crosscultural and Interdisciplinary Feminist Research: Far to Near East: Contemporary and Prehistory)*. Poznań: UAM, pp. 65–98.

Brown, R.H. (ed.) (1998) *Toward a Democratic Science: Scientific Narration and Civic Communication*. Yale: Yale University Press.
Brown, S.D. (2002) Michel Serres: Science, Translation and the Logic of the Parasite. *Theory, Culture & Society*, 19/3, pp. 1–27.
Bruni, A., Gherardi, S. and Poggio, B. (2005) *Gender and Entrepreneurship: An Ethnographical Approach*. London: Routledge.
Brunsson, N. and Sahlin-Andersson, K. (2000) Constructing Organizations: The Example of Public Sector Reform. *Organization Studies*, 21/4, pp. 721–47.
Bryman, A. (1992) *Leadership and Charisma in Organizations*. London–Newbury–New Delhi: Sage.
Burkert, W. (1985) *Greek Religion*. Cambridge, MA: Harvard University Press.
Burrell, G. and Morgan, G. (1979/1994) *Social Paradigms and Organisational Analysis: Elements of the Sociology of Corporate Life*. Aldershot–Brookfield: Arena.
Butler, J. (1991) 'I'm Not a Doctor, but I Play One on TV': Characters, Actors, and Acting in Television Soap Opera. *Cinema Journal*, 30/4, pp. 75–91.
Campbell, J. (1949/1993) *The Hero with a Thousand Faces*. New Jersey: Princeton University Press.
Campbell, J. (1972/1988a) *Myths to Live by: How We Recreate Ancient Legends in Our Daily Lives to Release Human Potential*. New York–Toronto–Sydney–Auckland: Bantam Books.
Campbell, J. (1972/1988b) *The Inner Reaches of Outer Space: Metaphor as Myth and as Religion*. New York–Cambridge–Philadelphia–San Fransisco–London–Mexico City–Sao Paolo–Singapore–Sydney: Harper and Row.
Campbell, J. (2004) *Pathways to Bliss: Mythology and Personal Transformation*. Novato: New World Library.
Campbell, J. with Moyers, B. (1988) *The Power of Myth*. Flowers, B.S. (ed.) New York–London–Toronto–Sydney–Auckland: Doubleday.
Caraker, M. (1996) *Women of the Kalevala: Stories Based on the Great Finnish Epic*. St. Cloud: North Star Press of St. Cloud.
Carbonneau, Th. (1990) The Remaking of Arbitration: Design and Destiny. In Carbonneau, T. (ed.), *Lex Mercatoria and Arbitration*. New York: Dobbs Ferry Transnational Juris Publications, pp. 23–41.
Carlsen, A. (2006) Organizational Becoming as Dialogic Imagination of Practice: The Case of the Indomitable Gauls. *Organization Science*, 17/1, pp. 132–49.
Cascio, W. (1993) Downsizing: What Do We Know? What Have We Learned? *Academy of Management Executive*, 7/1, pp. 95–101.
Cassirer, E. (1946) *Language and Myth* (trans. Langer, S.). New York: Dover.
Cassirer, E. (1955) *The Philosophy of Symbolic Forms*. vol. 2: *Mythical Thought*. New Haven–London: Yale University Press.
CBOS (1999) *Prestiz zawodów: Komunikat nr 2086 issued 3/3/1999*. Retrieved on 13 April 2006 from: www.cbos.pl
CfK (2006) Nie lubimy prywaciarzy. *CfK report for Rzeczpospolita*. Retrieved on 20 February 2006 from: http://media.wp.pl/kat,38146,wid,8194053,wiadomosc.html?ticaid=1143a
Clark, J.M. (1950) *The Dance of Death in the Middle Ages and Renaissance*. Glasgow: Jackson.
Coetzee, J.M. (2003) *Disgrace (Hańba)*. Kraków: Znak.

Cohen L. and Mallon M. (1999) The Transition from Organizational Employment to Portfolio Working: Perceptions of 'Boundarylessness'. *Work, Employment and Society*, 13/2, pp. 329–52.
Conger, J.A. and Kanungo, R.N. (1987) Toward a Behavioral Theory of Charismatic Leadership in Organizational Settings. *Academy of Management Review*, 12/4, pp. 637–47.
Cooper, D., Hinnings, B., Greenwood, R. and Brown, J.L. (1996) Sedimentation and Transformation in Organizational Change: The Case of the Canadian Law Firms. *Organization Studies*, 17/4, pp. 623–47.
Cooper, J.C., (2004) *An Illustrated Encyclopaedia of Traditional Symbols*. London: Thames & Hudson.
Corrie Blog (2006) *William Roache Reports no Plans to Retire*. Retrieved on 7 April 2007 from http://www.corrieblog.tv/2006/12/william_roache_.html
Corvellec, H. (2006) *Elements of Narrative Analysis*. Gothenburg: Gothenburg Research Institute.
Cronenberg, D. (1993) *M. Butterfly* (film by Geffen Pictures)
Crossan, M., Lane, H., White, R. and Klus L. (1996) The Improvising Organization: Where Planning Meets Opportunity. *Organizational Dynamics*, 24/4, pp. 20–35.
Cuff, D. (1991) *Architecture: The Story of Practice*. Cambridge: MIT Press.
Cullen, J.P. (2003) *American Dream: A Short History of an Idea that Shaped a Nation*. Cary: Oxford University Press.
Czarniawska, B. (1997a) *Narrating the Organization: Dramas of Institutional Identity*. Chicago: The University of Chicago Press.
Czarniawska, B. (1997b) *A Narrative Approach to Organization Studies*. London–New Delhi: Sage.
Czarniawska, B. (2004a) *Narratives in Social Science Research*. Thousand Oaks–London–New Delhi: Sage.
Czarniawska, B. (2004b) The Uses of Narrative in Social Science Research. In Hardy, M. and Bryman, A. (eds), *Handbook of Data Analysis*. London: Sage, pp. 649–66.
Czarniawska, B. and Calás, M. (1998) Another Country: Explaining Gender Discrimination with 'Culture'. *Administrative Studies*, 4, pp. 326–41.
Czarniawska, B. and Guillet de Monthoux, P. (1994) *Good Novels, Better Management: Reading Organizational Realities*. London: Routledge.
Dabrowska D. (2004) *Udomowiony świat: O kobiecym doświadczaniu historii*. (*The Domesticated World: On the Way Women Experienced History*). Szczecin: Wyd. Uniw. w Szczecinie.
Dachler, H.P., Gergen, K.J. and Hosking, D.-M. (eds) (1995) *Management and Organization: Relational Alternatives to Individualism*. Aldershot: Avebury.
Dallapiccola, A.L. (2003) *Hindu Myths*. Austin: University of Texas Press.
Dandridge, T.C., Mitroff, I. and Joyce, W.F. (1980) Organisational Symbolism: A Topic to Expand Organisational Analysis. *The Academy of Management Review*, 5/1, pp. 77–82.
De Ly, F. (1992) *International Business Law and Lex Mercatoria*. The Hague: T.M.C. Asser Instituut.
Deleuze, G. (1994) *Difference and Repetition*. London: Continuum.
Deleuze, G. and Guattari, F. (1994) *What is Philosophy?* London: Verso.

Deutsche Literaturgesischte (1905) *Bibliothek des allgemeinen und praktischen Wissens. Bd. 5*, p. 60, online image, copyright expired, Retrieved on 1 April 2007 from http://en.wikipedia.org/wiki/Image:Till_Eulenspiegel.jpg

Dickstein, M. (1998) *The Revival of Pragmatism: New Essays on Social Thought, Law, and Culture* (*Post-Contemporary Interventions*). Durham: Duke University Press.

Ditchev, I. (2002) The Eros of Identity. In *Balkan as Metaphor: Between Globalization and Fragmentation*. London: MIT Press, pp. 235–50.

Dobosz, D. and Jankowicz, A.D (2002) Knowledge Transfer of the Western Concept of Quality. *Human Resource Development International*, 5/3, pp. 353–67.

Douglas, M. (1963/1999) The Meaning of Myth. In *Implicit Meanings: Selected Essays in Anthropology*. London–New York: Routledge, pp. 131–45.

Douglas, M. (1966/2006) *Purity and Danger*. London: Routledge.

Dourish, P. (2001) *Where the Action Is: The Foundations of Embodied Interaction*. Cambridge: MIT Press.

Drahozal, Ch.R. and Naimark, R.W. (eds) (2005) *Towards a Science of International Arbitration: Collected Empirical Research*. The Hague–Boston: Kluwer Law International.

Dubin, R. (1970) Management in Britain: Impressions of a Visiting Professor. *Journal of Management Studies*, 7/2, pp. 184–98.

Durkheim, E. (1895/1938) *The Rules of Sociological Method*. Glencoe: Free Press.

Eliade, M. (1961) *The Sacred and the Profane: The Nature of Religion*. New York: Harper and Row.

Eliade, M. (1963/1998) *Aspekty mitu*. (*Myth and Reality*). (trans. Mrówczynski, P.) Warszawa: KR.

Empson, L. (ed.) (2001) Knowledge Management in Professional Service Firms. *Human Relations*, 54/7, pp. 811–963.

Eskridge, W.N., Frickey Ph.P. and Garrett, E. (2000) *Legislation and Statutory Interpretation*. New York: Foundation Press.

Fama, E.F. (1980) Agency Problems and the Theory of the Firm. *Journal of Political Economy*, 88, pp. 288–307.

Feldman, M.S. and Skölberg, K. (2002) Stories and the Rhetoric of Contrariety: Subtexts of Organizing (Change). *Culture and Organization*, 8/4, pp. 275–92.

Finkel, I.L. and Geller, M.J. (eds) (1997), *Sumerian Gods and their Representations*. Groningen: STYX Publications.

Fisher, W.R. (1987) *Human Communication as Narration: Toward a Philosophy of Reason, Value, and Action*. Columbia: The University of South Carolina Press.

Forbes, G. (1980) Goddesses or Rebels? The Women Revolutionaries of Bengal. *The Oracle*, 2/2, pp. 1–18.

Fournier, V. (1999) The Appeal to 'Professionalism' as a Disciplinary Mechanism. *Sociological Review*, 47/2, pp. 280–308.

Frazer, J.G. (1913/1951) *The Golden Bough: A Study in Magic and Religion. The Scapegoat*. Basingstoke: Palgrave Macmillan.

Freidson, E. (1986) *Professional Powers: A Study of the Institutionalization of Formal Knowledge*. Chicago: The University of Chicago Press.

Freidson, E. (2001) *Professionalism: The Third Logic*. Chicago: The University of Chicago Press.

Freud, S. (1963) *Civilization and its Discontents*. London: Hogarth Press.

Frommel, S.N. (ed.) (1999) *Conflicting Legal Cultures in Commercial Arbitration: Old Issues and New Trends*. The Hague: Kluwer.

Frye, N. (1990) Literary and Linguistic Scholarship in a Postliterate World. In Denham, R.D. (ed.), *Myth and Metaphor: Selected Essays 1974–1988*. Charlottesville: University Press of Virginia.
Furusten, S. (1992) *Management Books: Guardians of the Myth of Leadership*. Uppsala: Uppsala University.
Furusten, S. (1995) *The Managerial Discourse: A Study of the Creation and Diffusion of Popular Management Knowledge*. Uppsala: Uppsala University.
Gabriel, Y. (2000) *Storytelling in Organizations: Facts, Fictions and Fantasies*. Oxford: Oxford University Press.
Gabriel, Y. (2004a) (ed.) *Myths, Stories and Organizations: Premodern Narratives for our Times*. Oxford: Oxford University Press.
Gabriel, Y. (2004b) Introduction. In Gabriel, Y. (ed.), *Myths, Stories and Organizations: Premodern Narratives for Our Times*. Oxford: Oxford University Press, pp. 1–10.
Gaillard, E. and Savage, J. (eds) (1999) *Fouchard Gaillard Goldman on International Commercial Arbitration*. The Hague-Boston: Kluwer Law International.
Garratt, R. (1990) *The Learning Organisation*. London: Fontana/Collins.
Gartner, W.G., Bird, B.J. and Starr, J.A. (1992) Acting As If: Differentiating Entrepreneurial Behaviour from Organizational Behaviour. *Entrepreneurship Theory and Practice*, 16/3, pp. 13–30.
Gaustadt, J.M. and Vogdes, W. (1998/1999) Till Eulenspiegel – The Merry Prankster, Prosit. Retrieved on 1 January 2007 from http://www.steincollectors.org/library/articles/Eulenspiegel/Eulenspiegel.html
Geertz, C. (1973) *The Interpretation of Cultures*. New York: Basic Books.
Gehlen, A. (1940) *Der Mensch. Seine Natur und seine Stellung in der Welt*. (*Man, His Nature and Place in the World*). Berlin: Junker & Dünnhaupt.
Gemmill, G. and Oakley, J. (1992) Leadership: An Alienating Social Myth. *Human Relations*, 45/2, pp. 113–29.
Gherardi, S. (1995) *Gender, Symbolism, and Organizational Culture*. London–Newbury Park–New Delhi: Sage.
Ghosh, A. (2000) Spaces of Recognition: Puja and Power in Contemporary Calcutta. *Journal of South African Studies*, 26/2, pp. 289–99.
Giddens, A. (1990) *The Consequences of Modernity*, Cambridge: Polity.
Giddens, A. (1996) Affluence, Poverty and the Idea of a Post-Scarcity Society. *Development and Change*, 27, pp. 365–77.
Giddens, A. (1999) *Runaway World: How Globalisation is Reshaping Our Lives*. London: Profile Books.
Gill, M.J. (2003), Biased Against 'Them' More than 'Him': Stereotype Use in Group-directed and Individual-directed Judgments. *Social Cognition*, 21/5, pp. 321–48.
Girard, R. (1977/2005) *Violence and the Sacred*. London: Continuum.
Goffman, E. (1959) *The Presentation of Self in Everyday Life*. New York: Doubleday Anchor.
Goffman, E. (1963/1986) *Stigma: Notes on the Management of Spoiled Identity*. New York: Touchstone Books.
Goldman, B. (1983) Lex Mercatoria. *Forum Internationale*, 3/3, p. 24.
Goldsworthy, V. (2002) Invention and In(ter)vention: The Rhetoric of Balkanization. *Balkan as Metaphor: Between Globalization and Fragmentation*. London: MIT Press, pp. 25–8.

Grant, M. (1995) *Myths of the Greeks and Romans*. New York: Plume.
Green, R. (1992) *Women in American Indian Society*. New York–Philadelphia: Chelsea House.
Greenwood, R. (ed.) (2007) Special Issue on Professional Service Organizations, *Journal of Behavioral Studies*, in process.
Greenwood, R., Hinnings, B. and Brown, J. (1990) 'P^2-form' Strategic Management: Corporate Practices in Professional Partnership. *Academy of Management Journal*, 33, pp. 723–55.
Grey, C. (1997) Management as a Technical Practice: Professionalization or Responsibilization? *System Practice*, 10/6, pp. 703–25.
Grey, C. (1998) On Being Professional in a Big 'Six' Firm. *Accounting, Organization and Society*, 23, pp. 569–87.
Grimshaw, D., Ward, K., Rubery, J. and Beynon, H. (2001) Organisations and the Transformation of the Internal Labour Market. *Work, Employment and Society*, 15/1, pp. 25–54.
Grint, K. and Woolgar, S. (1997) *The Machine at Work*. Cambridge: Polity Press.
Grzeszczyk, E. (2003) *Sukces: Amerykańskie wzory – polskie realia*. Warszawa: IFiS PAN.
Guillén, M.F. (1997) Scientific Management's Lost Aesthetic: Architecture, Organization, and the Taylorized Beauty of the Mechanical. *Administrative Science Quarterly*, 42, pp. 682–715.
Guillet de Monthoux, P., Gustafsson, C. and Sjöstrand, S.-E. (2007) Aesthetic Leadership and its Triadic Philosophy. In Guillet de Monthoux, P. Gustafsson, C. and Sjöstrand, S.-E. (eds), *Aesthetic Leadership*. Basingstoke: Palgrave Macmillan, pp. 251–78.
GUS (1998) *Statistical Yearbook of the Republic of Poland*. GUS: Główny Urząd Statystyczny.
Gutman, R. (1988) *Architectural Practice: A Critical View*. Princeton: Princeton Architectural Press.
Halpern, B. (1961) Myth and Ideology in Modern Usage. *History and Theory*, 1/2, pp. 129–49.
Hammersley, M. and Atkinson, P. (1995/2000) *Metody badań terenowych*. Poznań: Zysk i S-ka.
Hampshire, S. (1965) *Thought and Action*. London: Chatto & Windus.
Hancock, M. (1995) Hindu Culture for an Indian Nation: Gender, Politics and Elite Identity in Urban South India. *American Ethnologist*, 22/4, pp. 907–26.
Handy, C. (2002) *The Elephant and the Flea*. London: Arrow Books.
Harley, D. (1990) Historians as Demonologists: The Myth of the Midwife-Witch. *Social History of Medicine*, 3/1, pp. 1–26.
Harré, R. and Secord, P. (1972) *The Explanation of Social Behaviour*. Oxford: Blackwell.
Hatch, M.J. (1983) The Dynamics of Organizational Culture. *Academy of Management Review*, 18/4, pp. 657–93.
Hatch, M.J. (1998) Jazz as a Metaphor for Organizing in the 21st Century. *Organization Science*, 9/5, pp. 556–7.
Hatch, M.J., Kostera, M. and Koźmiński, K. (2005) *The Three Faces of Leadership: Manager, Artist, Priest*. Malden–Oxford–Carlton: Blackwell Publishing.
Hatch, M.J., Kostera, M. and Koźmiński, A.K. (2006) Three Faces of Leadership: Manager, Artist, Priest. *Organization Dynamics*, 35/1, pp. 49–68.

Hillman, J. (ed.) (1980) *Facing the God*. Dallas: Spring Publications.
Hills, C. and Silverman, D.C. (1993) Nationalism and Feminism in Late Colonial India: The Rani of Jhansi Regiment, 1943–1945. *Modern Asia Studies*, 27/4, pp. 741–60.
Hjorth, D. and Johannisson, B. (2003) Conceptualising the Opening Phase of Regional Development as the Enactment of a 'Collective Identity'. *Concepts and Transformation*, 8, pp. 69–92.
Hobsbawm, E. and Ranger, T. (eds) (1983) *The Invention of Tradition*. Cambridge– New York: Cambridge University Press.
Hodgson, D. (2005) 'Putting on a Professional Preformance': Performativity, Subversion and Project Management. *Organization*, 12/1, pp. 51–68.
Hodgson, P. (1999) Leadership, Teaching and Learning. In *The Royal Society (RSA) on Work and Leadership*. Aldershot: Gower, pp. 129–33.
Hogg, M.A. and Vaughan, G.M. (2005) *Social Psychology*. Harlow, UK: Pearson Education Limited.
Holbek, B. (1987) *Interpretation of Fairy Tales: Danish Folklore in a European Perspective*. Helsinki: Academia Scientiarum Fennica.
Holland, D., Lachiotee, Jr. W., Skinner, D. and Cain, C. (1998) *Identity and Agency in Cultural Worlds*. Cambridge: Harvard University Press.
Holmberg, I., Salzer-Mörling, M. and Strannegård, L. (eds), (2002) *Stuck in the Future: Tracing the 'New Economy'*, Stockholm: Bookhouse Publishing.
Hood, C. (1991) A Public Management for all Seasons. *Public Administration*, 69, pp. 3–19.
Hopkins, E.W. (1901) *The Great Epic of India: Character and Origin of the Mahabharata*, New Delhi: Motilal Banarsidass Publishers.
Höpfl, H. (2007) Good Order: Ethics and Disposition. In Boje, D. *et al.* (eds), *Critical Theory Ethics for Business and Administration*, Greenwich, CT: Information Age Publishing.
Houghton, J.D., Neck, C.P. and Manz, C.C. (2003) Self-leadership and Superleadership: The Heart and Art of Creating Shared Leadership in Teams. In Pearce, C.L. and Conger, J.A. (eds), *Shared Leadership: Reframing the How's and Why's of Leadership*. Thousand Oaks, CA: Sage.
Iacocca, L. (1984) *Iacocca: An Autobiography*. New York: Bantam.
Ions, V. (1983) *Egyptian Mythology*. New York: P. Bedrick Books.
Ispirescu, P. (2004) *Fairytales: Romania*. Hera Publishing House.
Ivory, Ch. (2004) Client, User, and Architect Interactions in Construction: Implications for Analyzing Innovative Outcomes from User-Producer Interactions in Projects. *Technology Analysis and Strategic Management*, 16/4, pp. 495–508.
James, R.C. (1962) Discrimination against Women in Bombay Textiles. *Industrial and Labour Relations Review*, 15/2, pp. 209–20.
Janion, M. (1996) *Kobiety i duch inności*. (*Women and the Spirit of Otherness*). Warszawa: Sic!.
Jankowicz, A.D. (1994) The New Journey to Jerusalem: Mission and Meaning in the Managerial Crusade to Eastern Europe. *Organization Studies*, 15/4, pp. 479–507.
Jankowicz, A. D. (1999) "Planting a Paradigm in Central Europe: Do We Graft, or Must We Breed the Rootstock Anew?" *Management Learning* 1999; vol. 30 (3); pp. 281–99.

Jejeebhoy, S.J. (2002) Convergence and Divergence in Spouses' Perspectives on Women's Autonomy in Rural India. *Studies in Family Planning*, 33/4, pp. 299–308.
Jemielniak, D. (2005) Time for IT: Timing in Software Projects. In Khosrow-Pour, M. (ed.), *Managing Modern Organizations with Information Technology*. Hershey: Idea Group, pp. 1199–201.
Jemielniak, J. (2002) Just Interpretation: The Status of Legal Reasoning in the Continental Legal Tradition. *International Journal for the Semiotics of Law*, 15/4, pp. 325–35.
Johannisson, B. and Olaison, L. (2006) *Emergency Entrepreneurship – Creative Organising in the Eye of the Storm*. Paper presented at RENT XX, Brussels, Belgium, November 22–24, 2006.
Johansson, A.W. (2004) Narrating the Entrepreneur. *International Small Business Journal*, 22/3, pp. 273–93.
Jones P.R. (2006) The Sociology of Architecture and the Politics of Building: The Discursive Construction of Ground Zero. *Sociology*, 40/3, pp. 549–65.
Jones, T.M. (1995) Instrumental Stakeholder Theory: A Synthesis of Ethics and Economics. *Academy of Management Review*, 20/2, pp. 404–37.
Josephson, M. (1934) *The Robber Barons: The Great American Capitalists 1861–1901*. New York, Harcourt: Brace and Company.
Julier, G. (2000) *The Culture of Design*. London–Thousand Oaks–New Delhi: Sage.
Jung, C.G. (1966/1992) *Two Essays on Analytical Psychology*. vol 7. (trans. Hull, R.F.C.). London: Routledge.
Jung C.G. (1968) *Man and His Symbols*. Garden City, NY: Doubleday.
Kakabadse, A. and Kakabadse, N. (1999) *Essence of Leadership*. London: Thomson Business Press.
Kalevala, The (1999) *An Epic Poem after Oral Tradition* (trans. Lönnrot with an introduction and notes by Bosley, K.). New York: Oxford University Press.
Kärreman, D. and Alvesson, M. (2004) Cages in Tandem: Management Control, Social Identity, and Identification in a Knowledge-Intensive Firm. *Organisation*, 11, pp. 149–77.
Kesić, V. (2002) Muslim Women, Croatian Women, Serbian Women, Albanian Women.... In *Balkan as Metaphor: Between Globalization and Fragmentation*. London: MIT Press, pp. 311–22.
King Z., Burke S. and Pemberton J. (2005) The 'Bounded' Career: An Empirical Study of Human Capital, Career Mobility and Employment Outcomes in a Mediated Labour Market. *Human Relations*, 58/8, pp. 981–1007.
Kniveton, B. (2004) Managerial Career Anchors in a Changing Business Environment. *Journal of European Industrial Training*, 28/7, pp. 564–73.
Kociatkiewicz, J. (1997) Organizacje, komputery, ludzie: Studium idei postepu technicznego. (Organizations, computers, people: A study of the idea of technological progress.) unpublished Master's thesis, Warszawa: Warsaw University, Faculty of Management.
Kociatkiewicz, J. and Kostera, M. (2002) When Reality Fails: Science Fiction and the Fall of Communism in Poland. In Kostera, M. and Kelemen, M. (eds), *Managing the Transition: Critical Management Research in Eastern Europe*. Basingstoke: Palgrave, pp. 217–38.
Kołakowski, L. (1989) *Obecność mitu*. (*The Presence of Myth*). Warszawa: Prószyński i S-ka.

Koolhaas, R. (1978) *Delirious New York*. New York: The Monticelli Press.
Kopaliński, W. (1995) *Encyklopedia 'drugiej płci'*. (*Encyclopedia of 'the Second Sex'*.) Warszawa: Rytm.
Kostera, M. (1995a) The Modern Crusade: Missionaries of Management Come to Eastern Europe. *Management Learning*, 26/3, pp. 331–52.
Kostera, M. (1995b) Differing Managerial Responses to Change in Poland. *Organization Studies*, 16/4, pp. 673–97.
Kostera, M. (1996) *Postmodernizm w zarządzaniu* (*Postmodernism and management*), Warszawa: PWE.
Kostera, M. (2003) Od aktywisty do bossa: Historia polskiego kierownika 1950–2000. In Sulima, R. (ed.), *Zycie codzienne Polaków*. Łomza: Oficyna Wydawicza 'Stopka', pp. 69–91.
Kostera, M. (2003/2005) *Antropologia organizacji: Metodologia badan terenowych*. (*Anthropology of Organization: Methodology of Field Research*). Warszawa: PWN.
Kostera, M. (2005) *The Quest for the Self-actualizing Organization*. Malmö: Liber.
Kostera, M. and Wicha, M. (1995) The Symbolism of the Communist Manager Roles: A Study of Scenarios. *Scandinavian Journal of Management*, 11/2, pp. 139–58.
Kostera, M. and Wicha, M. (1996) The 'Divided Self' of Polish State-owned Enterprises: The Culture of Organizing. *Organization Studies*, 17/1, pp. 83–105.
Kowalczyk, I. (2003) Matka-Polka kontra supermatka? *Czas kultury*, 113/5, pp. 11–21.
Koźmiński, A.K. (1993) *Catching up? Case Studies in Organizational and Management Change in the Former Socialist Block*. Albany, NJ: SUNY Press.
Koźmiński, A.K. (1995) From the Communist Nomenklatura to Transformational Leadership: The Role of Management in the Post-Communist Enterprises. In Grancelli, B. (ed.), *Social Change and Modernization: Lessons from Eastern Europe*. Berlin: Walter de Gruyter, pp. 83–105.
Kunda, G. (1992) *Engineering Culture*. Philadelphia: Temple University Press.
Kurunmäki, L. and Miller, P. (2006) Modernising Government: The Calculating Self, Hybridisation and Performance Measurement. *Financial Accountability & Management*, 22/1, pp. 87–106.
Kvale, S. (1996) *InterViewing*. London: Sage.
Laclau, E. (1990) *New Reflections on the Revolution of our Time*. London: Verso.
Laclau, E. (2005) *On Populist Reason*. London: Verso.
Lanz, J. (2007) Gendered Textbook Filmmakers. In Guillet de Monthoux, P. Gustafsson, C. and Sjöstrand, S.-E. (eds), *Aesthetic Leadership*. Basingstoke: Palgrave Macmillan, pp. 51–71.
Lapierre, L. (2001) Leadership and Arts Management. *International Journal of Arts Management*, 3/3, pp. 4–12.
Larson, M.S. (1977) *The Rise of Professionalism*. Berkeley: University of California Press.
Latusek, D. (2007) When Trust Does Not Matter: The Study of Communication Practices between High-Tech Companies and Their Clients in the Environment of Distrust. In Brennan, L. and Johnson, V. (eds), *Computer-Mediated Relationships and Trust: Managerial and Organizational Effects*. Hershey, PA: Idea Group Publishing, forthcoming.
Le Corbusier (1946) *Towards a New Architecture* (trans Etchell, F.). London: The Architectural Press.

Lenchek, S. (1997a) *La Malinche – Unrecognized Heroine*. Retrieved 22 February 2007 from http://www.mexconnect.com/mex_/history/malinche.html
Lenchek, S. (1997b) La Malinche – Harlot or Heroine? El Ojo del Lago. *Guadalajara-Lakeside*, 14/4, pp. 7–12.
Lenk, H. (1982) Towards a Philosophical Anthropology of the Olympic Athlete and/as the Achieving Being: Can and/or How a Philosopher Can Understand Athletes and Olympic Athletics. *Proceedings of the Twenty-second Summer Session of the International Olympic Academy*.
Łętowska E. (2005) Multicentryczność współczesnego systemu prawnego i jej konsekwencje. *Państwo i Prawo*, 4/4, pp. 3–10.
Lévi-Strauss, C., (1979) *Myth and Meaning: Cracking the Code of Meaning*. New York: Shocken Books.
Lévi-Strauss, C. (1981) *Introduction to a Science of Mythology*. London: Cape.
Lew, J.D.M., Mistelis, L.A. and Kroll, S. (2003) *Comparative International Commercial Arbitration*. The Hague–Boston: Kluwer Law International.
Lindemans, M.F. (1998) Emma-o. In Lindemans, M.F. (ed.), *Encyclopedia Mythica*. Retrevied on 28 February 2007 from http://www.pantheon.org/articles/e/emma-o.html
Lindemans, M.F. (2000) Jalal. In Lindemans, M.F. (ed.), *Encyclopedia Mythica*. Retreived on 28 February 2007 from http://www.pantheon.org/articles/j/jalal.html
Linstead, S. and Höpfl, H. (eds) (2000) *The Aesthetics of Organization*. London–Thousand Oaks–New Delhi: Sage.
Long, J.L. (1903) *Madame Butterfly*. Grosset & Dunlop.
López Rodríguez, A.M. (2003) *Lex Mercatoria and Harmonization of Contract Law in the EU*. Copenhagen: DJØF Publishing.
Loti, P. (1887/ 2007) *Madame Chrysanthème*. BiblioBazaar.
Lurker, M. (2004) *The Routledge Dictionary of Gods, Goddesses, Devils and Demons*. London–New York: Routledge.
Lyotard, J.F. (1979/1984) *The Postmodern Condition: A Report on Knowledge*. Minneapolis: University of Minnesota Press.
Lyotard, J.F. (1983) *Le différend*. Paris: Editions de Minuit.
Macaloon, J. (1982) The Position of the Olympic Athlete in Society. *Proceedings of the Twenty-second Summer Session of the International Olympic Academy*.
MacIntyre, A. (1981) *After Virtue*. London: Duckworth.
MacIntyre, A. (1985) *After Virtue: A Study in Moral Theory*. London: Duckworth.
Mahabharata, The (1973) (trans. van Buitenen, J.A.B.) Chicago: University of Chicago Press.
Malinowski, B. (1955) *Myth in Primitive Psychology*. New York: Harper & Row.
Marody, M. (ed.) (1991) *Co nam zostalo z tych lat... Spoleczenstwo polskie u progu zmiany systemowej*. London: Aneks Publishers.
McClintock, A. (1995) No Longer in a Future Heaven: Nationalism, Gender and Race. In McClintock, A. (ed.), *Imperial Leather: Race, Gender and Sexuality in the Colonial Context*. New York–London: Routledge, pp. 352–89.
Memorable Quotes from 'Dynasty' 1981 (n.d.) *IMDb Earth's Biggest Movie Database*. Retrieved on 15 February 2007 from: http://www.imdb.com/title/tt0081856/ quotes

Merton, R.K. (1973) *The Sociology of Science: Theoretical and Empirical Investigations*. In Storer, N.W. (ed.), Chicago: The University of Chicago Press.
Meyer, G. (1941/1955) The Urban Pattern of Success. In Stanford, C.L. (ed.) (1955) *Benjamin Franklin and the American Character*. Boston: D.C. Heath & Company, pp. 48–53.
Mikołajczakowie, M. and A. (2001) *Bajeczne dzieje Polski*. (*Fabulous Past of Poland*). Wrocław: Wyd. Dolnośląskie.
Milburn, C. (2004/2005) Nanotechnology in the Age of Posthuman Engineering: Science Fiction as Science. In Hayles, N.K. (ed.) (2005) *Nanoculture: Implications of the New Technoscience*. Bristol: Intellect Books, pp. 109–29.
Miller, D.L. (1974) *The New Polytheism: Rebirth of the Gods and Goddesses*. New York–Evanson–San Fransisco–London: Harper & Row.
Miller, G. (1996) *The Legal and Economic Basis of International Trade*. Westport, CT: Quorum Books.
Milton, J. (1667/2007) *Paradise Lost*. New York: Longman.
Mistrz Wincenty (Kadłubek) (1992) *Kronika polska*. (*Polish Chronicle*). Wrocław–Kraków: Ossolineum.
Mitchell, T.R., Holtom, B.C., Lee, T.W., Sablynski, C.J., and Erez, M. (2001) Why People Stay: Using Organizational Embeddedness to Predict Voluntary Turnover. *Academy of Management Journal*, 44/6, pp. 1102–21.
Montesquieu, Ch. (1748/1989) *The Spirit of the Laws*. Cambridge: Cambridge University Press.
Moorman, C. and Miner, A. (1998) Organizational Improvisation and Organizational Memory. *Academy of Management Review*, 23/4, pp. 698–724.
Ng, T. and Feldman, D. (2007) Organizational Embeddedness and Occupational Embeddness across Career Stages. *Journal of Vocational Behavior*, 70/2, pp. 336–51.
Nietzsche, F. (1886/1966) *Beyond Good and Evil*. (trans. Kaufman, W.). New York: Vintage.
Nisbet, R. (1970) *The Sociological Tradition*. London: Heinemann.
Nixon, S. (2005) *Advertisement Culture*. London–Thousand Oaks–New Delhi: Sage.
Obrist, H.Ul. and Koolhaas, R. (2001) Relearning from Las Vegas: An Interview with Denise Scott Brown and Robert Venturi. In Chung, Ch.J., Inaba, J., Koolhaas, R. and Leong, S.T. (eds), *Harvard Design School Guide to Shopping*. Köln: Taschen.
Office of National Statistics (2003) Length of Service of Employees, 2002 *Social Trends 33*. Office of National Statistics. Retrieved on 9 April 2007 from http://www.statistics.gov.uk/StatBase.
Ogbor, J.O. (2000) Mythicizing and Reification in Entrepreneurial Discourse: Ideology-Critique of Entrepreneurial Studies. *Journal of Management Studies*, 37/5, pp. 605–35.
Oleksy, E.H. (1998) *Kobieta w krainie Dixie*. (*Woman in Dixie Land*). Łódź: Wyd. UŁ.
Olympic Charter (2004). International Olympic Committee (IOC). Retrieved on 15 October 2006 from http://multimedia.olympic.org/pdf/en_report_122.pdf.
Oppenheimer, P. (1995) *Till Eugenspiegel, His Adventures*. Oxford: Oxford University Press.
Ostrowska, E. (2004) Matki Polki i ich synowie: Kilka uwag o genezie obrazów kobiecości i męskości w kulturze polskiej. (Mother Poles and their Sons: Some Remarks on the Genesis of Femininity and Masculinity Pictures in

Polish Culture). In Radkiewicz, M. (ed.), *Gender, Konteksty*. Kraków: Rabid, pp. 214–27.

Owens, J. (1969) A Pedagogical Evaluation of the Olympic Games from the Point of View of the Athletes. *Proceedings of the Ninth Summer Session of the International Olympic Academy*.

Pakszys, E. (ed.) (2005) *Międzykulturowe i interdyscyplinarne badania feministyczne. Daleki – Bliski Wschód: Współczesność i prehistoria*. (*Crosscultural and Interdisciplinary Feminist Research: Far to Near East: Contemporary and Prehistory*). Poznań: UAM.

Paleologos, C. (1964) The Ancient Olympics. *Proceedings of the Fourth Summer Session of the International Olympic Academy*.

Parsons, T. (1939) The Professions and Social Structure. *Social Forces*, 17/4, pp. 457–67.

Patient, D., Lawrence, T. and Maitlis, S. (2003) Understanding Workplace through Narrative Fiction. *Organization Studies*, 24/7, pp. 1015–44.

Peiperl, M. and Baruch, Y. (1997) Back to Square Zero: The Post-Corporate Career. *Organizational Dynamics*, 25/4, pp. 7–22.

Perera, S.B. (1986) *The Scapegoat Complex*. Toronto: Inner City Books.

Peters, T. (1989) *Thriving on Chaos*. Basingstoke: Palgrave Macmillan.

Peters, T. and Waterman, R. (1982) *In Search of Excellence*. New York: Harper & Row.

Pettersson, K. (2002) *Företagande män och osynliggjorda kvinnor: diskursen om Gnosjö ur ett könsperspektiv*. Uppsala: Uppsala University.

Pinnington, A. and Morris, T. (2002) Transforming the Architect: Ownership from the Archetype Change. *Organization Studies*, 23/2, pp. 189–210.

Platman, K. (2004) 'Portfolio Careers' and the Search for Flexibility in Later Life. *Work, Employment and Society*, 18/3, pp. 573–99.

Plato (1984) *Uczta*. (*Symposium*). Warszawa: PWN.

Pocahontas (1995) (film by Walt Disney).

Postiglione, G. (2004) *100 Houses – One Hundred European Architects of the Twentieth Century*. Köln: Taschen.

Pratchett, T. (2004) *A Hat Full of Sky*. London: Corgi Books.

Pratley, N. (2004) On His Marks, *The Guardian*, 5 June. Retrieved on 9 April 2007 from http://www.guardian.co.uk/marks

Puccini, Giacomo (1904) *Madama Butterfly* (17.2.1904 Teatro alla Scala, Milan).

Quillen, C. (2001) Feminist Theory, Justice, and the Lure of the Human: Rey Chow, Contextualizing the Human. *Signs*, 27/1, pp. 87–22.

Ramayana, The (1975) (trans. Narayan, R.K.) London: Penguin.

Revised English Bible with Apocrypha (1996) Cambridge: Cambridge University Press.

Richman, M. (2003) Myth, Power and the Sacred: Anti-Utilitarianism in the Collège de Sociologie 1937–9. *Economy & Society*, 32/1, pp. 29–47.

Rob (2003) *Clients Are Stupid*. Retrieved on 11 November 2006 and 1 April 2007 from http://www.b3ta.com/questions/clientsarestupid

Rogers, E.M. (1962/1995) *Diffusion of Innovations*. Glencoe IL: The Free Press.

Rollinson, D. (1998/2005) *Organizational Behaviour and Analysis: An Integrated Approach*. London: Prentice Hall.

Rombach, B. and Solli, R. (2006) *Constructing Leadership: Reflections on Film Heroes as Leaders*. Stockholm: Santérus.

Ronell, A. (2002) *Stupidity*. Urbana/Chicago: University of Illinois Press.

Rorty, R. (1982) *Consequences of Pragmatism: Essays, 1972–1980.* Minneapolis: University of Minnesota Press.
Rose, N. and Miller, P. (1992) Political Power beyond the State: Problematics of Government. *British Journal of Sociology,* 43, pp. 173–205.
Rothenbuhler, E.W. (1998) *Ritual Communication: From Everyday Conversation to Mediated Ceremony.* London–New Delhi: Sage.
Roy, M. (1975) *Bengali Women.* Chicago: Chicago University Press.
Sawin, P.E. (1990) Kalevalan naishahmot Lönnrotin hengentuotteina. (*Kalevala's* female figures according to Lönnrot). In Nenola, A. and Timonen, S. (eds), *Louhen sanat (Louhi's words).* Helsinki: Suomalaisen Kirjallisuuden Seuran toimituksia 520, pp. 45–69.
Scase, R. and Goffee, R. (1989) *Reluctant Managers: Their Work and Lifestyles.* London: Unwin Hyman.
Schein, E. (1992) *Organizational Culture and Leadership.* 2nd edn, San Francisco, CA: Jossey Bass.
ScuttleMonkey (2005) *Your Favorite Support Anecdote.* Retrieved on 11 November 2006 and 1 April 2007 from http://it.slashdot.org/article.pl?sid=06/07/05/1527200
Sennett R. (1998) *The Corrosion of Character.* New York: Norton.
Serres, M. (1982, 2007) *The Parasite.* Baltimore: Johns Hopkins University Press.
Serres, M. (1995) *Genesis.* Ann Arbor: University of Michigan Press.
Sievers, B. (1994) *Work, Death, and Life Itself: Essays on Management and Organization.* Berlin–New York: Walter de Gruyter.
Siikala, A.-L. (2002) Myth and Mentality: Studies in Folklore and in Thought. *Studia Fennica Folkloristica,* 8. Helsinki: Finnish Literature Studies.
Silva, E.B. (2000) The Cook, the Cooker and the Gendering of the Kitchen. *The Sociological Review,* 48/4, pp. 612–28.
Silverman, D. (1993) *Interpreting Qualitative Data.* London: Sage.
Singh, K. and Gupta, S. (2006) Woman Army Officer in J&K Shoots Herself. *The Times of India,* 17 June, p. 1.
Smith, C. and Thompson, P. (eds) (1992) *Labour in Transition: The Labour Process in Eastern Europe and China.* London: Routledge.
Smith, P.C. (1909) *The Fool in Rider Waite Smith Tarot.* Online image, drawing with GNU license. Retrieved on 1 April 2007 from http://en.wikipedia.org/wiki/Image:RWS-00-Fool.jpg.
Smith, R. and Anderson, A.R. (2004) The Devil is in the E-tale: Forms and Sructures in the Entrepreneurial Narratives. In Hjorth, D. and Steyaert, C. (eds), *Narrative and Discursive Approaches in Entrepreneurship: A Second Movements in Entrepreneurship Book.* Cheltenham–Northampton: Edwar Elgar, pp. 125–43.
Śniadecka-Kotarska, M. (2003) *Być kobieta w Ekwadorze.* (*Being a Woman in Equador*) Warszawa: Celsa.
Söderbergh Widding, A. (1996) *Sätt att se.* Stockholm: T. Fischer & Co.
Soila-Wadman, M. (2003) *Kapitulationens estetik: Organisering och ledarskap i filmprojekt.* (*The aesthetics of capitulation: Organizing and leadership in a film project*). Stockholm: Arvinius.
Soila-Wadman, M. (2007) Film producer, Entrepreneurship and The Experience Economy. In Hjorth, D. and Kostera, M. (eds), *Entrepreneurship and Experience Economy.* Copenhagen: Copenhagen Business School Press, pp. 55–71.

Soila-Wadman, M. and Köping, A.-S. (2005) Stories of Leadership in Art and Culture Creating Organizations. Paper presented at 8th International Conference on Arts & Cultural Management. Montreal.

Sommers, M. (1994) The Narrative Construction of Identity. *Theory and Society*, 23/5 pp. 605–49.

Spinosa, C., Flores, F. and Dreyfus, H.L. (1997) *Disclosing New Worlds: Entrepreneurship, Democratic Action, and the Cultivation of Solidarity*. Cambridge MA: MIT Press.

Steyaert, C. and Hjorth, D. (eds) (2006) *Entrepreneurship as Social Change: A Third Movements in Entrepreneurship Book*. Cheltenham: Edward Elgar Publishing.

Strati, A. (1999) *Organization and Aesthetics*. London–Thousand Oaks–New Delhi: Sage.

Sutherland, S.J. (1989) Sita and Draupadi: Aggressive Behaviour and Female Role Models in the Sanskrit Epics. *Journal of the American Oriental Society*, 109/1, pp. 63–79.

Szacka, B. (2006) *Czas przeszły: pamięć – mit*. (*The Past: Memory – Myth*). Warszawa: Scholar.

Szczuka, K. (2001) *Kopciuszek, Frankenstein i inne: Feminizm wobec mitu*. (*Cinderella, Frankenstein and Others: Feminism and myth*). Kraków: eFKa.

Teather, D. (2007) Profile: Tony Hayward. *Guardian Unlimited*. 12 January. Retrieved on 8 April from http://business.guardian.co.uk/story/0,1989300, 00.html.

Teubner, G. (1997) 'Global Bukowina': Legal Pluralism in the World Society. In Teubner, G. (ed.), *Law without a State*. Aldershot–Brookfield–Singapore–Sydney: Dartmouth, pp. 3–28.

The New American Bible. Reader's Edition (2006) New York: Oxford University Press.

Thylefors, I. (1987) *Syndabockar*. (*Scapegoats*). Stockholm: Natur och Kultur.

Todorov, Tz. (1991) *Podbój Ameryki: Problem innego*. (*La conquete de l'Amerique: La question du l'autre*). Warszawa: Alethea.

Tokarczuk, O. (2006) *Anna In w grobowcach świata*. (*Anna In Tombs of the World*). Kraków: Znak.

Trzciński, Ł. (2006) *Mit bohaterski w perspektywie antropologii filozoficznej i kulturowej*. (*The Myth of the Hero from the Philosophical and Anthropological Perspective*). Kraków: Wydawnictwo Uniwersytetu Jagiellońskiego.

Turner, V. (1967) *The Forest of Symbols: Aspects of Ndembu Ritual*, Ithaca: Cornell University Press.

Tyler A. (2006) Malinche and Matriarchal Utopia: Gendered Visions of Indigeneity in Mexico. *Signs*, 31/3, pp. 817–40.

Tziotis, D. (ed.) (2001) *The International Olympic Academy*. The IOC Publications: Ancient Olympia, Greece.

Vail, P. (1996). *Learning as a Way of Being: Strategies for Survival in a World of Permanent White Water*. San Francisco: Jossey-Bass.

Vakimo, S. (1999) Louhi – sopimaton nainen? (Louhi – A Woman Who Does Not Fit?) In Piela, U., Knuuttila, S. and Kupiainen, T. (eds), *Kalevalan hyvät ja hävyttömät* (*Kalevala's Good and Indecent*). Helsinki: Suomalaisen Kirjallisuuden Seuran toimituksia 746, pp. 56–75.

Van Maanen, J. (1988) *Tales of the Field: On Writing Ethnography*. Chicago–London: University of Chicago Press.

Varady, T., Barcelo, J.J. and von Mehren, A.T. (2002) *International Commercial Arbitration*. St. Paul, MN: West Publishing Company.

Venturi, R., Scott Brown, D. and Izenour, S. (1977) *Learning from Las Vegas: The Forgotten Symbolism of Architectural Form*. Cambridge: MIT Press.
Vico, G. (1999) *New Science*. London: Penguin.
Voßkamp, A. and Wittke, V. (1990) Aus Modernisierungsblockaden werden Abwärtsspiralen. *Berliner Journal fuer Soziologie*, 1/1, pp. 17–40.
Wadley, S. (1975) *Shakti: Power in the Conceptual Structure of Karimpur Religion*. Chicago: University of Chicago Press.
Wærn, R. (2001) *Gert Wingårdh, Architect*. Birkhäuser: Publishers for Architecture.
Wajcman, J. and B. Martin, (2001) My Company or My Career: Managerial Achievement or Loyalty. *British Journal of Sociology*, 52/4, pp. 559–78.
Wajcman, J. and B. Martin, (2002) Narratives of Identity in Modern Management: The Corrosion of Gender Difference? *Sociology*, 36/4, pp. 985–1002.
Watson, T.J. (1994/ 2001) *In Search of Management: Culture, Chaos and Control in Managerial Work*. London: Thomson.
Watson, T.J. (2000) Ethnographic Fiction Science: Making Sense of Managerial Work and Organisational Research Processes with Caroline and Terry. *Organisation*, 7/3, pp. 513–34.
Watson, T.J. (2004) Shy William and the Gaberlunzie Girl. In Gabriel, Y. (ed.), *Myths, Stories and Organizations: Premodern Narratives For Our Times*. Oxford: Oxford University Press, pp. 223–35.
Weber, M. (1999) *Essays in Economic Sociology*. Swedberg, R. (ed.), Princeton: Princeton University Press.
Weick, Karl E. (1969/79) *The Social Psychology of Organizing*. Reading, MA: Addison-Wesley.
Weinert, R. (1995) Wirtschaftsführung unter dem Primat der Parteipolitik. In Pirker, T., Lepsius, M.R. and Weinert, R. (eds), *Der Plan als Befehl und Fiktion – Wirtschaftsführung in der DDR*, Opladen: Westdeutscher Verlag, pp. 285–308.
Wiley, I. (2006) The Unstoppables. *The Guardian (Work Weekly)*, 16 September, pp. 1–3.
Wilshire, D. (1992) The Uses of Myth, Image, and the Female Body in Re-visioning Knowledge. In Jaggar, A.M. and Bordo, S. (eds), *Gender/Body/Knowledge: Feminist Reconstructions of Being and Knowing*. New Brunswick, NJ: Rutgers University Press, pp. 92–114.
Winch, G. and Schneider, E. (1993) Managing the Knowledge-Based Organization: The Case of Architectural Practice. *Journal of Management Studies*, 30/6, pp. 923–37.
Wiseman, T.P. (2004) *The Myths of Rome*. Exeter: University of Exeter Press.
Wolanik Boström, K. (2005) *Berättade liv, berättat Polen: En etnologisk studie av hur polska högutbildade gestaltar identitet och samhälle*. (Narrated Lives, Narrated Poland: An Ethnographic Study on How Highly Educated Poles Construct Identity and Society.) Umeå: Umeå University Press.
Woman's Hour (2007) Radio 4. 9 January 2007, 10:00.
Yammarino, F.J., Dionne, S.D., Uk Chun, J. and Dansereau, F. (2005) Leadership and Level of Analysis: A State-of-the-Science Review. *Leadership Quarterly*, 16/6, pp. 879–919.
Zaleska, K.J. (1998) Polish Managers in Subsidiaries of Multinational Corporations: International Business as an Agent of Change. PhD thesis, Cantenbury: University of Kent at Canterbury.

Index

abandonment 110–11
Abbott, A. 187
absolute justice 166–9
actors 137–8, 140
Adam and Eve 103
admiration 98, 100
adulation 109–10
aggression 109–10, 113–14
  Indian women 116–18
alcoholism 91
altruism 186
Ambjörnsson, R. 12
American dream 14, 59, 60, 67–8, 69
amputation 111–14
Apollo 11
arbitrators 15, 165–74
  impartiality 165, 166, 171–3
  international commercial
    arbitration 165–6, 169–71, 173
architectural journals 161–2
architecture 15, 155–64
  nature of 156–8
  and symbolic capital 159–62
Arjuna 112, 113, 116
Armstrong, K. 152–3
art work 179–80, 181
  see also film producers
artist (leadership type) 41
  General Motors 45–7
Asplund, J. 190, 194
assistants 98, 99

Bai, Laxmi (Rani of Jhansi) 116–17
baker 96–7
bankruptcy 66, 67
Barlow, Ken 14, 71, 72, 75–6, 79
Baruch, Y. 76
Batman/Bruce Wayne 51–2, 53–4
Bauman, Z. 72, 79
Berger, P. 145–6
Bettelheim, B. 121
Bhattacharji, S. 109

Bhima 113
Bible 103, 167–8, 177
Bismarck, Otto von 163
Bloom, S.S. 114, 115
Boesky, Ivan 54
Bombay textile workers 117
Bond, James 12
Bourdieu, P. 156, 159
Bowles, M.L. 1–2, 3, 4, 9, 11, 92, 93, 178
BP 74
Brante, T. 186
Browne, Lord 74
Bruni, A. 100–1
Brunsson, N. 188
businesswoman phantom 139
Byrne, J. 56

Campbell, J. 2, 3, 9–10, 121, 153, 159
capitalism 137–8
capturing 151–2
careerist 138–9
caretaker (disciplinary) professional 189, 190–1
cassettes 62
Cassirer, E. 5
Centrala Handlu Zagranicznego (CHZ) (Centre for Foreign Trade) 62
CEPECA 123
Chakravarty, Lieutenant Sushmita 114–16
challenges 135–8
charisma 158–9, 163–4
  see also symbolic capital
chastity 110–11
Christianity 102, 103, 104, 167–8
Cio-Cio-San 106–7
comic books 14, 50–8
  Batman/Bruce Wayne 51–2, 53–4
  Iron Man/Tony Stark 54–5, 55–6
  Superman 51–2, 56–7
  universes 50, 51–2

commoditization of expertise 187
communication 161
Communist Party
  Poland 134, 135, 141
  Romania 120, 123–4, 126–7, 127–8
computer users 11, 14, 80–91
conduct, professional 189
conflicting interests 157
Conrad, Joseph, *Heart of Darkness* 153
continuity 51–2
Controller entrepreneur 96–7, 99–100
Coronation Street 14, 71, 72, 75–6, 79
Cortes, Herman 105
Coubertin, Pierre de 34
creation myths 102–3
cross-overs 51–2
'crusaders' 40–1
Cuff, D. 157
cultural bias 58
culture 4–5, 144
  organizational 13–14, 40–9
  popular 52, 58; *see also* comic books; soap operas

dairy farmer 94–5
Daredevil 57
dark forces 135–8
DC comics 50, 52, 53
death 167–8
definition 117–18
Deleuze, G. 179
demission 127
denim 62, 63
Devi, Phoolan 105
devils 52
directors
  film directors 175–6, 180
  Romanian socialist directors 15, 119–31
disciplinary professional 189, 190–1
disk drives 85, 86–7
distribution 64–5
divine judges 168–9
Divine Mother 109–10, 115
Donors 133–5

Douglas, M. 178
Draupadi 111–14, 115–16
Dubin, R. 77
Dunlap, Al 57
Durga 14, 109–10, 115, 116
Duryodhana 112

EastEnders 77–8, 79
economic transformation 59–60, 62–6
Eleithya 182
Eliade, M. 108
emerging myths 93–4
  Kosovar heroine 97–101
emotions 98, 100
engaged leadership 13, 30–9
  virtues of 31–3
entrepreneurship 92
  female entrepreneurship in Kosovo 14, 92–101
  Polish 14, 59–70
epic drama 98
ethnography 61–2
exclusivity rights 65–6
expatriate managers 40–1

fairytales, Romanian 14, 119, 120, 121–2, 129–31
family 103–4
Feldman, D. 74–5
female entrepreneurs 14, 92–101
femina curans 14, 99–100
'fighting well' 34–6
figures of thought 190–4
film directors 175–6, 180
film producers 15, 175–83
  as midwives 15, 181–2, 183
  as scapegoats 15, 176, 180–1, 182–3
finance, film 176, 180, 181, 182–3
fit 74
five-year plan 123–4
flexibility 126
florist 95–6
folk mother (*volksmoeder*) 105
folkloristic professional 185, 190–1
Fool, The (from Tarot) 14, 88, 89, 91
Fournier, V. 189

Index 215

Fowler, Pauline 77–8, 79
Franklin, Benjamin 59
Frazer, J.G. 176–7
Freud, S. 164
Furusten, S. 5–6

Gabriel, Y. 6–7, 10, 147, 154
Gandhi, Indira 105, 116
Gartner, W.G. 100
Gates, Bill 57
Gehlen, A. 145–6
Gehlen, R. 145
geisha 106–7
gender-content myths 14, 102–7
General Electric 57
General Motors 13–14, 40–9
  leadership types 43–8
  plants in Poland and UK 13–14, 42–3
Gherardi, S. 10, 18
Girard, R. 177, 178
Gliwice Opel Polska plant 40–9
global professional network (GPN) 187
gods
  divine judges 168–9
  judgmental 166–8
  McManus 149, 151
  modernity and demise of 152
Greek mythology 5, 11–12, 13
  goddesses 10, 18, 166–7
  Eleithya 182
  judgmental deities 166–7
  loyalty 72
  scapegoat 176–7
Greuceanu (The Heavy and The Great Man) 122, 129–31
Grzeszczyk, E. 60, 67, 68
Guattari, F. 179
Guillet de Monthoux, P. 181
Gupta, S. 114–15

Halpern, B. 108
Hancock, M. 116
Handy, Charles 73–4
harassments 135–8
hard-working heroes/heroines 132–41

Hatch, M.J. 10, 18–19, 41, 98, 100, 177
Hayward, Tony 74
head teacher 137
Helpers 133–5
heroes
  hard-working 132–41
  McManus myth 15, 142–54
  modernity and demise of 152
  scientific hero ideal type 185–6, 190–1
  and villains 9–16
Hills, C. 116–17
Holmes, Sherlock 12
Homo Sovieticus 139–40
Höpfl, H. 117, 118
hospitals 188

Iacocca, Lee 54
Icahn, Carl 57
ideal types
  organizations 187
  professions 16, 184–94
ideals, Olympian 34–6
ideas 160–1
idiots 14, 80–91
Ilmarinen 19, 20–3, 24, 27
immobility 14, 71–9
immortality 5
impartiality 15, 186
  arbitrators 165, 166, 171–3
  judges 165, 167, 169
improvization 34, 125
incompetence of PC users 82–7
India 105
  Vedic mythology see Vedic mythology
individualism 68
inspiration 98, 100, 162
international commercial arbitration 165–6, 169–71, 173
International Service Personnel (ISP) 43, 46
intersubjectivity 178–9
Intrapreneur 94–5, 99
involvement see mode of involvement
Iron Man/Tony Stark 54–5, 55–6

Ispirescu, P. 121, 122
IT specialists 14, 80–91
Ivory, Ch. 157–8

Jakubas, Zbigniew 69
Jalal 166
James, R. 117
Japan 43, 106–7
Jayadratha 113
Jehovah 166
Jejeebhoy, S.J. 114
Jesus of Justice 167–8
Jhansi 116–17
journalism 15, 142–54
Juan, Don 12
Judaeo-Christian myths 102, 103
judgmental deities 166–8
judges 15, 165, 172
  divine 168–9

Kalevala 13, 17–29
  as spoken tradition 18–19
Kauravas, the 112–13
Kingpin 57
knowledge 186, 191
  as a bits and pieces 186–8
  attractiveness of scientific knowledge 192–3
Kociatkiewicz, J. 11, 59–60, 91
Kosovo 14, 92–101
  tracing the legend of a Kosovar heroine 97–101
  types of female entrepreneur 94–7
Kostera, M. 10, 18–19, 59–60
Koźmiński, A. K. 10, 18–19, 40–1
Krakow Militia Hospital 136–7

Laclau, E. 93–4
Lakshmana 111
language forms 119–20
Lanz, J. 180, 181
Lapierre, L. 179
late modern professional 186–8, 190–1
Latin America 105

leadership 10–11
  context of Romanian economic leadership 120–1
  development 13–14, 40–9
  engaged *see* engaged leadership
  style: and organizational culture 13–14, 40–9; Romanian directors 123, 125
  virtues of 32–3
learning leadership *see* engaged leadership
leaving 14, 71–9
  attitudes to 73–6
lecturer 134–5, 135–6, 140
Lemminkäinen 19, 22–3, 24, 27–8
Lévi-Strauss, C. 158, 162
lex mercatoria 170–1, 173
links 74
'lone genius myth' 157
loner 3, 17–29
long-stayers 14, 71–9
Louhi 13, 17–29
  loneliness of 26–8
  relationships with other characters 27
  story of the Sampo 19–26
loyalty 14, 71–9
Luckmann, T. 145–6
Luthor, Lex (Superman's rival) 56–7
Luton Vauxhall GM plant 40–9
lying 126

Macaloon, J. 37
MacIntyre, A. 121
Madame Butterfly 106–7
Mahabharata 111–14
Mahishasura 109
male social roles 12
Malinche, la 105
Malinowski, B. 108
management
  changing public view of 54
  comic book superheroes and 50–8
  as modern myth 4
manager (leadership type) 41
  General Motors 43–5
managerial professional business (MPB) 187

Maria-Vittoria 149–51, 154
Marina, dona 105
marketing 64
Marks & Spencer 78
martial law 136
Martin, B. 76
Marvel comics 50, 52, 53, 54
Mary, the Virgin 104, 105
masculinity 151–2
mass media 67–8
  see also comic books; soap operas
Matthew effect 163
McManus myth 15, 142–54
'mercenaries' 40
Merchant Law 170–1, 173
Merton, R. 163
Mexico 105
midwife, film producer as 15, 181–2, 183
Militia Hospital, Krakow 135–7
Milken, Michael 57
Milton, J. 165
mode of involvement 186, 191
  attractiveness of 193
modernism/modernity 152–4
  and continuing role for the mythical 152–4
  and demise of gods, heroes and devils 152
  and professionalism: late modernity's organizational man 186–8, 190–1; scientific hero 185–6, 190–1
modernization 126
Montesquieu, Ch. 169
Morris, T. 156–7
Mother Pole myth 104
motherhood 104–5
  cult of the mother in India 116
  Vedic mythology 109–10, 115, 116
mouse clicking 82–3
myths 1–8, 10
  emergence of 93–4; Kosovar heroine 97–101
  and human beings 2–4
  modernity and continuing role for the mythical 152–4
  organizational mythmaking 4–7
  and sacred forces 146–7
  and the shield against terror 144–5
  symbolic capital 158–9

Nabisco 57
narcissism of minor differences 164
nation forming 102–7
Native Americans 106
negotiation 123–4
networking 123–4, 133–4
neutrality see impartiality
New Merchant Law 170–1, 173
New Public Management 188
Ng, T. 74–5
nostalgia 98, 100
novels 153

Olympian athlete 13, 30–9
  living the myth of 36–8
  Olympian ideals and as vision for leadership 34–6
Olympic Charter 34
Opel Polska 40–9
organizational culture 13–14, 40–9
organizational embeddedness 74–5
organizational expertise 187–8
organizational ideal types 187
organizational man 186–8, 190–1
organizational mythmaking 4–7
'Oriental woman' 106–7
other characters 98, 99–100
Owens, J. 34

paediatrician 133–4, 136–7, 138
paints 62, 63–6
Pandavas, the 112–13, 116
paradise, images of 140–1
parents 84
Parsons, T. 186
participation 5
PC users 14, 80–91
Peacemaker entrepreneur 97
Peiperl, M. 76
Perera, S.B. 177, 178
phantoms 138–40
pharmakon 177
photographer 15, 142–54
phronesis (practical judgment) 32–3

Piast myth 103–4
Pinnington, A. 156–7
plastic bag manufacturer 97
plot focus 98
Pocahontas 106
Poland
 economic transformation of 1989 59–60, 62–6
 leadership in General Motors 13–14, 40–9
 pre-historic myth 103–4
Polish entrepreneurship 14, 59–70
 millennium-era entrepreneurs 61, 66–8, 68, 69
 1989 entrepreneurs 61, 62–6, 68–9
Polish professionals 15, 132–41
 favourite phantoms 138–40
 Helpers and Donors 133–5
 images of paradise 140–1
 trials, challenges and harassments 135–8
popular culture 52, 58
 see also comic books; soap operas
popular management books 5–6
practical judgment (phronesis) 32–3
practising 33–4
Pratchett, T. 182, 184–5
predicament 98
priest (leadership type) 41
 General Motors 47–8
primary reality 17
producers *see* film producers
professional partnerships 187
professionalism 16, 184–94
 disciplinary 189, 190–1
 folkloristic 185, 190–1
 organizational man 186-8, 190–1
 Polish professionals *see* Polish professionals
 professionalization of vocational groups 190–4
 scientific hero 185–6, 190–1
protagonists 98–9
protest 117
public sector 188
Puccini, Giacomo 106

qualifications 186

quasi-object 178–9
quest, heroic 10

Ramayana 110–11
rationality 186
Ravana 110
Reid, Anne 75
religion 145
 see also Christianity; Greek mythology; Roman mythology
repetition 33
reputation 157–8, 161–2, 163–4
rescue objects 98, 99
Richard, Wendy 77–8, 79
ritual 176–9
Roache, William 14, 71, 72, 75–6, 79
Rockefeller, John D. 59
Roman mythology 166–7, 168
Romanian fairytales 14, 119, 120, 121–2, 129–31
Romanian managers 15, 119–31
 context of Romanian economic leadership 120–1
 self-portraits 123–8
Rombach, B. 11
Ronell, A. 88
Rose, Stuart 78
Roy, M. 114
Rushdie, Salman 116

Sacagawea 106
sacred forces 146–7
sacrifice 74–5, 177
Sahlin-Andersson, K. 188
Sampo 19–26, 26, 27
scapegoat 176–9
 film producer as 15, 176, 180–1, 182–3
scientific hero 185–6, 190–1
scientific knowledge *see* knowledge
secondary reality 17
self-made man 14, 59, 60, 67–8, 69
Sennett, R. 73
Serres, M. 178, 179
Shamash 166
Shepherdson, Jane 74
shield against terror 144–5
Shinto myth 102

shooting 151–2
shortages 125–6
Sievers, B. 5
Silva, E.B. 91
Silverman, D.C. 116–17
Singh, K. 114–15
Sita 14, 110–11, 116
  role model for Indian women 114–16
Smith, C. 124
Smith, Captain John 106
soap operas 76, 79
  Coronation Street 14, 71, 72, 75–6, 79
  EastEnders 77–8, 79
social facts 155
socialism
  Poland 135, 136, 137, 139–40, 140
  Romania 119–31
software engineers 14, 80–91
Solli, R. 11
South Africa 105
Spirit entrepreneur 95–6
spoken tradition 18–19
Stane, Obadiah (Iron Man's rival) 55–6
Stark, Tony/Iron Man 54–5, 55–6
status 191
  attractiveness of 192
  staying 14, 71–9
  attitudes to 73–6
stories 6–7
  and myths 10
  spoken tradition 18–19
stupidity 14, 80–91
superhero myths 14, 50–8
Superman 51–2, 56–7
surveillance 128
Sutherland, S.J. 111, 115
Sweden 185, 190–4
Swedish Embassy, Berlin 160, 161
symbolic capital 15, 155–64
  architecture and 159–62
  myth and charisma as 158–9
symbolic universes 146

taking (photographs) 151–2, 153
targets 123–4

Tarot (The Fool) 14, 88, 89, 91
technocracy 186
television 67–8
  soap operas *see* soap operas
terror, shield against 144–5
textile workers 117
Thompson, P. 124
Thylefors, I. 178
Till Eulenspiegel 88–91
Topshop 74
trade dispute resolution 165–6, 169–71, 173
transformation, economic 59–60, 62–6
trials 135–8
trickstery 15, 125–6, 128, 130–1

universes
  comic books 50, 51–2
  symbolic 146
users, computer 11, 14, 80–91

Väinämöinen 19, 19–20, 22–6, 27
Valmiki 110, 111
Vauxhall GM plant 40–9
Vedic mythology 14, 108–18
  Draupadi 111–14, 115–16
  Durga 14, 109–10, 115, 116
  implications for Indian women 114–18
  Sita 14, 110–11, 114–16, 116
vengeance 113–14
Vico, G. 158
villains
  hard-working heroes and 135–8
  heroes and 9–16
  Kosovar heroines and 98, 99
  McManus 147–9
vocational groups 185, 190–4
Vulcan-Hephaestus 72

Wajcman, J. 76
Wayne, Bruce/Batman 51–2, 53–4
Weber, M. 159
Welch, Jack 57
West, the 140
Wiley, I. 73
Wilhelm I 163

Wingårdh, Gert 159, 160, 161, 162, 163
Wingårdh Architect Firm 155, 156, 159–62, 163–4
witches 182, 184–5
  folkloristic professional 185, 190–1
women
  female entrepreneurs in Kosovo 14, 92–101
  gender-content myths and nation forming 104–7
  incompetence in PC use 82–5
  Louhi 13, 17–29
  Vedic mythology *see* Vedic mythology
  writer 134, 136

Yudhisthira 112, 113

Zaleska, K.J. 40
Zeus 11